Crisis — The Inside Story of the Suez Conspiracy (1965)

The Shame and the Glory — Dieppe (1962)

Full Speed to Heaven (1960)

Channel Dash (1959)

The Ship with Two Captains (1957)

Walker, R.N. (1957)

Night Raider of the Atlantic (1956)

CRISIS

The Inside Story of the Suez Conspiracy

TERENCE ROBERTSON

CRISIS

The Inside Story of
the Suez Conspiracy

ATHENEUM NEW YORK 1965

For the Peace-keepers

CONTENTS

ACKNOWLEDGEMENT

Researching the Crisis

WRITERS of contemporary history are handicapped by the confidential nature of their source material. Documents are often classified, and if the participants are political leaders still in office or highly placed government officials, they will tend to provide information on a confidential basis only. This means that the writer, confident as he may be that his narrative is factually correct, cannot always document it as completely as he would wish.

My case is no exception. Documentation from official and private sources was made available to me in all the countries intimately involved in the Suez crisis, but always for my guidance and not for publication. In some instances, interviews were granted on condition that the information was treated as private and confidential. As one statesman put it, "I don't mind telling you what I know, providing I am not named as your source. You will have to be responsible for what you say in this book."

In view of this responsibility I have taken precautions to protect the integrity of the story. The facts and conclusions are supported by a formidable collection of records, papers, and diaries. The manuscript was read by officials of Canada's Department of External Affairs who corrected it in detail where Canadian participation is concerned.

It was also read by Christian Pineau, former Foreign Minister of France, who checked it for accuracy in terms of French participation, and by Robert Murphy, former United States Under Secretary of State, who provided invaluable advice on the policies and attitudes of official Washington during the crisis.

After commenting on the "obvious and successful effort to be fair and impartial to all concerned on a subject which aroused so much bitterness and emotion," Mr. Murphy said: "That part of the text relating to the chronology of events in the United Nations is especially valuable. Your account reveals the scope and importance of the constructive, dramatic role played by our good friend, Mike Pearson. This is long overdue and will be the source of satisfaction to his many friends among whom I like to count myself. I am reminded too of Arnold Heeney's intelligent and invaluable support during those difficult days."

Apart from confidential material and the bibliography, the story relies heavily upon information supplied through a series of exhaustive interviews. Part One is based upon conversations with David Ben-Gurion, former Prime Minister of Israel; Mrs. Golda Meir, Foreign Minister of Israel; Shimon Peres, Deputy Defence Minister of Israel; Abba Eban, Deputy Prime Minister of Israel; Christian Pineau, former Foreign Minister of France; Guy Mollet, former Prime Minister of France; Maurice Bourgès-Maunoury, former Defence Minister of France; and Abel Thomas, former Director General of the French Defence Ministry.

Part Two is substantiated primarily by the Right Honourable Lester B. Pearson, Prime Minister of Canada; Norman Robertson, former Canadian Under-Secretary of State for External Affairs; Arnold Heeney, former Canadian Ambassador to the United States; Pierre Dupuy, former Canadian Ambassador to

France; Geoffrey Murray, now Deputy High Commissioner for Canada in London; John Holmes, former Canadian assistant Under-Secretary of State and now President of the Canadian Institute for International Affairs; Robert Murphy; and Hans Engen, now Norwegian Ambassador in Washington. I am grateful for the kind and generous assistance each gave me in the research stage of this book.

I must give particular thanks to Prime Minister Pearson for making so much of his time available to me for interviews, for discussions in which the process of developing Canadian policies was traced in detail, and for checking the accuracy of my descriptions dealing with the Canadian role.

For permission to quote from *Full Circle: The Memoirs of Sir Anthony Eden*, I wish to thank Cassell & Co., Ltd., of London, England, and Houghton Mifflin Company of Boston, U.S.A.

Some critics, particularly those with a conservative and academic background, may say that a history that cannot be fully documented because it is written so soon after the event is really no history at all. I disagree, if only because I do not believe the world can afford to wait for fifty years to absorb whatever lessons there are to be learned from the Suez crisis.

TERENCE ROBERTSON
Toronto, 1964

Background to the Crisis

DURING the course of a Dag Hammarskjold Memorial Lecture on recent conflicts and confrontations, Adlai Stevenson said: "I would suggest only in passing that perhaps . . . Suez was the end of the road for colonial-type military solutions . . . there is reason to hope that the aggressors are extending their doctrine of no-nuclear-war to a broader doctrine of no-conventional-war on the ground that you cannot be sure there will be no nuclear war unless you are sure there will be no conventional war."

For approximately twenty-one days in November 1956, no one could be sure that the Suez conflict would not develop into a conventional war, perhaps a nuclear war. This was the pressure under which Lester B. Pearson, then Canada's Secretary of State for External Affairs, conceived and created a United Nations emergency force in spite of assurances from the governments of the United States, France, and Britain that it could not be done quickly enough to resolve the immediate crisis.

It was his initiative and single-minded pursuit of peace that placed an embryonic international force on the ground in Egypt just fifteen days after he had proposed its formation.

As a result of this rapid intervention the major powers were disengaged and given time to digest the disquieting facts that missiles had been armed and aimed, that threats to use them had been made, and that in consequence use of the H-bomb in certain conditions was not so unthinkable as they had imagined. They were subsequently forced, when the last threats against Israel were more or less accompanied by the launching of Sputnik One, to drastically re-evaluate their political and military strategies, a process from which a climate of non-belligerent stand-off has emerged.

The Middle East is one of the most sensitive and critical areas in the world, and the pattern of events generated from Pearson's efforts to restore peace there has led directly to the present era of cease-fire among nations.

There is something curiously apt about the slender roots of an international police force being planted along the Suez Canal. When Professor Ernest Renan formally greeted the visionary builder, Ferdinand de Lesseps, to the French Academy in 1885, he said: "Now that you have cut across the Isthmus [of Suez] . . . you have created . . . a serious embarrassment. Not merely does the canal connect two inland seas, but it will also serve as a communicating passage to all the oceans of the globe. In case of a maritime war it will be of supreme importance, and everyone will be striving at top speed to occupy it. You have marked out a great battlefield for the future."

The "battlefield" is a ditch about a hundred miles long running north and south to link the Mediterranean at Port Said with the Red Sea at Suez. The narrow ribbon of grey-blue water stitched with machine-like precision for most of its length across the pale, sun-burned yellow of the desert is on the average five hundred feet wide at the surface between sloping banks which give a width at the bottom of about two hundred feet. As ships are limited to less than eight knots to avoid creating a heavy wash, it takes about twelve hours to make the trip from Port Said to Suez — two convoys of ten to twelve ships each travelling in both directions every day. By far the most intriguing sight is to drive towards the canal from the flat and barren Sinai and see in the distant, shimmering haze a level desert horizon dotted with the masts, funnels, and superstructures of a convoy moving slowly along it like targets at a fairground shooting gallery.

The ninety-nine-year concession granted to de Lesseps by the Viceroy of Egypt which, as part of the then Ottoman Empire, was under the suzerainty of the Sultan of Turkey, gave the Suez Canal Company the right to operate the canal in return for certain rents, taxes, and percentages of gross profits. The company itself was registered in Egypt, with head offices in Egypt and administrative offices in Paris. Throughout its many arrangements with successive Egyptian governments the canal was always acknowledged to be an integral part of Egypt.

France, though a major canal-user, had been more concerned with administrative and economic aspects of the company than with the security of the canal. A French conception originally, a French gamble financially, and a French triumph eventually, the company represented the faith of nearly a quarter of a million small investors – shopkeepers, civil servants, and middle income wage-earners. It became a custom in France for parents to give their children canal company shares as wedding and christening presents.

Britain's interest was the safety of the canal as the shortest, most economic route to India and the East. The British government owned 44 per cent of the shares, and British ships using the canal represented nearly 70 per cent of all traffic. The canal became, in Bismarck's words, "the spinal column of the British Empire."

When, in the early 'eighties, Egyptian nationalists revolted against Turkish domination, the Viceroy invited Britain to station troops at key points along the canal to prevent it from being blocked. This temporary occupation was to last seventy-four years.

The convention signed in 1888 between the major canal-users and the Turkish government guaranteed freedom of passage for all ships of all nations beyond the life of the company's concession. It made the company responsible for operating the canal impartially in war and peace and Egypt responsible for protecting the canal against aggression.

After the defeat of the Turks in the First World War and the collapse of the Ottoman Empire, the rights of the Sultan in terms of the Suez Canal were transferred under the armistice agreements to Britain, which then became the official custodian of the canal's safety. Whatever Egyptian objections at the time – and there were many – they were quietened in 1935 when the Italians complained that the cost of transiting troops and supplies through the canal for the annexation of Ethiopia was rendering its colonial war uneconomic. The prospect of the Italian fleet being sent to occupy the canal so alarmed the Egyptian government that a year later it signed a treaty with Britain providing for protection of the canal during the next twenty years.

The chief British negotiator was a relative newcomer to the political scene named Captain Anthony Eden; and among those diplomats at the League of Nations who were depressed by the lack of any collective action to stop the Ethiopian war was the Canadian representative, Lester B. Pearson. When we discussed this period recently, Pearson said: "I felt then, as I still do today, that when the League showed itself too weak and divided to respond collectively and effectively to Italy's action, the Second World War became inevitable."

By 1954, when all but the most die-hard imperialists were willing to concede that the advent of thermonuclear weapons made far-flung military bases such as that at Suez obsolete, Eden negotiated an Anglo-Egyptian treaty under which British troops would evacuate the Canal Zone by 1956. In June of that year the last British soldiers left Egypt, and a month later Colonel Nasser nationalised the Suez Canal Company. Egypt had been occupied because in effect it had belonged to the canal; now the canal would belong to Egypt.

The Anglo-French position that Nasser had acted illegally

in international law and had committed a breach of international agreements was too weak to attract general support, though it was admitted that the methods of the takeover and the intentions of the Egyptian government might be causes for concern. Expropriation, a legal procedure by which a state encroaches upon private property rights in order to place them at the disposal of its public services, is an established sovereign right under international law. During the Mexican oil expropriations in 1938 the United States Secretary of State, Cordell Hull, said, "This government has not undertaken and does not intend to undertake to question the right of the Mexican government, in the exercise of its sovereign power, to expropriate properties within its jurisdiction."

France and Britain put forward as their best legal point that Nasser had breached the concession to the Canal Company. In international law this was not even an issue. The concession was an agreement between the State and a private company, and therefore subject to Egyptian municipal law which could in no way detract from the sovereign rights of the State under international law.

The next point, that Nasser had breached the convention, was also invalid as the guarantees of free passage had not been flouted and there was no evidence that they would be. The case of Israel was an exception that had been tolerated by the Canal Company, by the United Nations, and by the world opinion generally for five years.

A third point, that the act of nationalisation menaced international rights derived from long and uninterrupted use of the canal, attempted to bring into play the discredited concept of acquired rights under international law. Codification conferences held under the auspices of the League of Nations and the United Nations during the past thirty years have consistently repudiated this concept as being too ambiguous, obscure, and indefinable to be raised to the dignity of a principle in law.

There were, in fact, only two issues upon which Anglo-French intervention might be legally justified – if Nasser failed to maintain free and non-discriminatory flow of traffic through the canal, and if Egypt failed to pay adequate compensation to the Suez Canal Company.

I have endeavoured in this book to reconstruct the events which led to nationalisation of the Canal Company, to describe the political manœuvrings which culminated in the Anglo-French-Israeli decision to fight, and to trace as fully as possible the unremitting efforts of a handful of diplomats at the United Nations to restore peace.

The origins of the Suez crisis lie in Israel, where the decision to fight a preventive war was deliberately timed to take advantage of what Israeli leaders thought to be widespread disenchantment with Colonel Nasser and his policies. That they were able to implicate two major powers in such a gamble would be less alarming if the world knew more about Israel's ultimate aims. Early in 1957 John Foster Dulles told the Israeli Foreign Minister, Mrs. Golda Meir, that there was little rapport between their two governments as the United States knew nothing of the long-range objectives of Israel. He said the United States administration would have greater sympathy for Israeli complaints against the Arab states if they were accompanied by evidence of a genuine desire to reach an enduring political settlement. Israeli policies remain as provocative today as they were in 1956, sincere attempts to reach an accommodation with the Arab states being conspicuously absent.

PART ONE

The Transgression

CHAPTER ONE

Circle of Change

THE British decision to withdraw from Egypt flowed naturally from the advent of the H-bomb, and the political conclusion that the principle of nuclear deterrence beginning to emerge in 1954 demanded a revision of defence policies. A vast, sprawling target such as the military base in the Suez Canal Zone was as much of a drain financially as it was a strategic liability, and its abandonment would save more than the cost of the proposed new Middle East base in Cyprus, then envisaged as a vital link in the NATO bomber and interceptor chain stretching from Germany through Greece to Turkey.

That summer, after months of protracted negotiation, the British and Egyptian governments agreed upon the terms for a treaty of withdrawal which, when submitted for ratification by Parliament in London, led to a strangely paradoxical scene in the House of Commons.

The British Empire, with all its triumphs and weaknesses, sat on the front bench of the government side of the House in the hunched figure of Prime Minister Sir Winston Churchill. In 1946 he had hurled his contempt at Attlee's Labour government for "scuttling" from the Empire. "Things are built up with great labour, and cast away with great shame and folly," he had said.

Now it was Attlee who rose to his feet, his voice harsh with anger, to flay the Conservatives with reminders that they had once claimed that only the presence of British troops in Egypt could protect the canal and keep it open. "What has become of all the talk of the Suez Canal as an international waterway that must be open and kept open?" he asked. "In the White Paper the 1888 Convention [by which the major maritime powers agreed that the canal should be open to all nations at all times] is invoked. . . . Egypt has been in default of that convention for a number of years and nothing has been done about it. It is not much good affirming a convention which is not observed. . . . There is an immense difference between the Prime Minister in office and the Prime Minister in Opposition. When he came to office he had to face reality instead of making fatuous attacks on those who were bearing the responsibility. For years we have borne his accusations of 'scuttling.' Now we have this agreement . . . which is certainly in the worst terms I have ever seen. . . . "

No one is more sentimental and emotionally atavistic than a hard, ruthless imperialist. Nearly forty of them, the extreme right wing of the Tory Party known as the "Suez Group," sat on the backbenches behind Churchill as Captain Charles Waterhouse, their spokesman, brandished the White Paper and began: "Here it is. . . . All we have got left of eighty years of British endeavour. . . . This is not a sellout. It is a give-away. Instead of having physical control of a great base, insteal of having troops on the major waterway of the world, we have got this piece of paper. What do we mean by saying we have gained the right of re-entry? If Egypt wants us in for some future emergency . . . she will invite us in, treaty or no treaty. If she does not want us in, this piece of paper will not get us in. I think this piece of paper is not worth anything at all."

Churchill sat, head down, eyes fixed on his knees; beside him Foreign Secretary Anthony Eden was relaxed, confident. On the Opposition side Richard Crossman, one of the ablest Labour critics, looked prophetically into the future. "It is touch and go," he said, "whether this Anglo-Egyptian agreement ends in complete chaos and collapse in the Middle East or whether it is the beginning of new relations with Egypt. It depends not only on Egypt but on the attitude of the British government."

The Prime Minister lumbered to his feet. "I have not in the slightest degree concealed . . . how much I regret the course of events in Egypt." His voice heavy with portent, he continued: "I have not held my mind closed to the tremendous changes which have taken place in the whole strategic position in the world which makes the thoughts which were well-founded and well-knit together a year ago obsolete – absolutely obsolete – and which have changed the opinions of every competent soldier I have been able to meet. I am not going to lay these arguments before the House . . . but I should be prepared to do so to show how utterly out of proportion the Suez Canal and the position which we hold in Egypt are to the appalling developments and the appalling spectacles which imagination raises before us.

"Merely to try to imagine in outline and to portray the first weeks of a war as it would be now . . . would I am sure convince [the House] of the obsolescence of the base. . . . "

The House approved and the Anglo-Egyptian treaty was signed in October 1954. Eighty thousand British troops would quit the Suez Canal Zone by 1956; the once mighty British hegemony was slipping into history, and for those who yearned for the days of the Empire's grandeur there was consolation in knowing that at the other end of its Mediterranean graveyard towered a brooding, immovable monument – Gibraltar, a rock in search of a navy.

On the night the treaty was signed in Cairo, Colonel Gamal Abdel Nasser addressed the crowds, saying: "The first stage of our struggle has ended and a new stage is about to begin."

II

THE "new stage" opened three weeks later. Mahmoud Younes, a marine engineer who had served with Nasser in the Israeli war, was instructed to undertake a secret survey of the Suez Canal Company's administrative, planning, and operational functions, and submit a comprehensive report on the entire complex organization. The company's concession was due to expire in 1968, and the future control and operation of the canal was beginning to concern the governments of Egypt, Britain, and France. To cover the clandestine activities of Younes, Nasser announced on November 17 that an agenda for discussions was being prepared.

"I am confident," he said, "that the company will continue to give their assistance to the government so that the remaining period of the concession will pass in the best possible manner. Let us remember that Egyptian rights have been shamefully usurped by foreigners who have used the canal as an excuse to occupy our land. We will not tolerate delays in their departure when the time comes."

The special position the Suez Canal Company enjoyed in Egypt for more than eighty years made it a natural target for nationalistic agitation. Its unique character, evident wealth, accumulation of acquired rights, corpus of privilege, and the disparity between the profits of European shareholders and those of the Egyptian government, were all calculated to excite the bitter envy of nationalists, particularly those of the Army Revolutionary Council that had overthrown Farouk. The members of this junta of impetuous, idealistic young officers led by Nasser were each personally and desperately involved in the search for national dignity and honour. If they were appalled at the evidence of the King's evil personal habits and the perversions of his Court, they were even more astounded at the extent to which corruption seeped into every crevice in the structure of government and society.

They discovered, for instance, that whereas friction between the Canal Company and the government had been present for years, successive Ministers of Commerce had always settled the issues with some mutually acceptable financial arrangement. Nasser himself was perpetually outraged by the physical presence of a closed foreign community with a standard of living which by comparison made the Arab worker appear less well cared for than his camel. And in any event the company had served as an instrument for colonialism for so long that it was blind to its own anachronistic nature in an anti-colonial climate.

There was a good chance that when serious negotiations began with the governments of countries dependent upon the canal for a substantial part of their trade, they would be protracted and difficult, and Nasser was relying upon Younes to provide him with information that might be otherwise concealed. The Egyptian leader's chauvinism was being replaced gradually by political maturity. His self-deprecating pose as a simple soldier inspired by high and noble motives but plagued by the duplicity of those around him was a political asset that at this stage he could afford to cultivate. He distrusted Western statesmen almost as much as he did his own people, and the mask of open, engaging innocence in affairs of state served to hide a conviction, so deeply rooted that it bordered on the pathological, that their actions were designed to undermine his authority. There was every reason for him to suspect the West, which had thrived in one way or another upon Arab ills for a century or more. Nasser's dream was of a new Egypt based upon the expulsion of Western influence and exculpation of the disgrace of the Palestine war.

By the end of that November he was being carried along to the next act by pressures beyond his control. He had been an Egyptian nationalist at the beginning, and his apparent success in nudging the British out of Suez had captured the imagination of the entire Arab world, with only a few notable exceptions in Iraq and Jordan. His reputation spread and external forces began to push him into the position of symbolizing all Arab aspirations.

For the son of a poor postman in an Upper Nile village, the prospect of leading a generation in revolt was irresistible.

David Ben-Gurion, Israel's physically diminutive, intellectually massive nation-builder, was living in retirement at Sde Boker, his settlement home in the Negev, watching with opportunistic eyes as the circle of change tightened like a noose about the Middle East.

He recognized that new dangers for Israel might follow from the British decision to withdraw from the Suez Canal and from the new stage of Anglo-Egyptian friendship it seemed to herald, while appreciating that there could be advantages, particularly for a policy of territorial expansionism.

Israel's security rested upon a tripod: the Tripartite Declaration of 1950 signed by the United States, Britain, and France to guarantee the armistice lines; the presence of eighty thousand British troops in the Canal Zone which lay like a buffer between Egypt proper and the Sinai Desert; and her own will to survive, expressed by a population of one and a half million and an army of one and a half million. There were forty million Arabs around her, but Israeli leaders considered these odds reasonable, given parity in arms. The disparity was alarming.

The Tripartite Declaration had served to maintain the nervous truce, because the British troops in Egypt were a tangible expression of an intent by the United States, Britain, and France to implement it if hostilities were resumed. Egypt, for instance, could not undertake the movements of men and supplies necessary to prepare for a war without crossing the canal in full view of the British. On the other hand, the British presence held in check Israeli ambitions to annex the adjacent Sinai and move into Jordan.

Britain's intention to withdraw her troops from Egypt changed the strategic positions of both sides. There would be nothing to prevent the Egyptian Army from moving into the Sinai Desert to establish forward lines hard against the Israeli border, and nothing to prevent Israel from launching a preventive war first. Israeli leaders, particularly Ben-Gurion, repeatedly asserted that they had no such intention.

With one leg of the tripod growing smaller as each British troopship sailed home from Egypt, the efficacy of the other two needed closer examination. And when it was made, no responsible Israeli leader would place the future of his country unreservedly in the hands of Washington, London, and Paris. Dulles, preoccupied with Soviet expansionism, would do nothing to anger Afro-Asian-Arab sensibilities, simply because his principal political weapon was identification of the United States with the surging streams of anti-colonial nationalisms. The State Department believed that the string of Strategic Air Command bases stretching across North Africa to Saudi Arabia, Turkey, and Pakistan required the best possible diplomatic relations with the nationalistic governments involved.

If the Israelis were dubious about relying upon Dulles to uphold the Tripartite Declaration, the flirtation between Eden and Nasser which followed the decision to withdraw British troops made it unlikely that Britain would act independently of the United States. France remained as a possible ally. Could France, submerged in the bitter Algerian conflict, answer an appeal for help with an armed force against the advice of the United States and Britain? In those early months of 1955, France, in Israeli eyes, was a question mark.

Nor could Israel place its faith in the United Nations. Repeated complaints to the Security Council about the blockade of Israeli shipping had produced resolutions and no relief.

The tripod tilted upon one leg, the restless bellicosity of the Israeli people in the face of Arab threats. In the circumstances, belligerent determination derived from centuries of spiritual attachment to have and hold all Palestine was not enough; it needed material reinforcement in the form of weapons.

The Tripartite powers, aware of the risks that an arms race might develop in an area of continuing hostility, had made a gesture towards the control of both demand and supply by writing into the Agreement a clause saying: "The three Governments recognize that the Arab States and Israel all need to maintain a certain level of armed forces for the purpose of assuring their internal security and their legitimate self-defence and to permit them to play their part in the defence of the area as a whole. All applications for arms or war material for these countries will be considered in the light of these principles."

Nevertheless Britain was contributing to the imbalance through special treaties with Iraq and Jordan, both of whom received regular military and financial aid outside the principles laid down by the Tripartite Declaration. Jordan's famed Arab Legion, then commanded by Glubb Pasha, was armed and maintained by annual British subsidies; and the Arab Legion occupied Old Jerusalem.

The United States made shipments of planes, artillery, warships, and light arms to Egypt and Iraq, and fulfilled lavish orders from Saudi Arabia, which included jet transports and bombers. Syria was able to buy arms from France and Italy, one order of thirty jet fighters being transferred on arrival from Damascus to Cairo. Britain provided more arms to Egypt than the United States and went beyond the intention of the Declaration by selling manufacturing licences and entire plants.

If the Tripartite powers had been inspired by the best of intentions, their methods of carrying them out provided a classic illustration of the little wisdom with which the world is governed. Their fears, involvements, obsessions, conflicts of interest, mutual agreement to disagree, and only dimly perceived objectives had brought about a state of tumult and anarchy from which there came but one cry loud enough to be heard – the call for arms and more arms.

In this tense political atmosphere the blow Ben-Gurion had expected came at night from the Gaza Strip. Specially trained

quasi-military sabotage gangs recruited from Palestinian refugees with known criminal records raced across the border in
small groups, shadows in rubber-soled shoes, to kill and burn
in the Israeli settlements. Hand grenades crashed through windows, sub-machine guns raked evening classes in the schools,
land mines laid in darkness took their toll in daylight. Nasser
had unleashed the fedayeen.

Threatened by a refinement of war against which there
appeared to be no defence, David Ben-Gurion came back from
the Negev early in 1955 to take charge of the nation's defence
forces, assisted by two young men he had long ago entrusted
with the defence of Israel – Moshe Dayan and Shimon Peres.

Dayan, the forty-year-old Chief of Staff, had grown up in
the Jewish kibbutz settlements of Palestine serving as a boy in
Haganah, the Jewish Defence Force, before the Second World
War and had become the deputy commander of Orde Wingate's "Special Night Squad," which prowled the desert ready
to intercept marauding Arabs. Wingate, then a young captain
with British Intelligence serving in Palestine, had told the kibbutz settlers: "If you want to stop Arab attacks, go out and
attack them. If they know you will kill two Arabs for every Jew
they kill, these raids will stop." Attack reprisal became Dayan's
creed. He was said to be brilliant; in eighteen months he would
have the chance to prove it.

Shimon Peres, Director General of the Defence Ministry,
commanded affairs inside Israel's borders or far beyond them
which were as concealed as his subdued personality.

Dayan – gay, picturesque, and belligerent; Peres – remote
and distant, less inclined to believe in militance as the sole
answer to the Arab threat.

When Ben-Gurion asked Dayan what could be done about
the fedayeen, the youthful Chief of Staff requested permission
to retaliate in strength. Peres advised caution, suggesting that
reprisals could be dangerous if kept up for too long or if they
were so heavy as to be out of proportion to the provocation.

Although Ben-Gurion needed the patience and restraining influence of Peres, Dayan's aggressiveness matched his own; he decided Israel could not afford to wait for the war it must one day fight. Dayan should have his way.

A week later, on February 28, an Israeli armoured column raced out of the Negev, crashed across the border into the Gaza Strip, entered the town of Gaza itself, and deployed outside fedayeen headquarters. When the column regrouped and left the scene, sixty-three Egyptians and Palestinians lay dead or dying, a dramatic, brutal warning to all Arab States that the law of reprisal had been established – five Arabs for every Israeli killed. If there had to be retaliation, and the question of whether it was really necessary is debatable, there was no reason for it to be carried out so savagely.

Reeling from the shock of the Gaza raid, Nasser announced that he would have to re-examine the "conditions of peace" – a curious statement, since he had repeatedly insisted that Egypt was in a state of war with Israel and that the armistice in no way affected his "rights of war." In this mood he set off for Indonesia to attend the Bandoeng Conference of Afro-Asian heads of state.

It was Colonel Nasser's first appearance among the dictators of neutrality, and their welcome was a heady experience. He discovered in Pandit Nehru not only an ally in his campaign against the Baghdad Pact, but a personal friend; Chou En-Lai of Red China listened intently to his tirade about the iniquitous conditions the West always attached to aid and arms agreements, and promptly offered to supply Egypt with all the arms she could afford, unconditionally.

Warmed and refreshed by his elevation to high estate in Asian circles, Nasser returned to Cairo and signed a "Treaty of Friendship" with India. If its intention was to keep the cold war out of Arab affairs, as both these devoutly sincere leaders said it was, then it was singularly unsuccessful. The cold war was already approaching Egypt – by air.

July 26 marked the anniversary of the Egyptian revolution. It was a spectacular national holiday, with speeches to the thousands in the streets, impressive fireworks displays, and a state banquet. When Nasser took his place on a flag-draped platform, he was followed by Dimitri Shepilov, soon to become foreign minister of the Soviet Union. Shepilov stayed so briefly in Cairo that his presence was little more than the caress of a chilling gust of wind. Yet it was enough to turn steaming Arab passions into dry, electric enmity. The call for arms had been heard.

III

EDEN'S health was gradually but steadily deteriorating. Recurring jaundice and three operations in 1953 had weakened him physically, and mental fatigue was inevitable after twenty years of struggle against ambitious dictators.

A quick, intense temper inherited from his eccentric father consumed vast quantities of his energy, but, if the fury still appeared from behind the public mask of well-bred urbanity to tongue-whip inept officials in the privacy of his office, it did so less frequenty and less violently.

When he returned to office in 1951, the towering stature of Churchill was still there to cast a protective shadow, to carry the weight of responsibility for decisions that grew increasingly difficult to make as the H-bomb loomed ahead to demand of men the sort of wisdom few, if any, possess. But Churchill too was tired, and in April 1955 Eden moved into No. 10 Downing Street, no longer protected, at long last a leader in his own right.

If, because he looked like one, Eden had always enjoyed a natural right to be Foreign Secretary, John Foster Dulles

could claim that his wide-jawed, rangy appearance made him
a natural United States Secretary of State.

Family connections with the State Department – his
grandfather had been Secretary of State in President Harrison's
cabinet – and minor extracurricular political chores when he
was practising law inspired him to write a turgid, unimpressive
book on international affairs which appeared in 1939. When
he took office thirteen years later, his friends wished he had
never written it. The wavering thesis led to the conclusion that
Nazi Germany and Fascist Italy represented the forces of
change which were being repressed by "satisfied" nations such
as Britain and France.

He brought the twin cults of "brinkmanship" and "massive
retaliation" into the world, and never understood why they
made him so disliked among the Allies. It bewildered him that
on occasion when he wanted to go to the brink, they sometimes
declined the privilege of keeping him company. The United
States was strong, they were weak; their pride was something
that wouldn't occur to him. On the other hand, he rightly
resented Eden's attitude of identifying British policy with that
of the United States and vice versa. He insisted that as United
States Secretary of State his sole concern was to do his best for
the American people, that there was no single Anglo-American
policy, no "splits," but simply divergences in their respective
policies. He suspected with good reason that the portrayal of
the Anglo-American alliance as being full partnership in all
aspects of foreign affairs was an Eden device to keep Britain in
the Big Power league.

Eden, with the attractive fragility of antique Chippendale,
and Dulles, the solid, forthright piece of Early American, had
to clash, and they did; and sometimes the impact stunned both
of them.

They collided over Indo-China, when Dulles, intending to
go to the brink, asked for British support. Eden refused, and
Dulles never forgave him. They collided again at the Geneva

Conference in 1954, when Eden distilled the "spirit of Geneva" from the brittle East-West conference and Dulles was so angry he packed his bags and went home.

On this unpromising plane the Secretary of State, who had chosen to lead a crusade against Communism, and the Prime Minister, who was haunted by memories of an unhappy past, went their separate ways in relentless pursuit of treaties.

They went by different routes, and treaties appeared in profusion in the wake of their attempts to freeze Afro-Asian nationalism into a solid bloc of anti-Communism. Dulles, finding the western approaches to the southern route through Egypt and Saudi Arabia impossible to negotiate, changed direction and came in from the Far East to Karachi, where he signed a military aid pact linking Pakistan to the South East Asia Treaty Organization.

Eden took the northern route, and by joining the Baghdad Pact brought Britain into a regional alliance with Iraq, Iran, Turkey, and Pakistan. In sum, their individual efforts had the political effect of making NATO, the Baghdad Pact, and SEATO extensions of each other.

One weakness in the chain was the conspicuous absence of the United States from the membership of the Baghdad Pact; another was the historical diplomatic truth that once a treaty is signed the signatories inherit each other's enemies without necessarily being more than friends of convenience themselves. When alliances are put together in series, the number of enemies is increased to the extent that the efficacy of the structure as a whole is thrown into doubt, which is precisely what happened.

Egypt, with the sycophantic Saudi Arabia, Syria, and Yemen following her lead, raged at Iraq's defection from the cause of Arab unity and branded the Baghdad Pact as an imperialistic device to ensnare the Arab world into committing itself to the West; Pandit Nehru echoed Nasser, and condemned Pakistan for betraying Asian neutrality; in the Far East,

Sukarno contented himself with disrespectful remarks about the
West in general.

The division of the Arab states was centred on Colonel
Nasser, whose support outside Egypt was the broad mass of
middle-class and peasant extremism, and Nuri es-Said, Prime
Minister of Iraq and elder Arab statesman, who emerged at this
moment of internal Arab crisis, as he had done many times
before, as the leader of the moderate, well-established sections.
All were nationalistic, all hated Israel, and all resented any
form of foreign pressures, the spectrum running from those
who wanted everything at once regardless of consequences, to
those who advocated cautious evolvement.

Behind Nasser's twisting and turning in his relations with
the rest of the world, which in fact followed a pattern well-
established by leaders of other non-aligned countries, lay the
Upper Nile, where, if a mighty dam were built, enough water
could be stored to treble the existing cotton crop, irrigate an
extra two million acres of desert, and supply hydro-electric
power for industry.

The project, born of necessity, was bold, imaginative, and
expensive. The estimated cost of $1,300 million was far be-
yond Egypt's capacity, yet the Minister of Finance, Dr. Abdul
Kaissouni, went in search of funds to be repaid by income
derived from cotton exports. Despite the dwindling Western
market for Egyptian cotton, the United States was asked to join
Britain in making a joint loan to Egypt, the figures discussed
then being $56 million for the United States and $14 million
for Britain.

Sympathy for the project depended logically on Nasser's
willingness to stay away from commitments with the East and
become, in a general sense, someone Dulles and Eden could
put down on the credit side of their political ledger.

The Egyptian government then applied to the World Bank
for a loan of $200 million which, so it appeared, they expected

to be granted with no further guarantees than a proposal to repay from cotton exports to the West.

Since Nasser's vehement campaign against the Baghdad Pact, and against Britain in particular, British interest had cooled, and Washington told Dr. Kaissouni that further reassurance was required of Egypt's ability to repay the loans. Nasser, furious that his request for loans had not been automatically granted as a gesture of the West's faith in his administration, regarded this Anglo-American attitude as another example of interference in Arab affairs.

Then, in late September, the entire military and political structure of the Middle East changed drastically, ominously. Colonel Nasser announced that Egypt had signed an agreement with the Soviet Union for the supply of Czech arms.

The mysterious visit of Shepilov to Cairo in July was suddenly explained. He was to be followed by destroyers, submarines, torpedo boats, minesweepers, MIG fighters, jet bombers, jet transports, heavy and medium tanks, anti-tank weapons, artillery of all calibres, light weapons by the thousands, and millions of rounds of ammunition. The MIGs alone were to arrive with half a million rounds.

Soviet technicians were to be sent to train the Egyptian armed forces in the use and maintenance of these arms; at the same time, Egyptian officers were to undergo special courses at a Warsaw Pact training ground in Poland.

No sooner had Nasser made his announcement than the Syrian government disclosed that it too had placed an order for Soviet bloc arms which, for convenience, had been packaged with the Egyptian.

The arms race was on. Reactions ranged from shocked disbelief by Dulles and Eden to frenzied excitement by Arab nationalists. The Tripartite Declaration was badly rent, the shaky Baghdad Pact threatened to come apart as its validity in terms of defence against Communist infiltration and subversion appeared largely mythical, and Anglo-American policies, evolved so laboriously from a multitude of differences, collapsed.

The arms deal brought the Soviet Union into the centre of Arab politics for the first time, and it arrived bearing gifts – offers of industrial aid, scientific assistance for weapons development, agricultural research experts, and, most important to Egypt, a proposal that should the West turn down the Aswan Dam loans, the Soviet Union would provide financial and technical assistance. The Middle East, now a cold war arena in which East and West competed with arms and money, was suddenly vital.

Eden and Harold Macmillan, who had been appointed Foreign Secretary, agreed that the Soviet move required a quick, effective counter in the nature of a major Churchillian-type rallying call for an Arab-Israeli settlement, perhaps a general rapprochement right across the Middle East.

Telegrams went out from the Foreign Office instructing British representatives to prepare the ground for a peace offensive. In the Arab capitals, heads of government suddenly became the most sought-after guests at British embassies.

In Washington, Dulles considered the harsh realities which conspired to thwart his plans to contain Communism, and re-evaluated the advice he was getting from Henry Byroade, the United States Ambassador in Cairo, and from George Allen, Assistant Under-Secretary in charge of Near Eastern Affairs at the State Department.

Byroade and Allen believed that sympathy for Arab nationalism could be best expressed by acts of friendship toward Nasser. They emphasized that the United States tended to be identified by Arabs as Britain's partner, that the most convincing rebuttal at this stage would be to stay clear of the Baghdad Pact, confine arms shipments to Egypt and Saudi Arabia, and give Nasser enough money to build his dam. Because they had persuaded him that Nasser would respond with co-operation in a pro-West, anti-Communist defence alliance, Dulles now felt in some way betrayed.

CHAPTER TWO

Desert Intrigue

THE Israeli village of Patish is a small farming outpost in the vast emptiness of the Negev. In March 1955 it was a new village built of sand and rough-hewn rock by a handful of recently arrived Yemenite Jews – a solemn, patient, leathery people whose lives are spent wresting food from the desert. On the 24th a wedding was taking place in the communal hall, a colourful, gay affair held in the late evening. Inside the hall, celebrations were hushed as the marriage ritual began; outside was the desert – cool, dark, and quiet.

The shadows moved quickly over the sand and crouched briefly outside the hall until a flashlight blinked twice. Windows crashed in, grenades exploded, and automatic weapons sputtered. Less than a minute later the shadows were gone, leaving behind twenty wedding guests dead, dying, and wounded, among them a sixteen-year-old bridesmaid.

Suffering is no novelty to the people of the desert, especially the Yemenite born in a cruel, barbaric kingdom where beheading is one of the more merciful judicial punishments. When the Israeli army patrol arrived four hours later, the rites of burial were being carried out with the stoical calm of a remote, Biblical people to whom disaster and tragedy are as inevitable as joy, gladness, and the heat of the desert sun.

While the fedayeen pillaged and killed, formal protests poured into the headquarters of the United Nations Truce Supervisory Commission, headed by Canada's General E. L. M. Burns. Each incident was investigated, and the Commission informed the Egyptian government that it "noted . . . and requests action be taken to prevent recurrences. . . ."

More than one hundred Israelis were killed or wounded in that winter wave of fedayeen terror, villages near the Gaza border were abandoned, and General Burns, armed with restrictive terms of reference, "noted . . . and requested."

The border was comparatively quiet for the early summer, but in August 1955 a new and different fedayeen appeared, an efficient commando trained as saboteur and intelligence agent. They moved across Israel, blowing up installations, capturing Israeli soldiers, extracting information, and completing their missions in Jordan or Syria, where they were re-equipped by Egyptian military attachés in Amman and Damascus and sent back through Israel to the Gaza Strip.

On August 31 Moshe Dayan ordered an Israeli armoured column to enter the strip and destroy fedayeen headquarters at Khan Yunis. When they returned with only one man lost against an estimated forty Egyptians killed, even Dayan must have thought that on a raid-for-raid basis the law of reprisal odds were getting a bit too lopsided.

A second reprisal involved the ejection of Egyptian battalions that were entrenched on the Israeli side of the demarcation line between the Sinai and Negev at El Auja. When United Nations observers arrived to check the positions of the empty gasoline cans which marked the border, some twenty of them were missing. Sir John Nicholls, British Ambassador to Israel, said in a later review of border conditions: "The first recognizable wave of fedayeen entered Israel . . . with the objective of disruption of settlements in the Negev. It immediately became apparent that for Nasser this was a highly profitable activity. Not only was it popular in Egypt and other Arab countries, but it even escaped censure. . . . A renewed wave was launched in August drawing another Israeli reprisal against Khan Yunis. . . . In scale the last of these reprisals [at El Auja] became almost an operation of war against a battalion of Egyptian infantry who had dug in inside the Israeli frontier. Partial mobilization had to be carried out three times as a precaution against Egyptian counterattacks. . . . If Egyptian provocation [continues] the next Israeli move might well be to launch a major attack on the Sinai. . . ."

Occupation of the El Auja demilitarized zone developed into an affair of honour and attrition, one side moving in and the other moving out, and with each change of occupancy the number of troops involved increased. General Burns demanded that Egypt keep out, and was then forced to make the same demand to the Israelis. The Egyptians occupied check posts and turned them into garrisons; so the Israelis established a fortified kibbutz in the zone. United Nations surveyors attempting to re-establish the border were shot at, and, as expected, each side accused the other of being responsible. Eventually, Burns reported to United Nations headquarters in New York that both Egypt and Israel were in flagrant breach of the armistice agreements.

The reason for such stubborn interest by both Israel and Egypt in this triangular no man's land was military. Inside it were the only main paved road junctions in the central Sinai, a desert gateway to Suez for the Israelis, and the mouth of a funnel into Israel for the Egyptians. Neither side could afford to let the other have unchallenged occupancy.

Early in September Shimon Peres placed on Ben-Gurion's desk a lengthy document, a summary of the pending arms deal between Egypt and the Soviet Union compiled by Israeli Intelligence. The weak Israeli Air Force, primarily designed for army co-operation, would be unable to stop the jet bombers listed in the Intelligence report; Jerusalem, Tel Aviv, and Haifa could be destroyed in half a dozen raids.

In all likelihood it was this evidence of an Egyptian military build-up that convinced Ben-Gurion that he would have to take military action quickly, that a preventive war was inevitable.

Israel needed help, and Ben-Gurion had felt for some time that the close friendship it enjoyed with France could be exploited more effectively to mutual advantage. The adhesive factors in their relationship were the common conflict with the Arabs, their common dislike of the Baghdad Pact with its implication of a possible Anglo-American rapprochement with the Arabs in the future, and the natural political sympathy of French socialists for Israel's efforts to build itself on socialist foundations. This affinity compensated to some degree for Britain's extensive treaty arrangements with Jordan and Iraq.

Israel had already made a $60-million offer to buy arms from the United States but, despite the pressure brought to bear by the Jewish lobby in Washington, Dulles had rejected it. He automatically shied away from any act that might place the United States in opposition to the Arab world.

Israel had then turned to Britain, but Eden, refusing to sell tanks, had merely approved the sale of six obsolete Meteor jet interceptors, useless against the Ilyushin bombers Egypt and Syria were to receive from the Soviet Union.

In late September the first hesitant approach was made to France. Peres flew to Paris to convince the French Minister of Interior, M. Maurice Bourgès-Maunoury, who was responsible for Algerian affairs, that Egypt was providing greater and more varied assistance to the Algerian rebels than France suspected, and that Nasser was just as much the enemy of France as he was of Israel. Bourgès-Maunoury agreed and, with a common identity of interests firmly established, offered to supply Israel with a consignment of arms which included aircraft, tanks, and anti-tank guns. The military aspects of the meeting were not so important as the political implications. The principle of a Franco-Israeli alliance against the Arabs was recognized, and Israel, confident of French assistance, could prepare for preventive war.

In November 1955 Ben-Gurion replaced Moshe Sharett as Prime Minister, and it was rumoured that France would divert Mystère jet interceptors from NATO production for delivery to Israel by April 1956.

Sudden thunder was in the desert air. In a timeless land, time had become more precious than water.

II

WITH a quarter of a million troops locked up in Algeria, France could not afford the luxury of Anglo-American ambivalence toward the Arabs. France was already at war in North Africa.

Cairo Radio inflamed Frenchmen of all shades of opinion by its constant appeals to Arabs everywhere to unite behind the Algerian rebels, and boasted that Egypt was giving moral and material aid to its brethren in their struggle to free themselves from French tyranny.

The mood of France in December was one of desperate yearning for a solution to a conflict that was draining her of youth and money, a wistful longing for an end to a state of war that had existed virtually since 1939. But no matter how deep and passionate their desires, they would not have them satisfied on terms dictated by Cairo.

In this mood the government fell, and France was once again plunged into an election. After the results in January 1956 the new government was headed by M. Guy Mollet, general secretary of the Socialist party who, after years of being a behind-the-scenes political strategist, now held office for the first time as the compromise choice of a coalition of right- and left-wing elements of the major parties. He appointed to the key ministries of Foreign Affairs and Defence two of the most potent men in French politics: Christian Pineau, resolute, and respected as the toughest minister intellectually in the new government, and the former Minister of the Interior, Maurice Bourgès-Maunoury.

Bourgès-Maunoury simply moved from one cabinet post to another, his fifteenth move in about ten years of political responsibility in one high office after another. A right-wing radical Socialist who sympathized with the intransigent *colons* of Algeria, he had already initiated the process of collaboration with Israel, and as Defence Minister would be able to carry it forward toward even closer military partnership. Pineau, on the other hand, was a shrewd, experienced Socialist who leant toward the right. Decisive, quick to recognize the critical core of complicated diplomatic problems, he was inflexible once persuaded that his course was right.

From January, then, Pineau was the architect of French foreign policy, Bourgès-Maunoury gave it military teeth, and Mollet kept the Assembly under control with soothing speeches.

Pineau's attitude toward the war in Algeria reflected the majority opinion in France – a solution, but an honourable one from which the Egyptian dictator could derive no pleasure. The violent abuse hurled at France received equal time on Cairo Radio with the campaigns against Britain and Israel, but there was the significant additional factor that since signing the arms deal with the Soviet Union, Nasser had started to send weapons no longed wanted by his own army to the Algerian Arab forces.

Pineau hoped that Nasser could be persuaded to disengage himself from the Algerian conflict, thereby creating an opportunity for France to come to terms with the rebels. He decided to visit Cairo and make a personal appeal to Nasser, but first he needed something to fall back on if the Egyptian refused to co-operate. In such an event the most effective method of dis-illusioning the rebels that they were fighting the crusades in reverse would be to impose a series of diplomatic and, if pos-sible, military defeats on Nasser. The only country in a position to inflict military indignities was Israel.

About a week later in Tel Aviv, the impenetrable Shimon Peres began clearing his desk at Defence Headquarters of un-finished routine business. It seemed to his colleagues that he expected to be away for some time, but there was not the slightest hint of where he was going.

III

NASSER's most volatile support in his campaign against British influence in Jordan came from the thousands of Palestinian Arabs absorbed into the country's small population. Most of them lived on the west side of the Jordan River against the Israeli border in towns and villages of their own making. Although nominally Jordanians since 1949, they tended to confine themselves to their own communities which were, in fact, better served with modern amenities than the older Jordanian settlements on the east side of the river.

Their newspapers wielded powerful influence in Amman, and their political activities extended into the Cabinet, in which four ministers were Palestinians, and their younger men, com-missioned in the Jordanian National Guard, were encouraged by the Egyptian military attaché in Amman to form their own "Society of Free Officers." They disliked the British-supported Arab Legion, a comparatively small force responsible for in-ternal security, a Praetorian Guard for the insecure young

King Hussein, and were determined to rid Jordan of its British commander, Glubb Pasha. An insidious campaign aimed at undermining Glubb's privileged position at Hussein's right began in the most trivial way.

Enthusiastic Western magazine writers often revived around Glubb's portly, unromantic figure the mystique of Beau Geste and Lawrence. Each time such a story was published, hundreds of copies of the magazine appeared in Amman, distributed with seeming casualness where the King would be sure to see them. Coincidentally, the bribed newspapers printed editorials accusing Glubb of portraying himself as the real ruler of Jordan. Palestinian politicians then launched whispering campaigns ridiculing the King as a weak, ineffective parody of a monarch who would not remain on his throne for a day if Glubb's Legion were not there to support him.

On the advice of Harold Macmillan, who was attending meetings in Baghdad, Eden decided to bludgeon Jordan into joining the Baghdad Pact. He says in his memoirs: "The Jordan government was ready to join the Baghdad Pact . . . providing it received the necessary backing from us. . . . At the same time I was anxious . . . about possible internal reactions fermented by Egyptian propaganda and Saudi money. . . . To meet this danger I felt sure that we should draw up an agreement, showing what we planned to do so that all Jordanians could see definite and tangible gains. . . . "

Britain immediately offered Jordan a free gift of ten jet interceptors, a supply of sundry other weapons, and an undertaking to revise the existing Anglo-Jordanian treaty to boost the annual subsidy. The offer failed to push Jordan into the Baghdad Pact, but it encouraged other Arab states to clamour for arms, with the implied threat that if refused, they might follow Nasser's example of appealing to Moscow. Lebanon, always friendly to the West, was the first to apply and received immediate approval for tanks and planes from the United

States. Iraq followed and received an undertaking from Britain to supply similar weapons.

The next step was tragically inept. Into this tiny, weak, and divided kingdom, where a king in his early twenties walked a tightrope with not merely his throne but his life at stake, stalked Field Marshal Sir Gerald Templer, Chief of the Imperial General Staff, whose iron-fisted tactics had subdued the Communists in Malaya. No other act on Britain's part could have been so guaranteed to whip Cairo and its ally, Damascus, into a new highly frenzied state of fury.

The Middle East had not yet thrown off the habit of viewing Britain's legendary imperialistic power with considerable respect. The legacy of a British military presence was a lingering tendency to consider political action in terms of how the British would react.

Throughout the long period of a British presence it had been rare for the Chief of the Imperial General Staff to visit an Arab country, and to Arabs generally he was a fabled, all-powerful military giant. Sending Templer to Jordan was tantamount to declaring war on Egypt, Syria, and Saudi Arabia. Hussein may have been impressed with this additional "tangible gain" to emerge from his interest in the Baghdad Pact, but Nasser was reported to be "speechless with rage." Anti-British riots broke out in Amman; the four Palestinian members of Hussein's Cabinet resigned; the Prime Minister also resigned; and the astonished Field Marshal, the unwitting cause of it all, thoroughly out of his depth amid such an unseemly demonstration of civil disorder, flew away from the scene, leaving behind several hundred worried British residents of Amman. Jordan was no longer able to join any alliance; for once in his distinguished career the Field Marshal had achieved precisely nothing. King Saud, hoping for a *coup d'état*, moved two thousand troops to his northern frontier close to Amman as support for the "Society of Free Officers" in the Jordanian

National Guard, and Eden flew paratroopers to Cyprus, ostensibly to protect British lives in the event of a revolt. Hussein telephoned his cousin, King Feisal of Iraq, to appeal for help, and Iraqi troops were alerted for possible intervention in Jordan.

Dulles sent a message to Eden deploring the movement of British troops, questioning the wisdom of Hussein's accepting Iraqi aid, but omitting any mention of Saudi Arabian troop movements. Eden, presumably stung into a rage of his own by this time, ignored it and informed King Saud that if his troops crossed the border, Britain would honour her treaty obligations to defend Jordan.

Macmillan gave no further advice as Foreign Secretary. Just before Christmas he was shuffled off to the Treasury as Chancellor of the Exchequer, and replaced by Selwyn Lloyd, the third Foreign Secretary in less than a year.

Lloyd, fifty years old, peacetime lawyer and wartime soldier, had entered politics in 1945, and after the Attlee government was ejected in 1951, he became a Minister of State at the Foreign Office and an occasional British spokesman at the United Nations. It was suggested, perhaps unkindly, that his most important asset was malleability, that he would likely do what Eden wanted as Eden had done for Churchill.

And as he took office in London, with little experience of the Middle East, the future of the Suez Canal suddenly became a major political issue in Cairo.

IV

───────

THE problem of the canal's future when the concession expired had dropped from sight after Nasser's announcement that he intended to invite "parties concerned" to begin discussions. In the autumn of 1955 it re-emerged, and it seemed that a serious beginning was at last possible.

For several days government and company representatives met in private, discussing proposals from British and American oil corporations for widening the canal; then the Egyptians unveiled their real intentions. One day they demanded that a harbour be constructed at Lake Timsah, near the company's operating headquarters at Ismailia; the next day they insisted that the number of Egyptian pilots should be doubled; and so it went on.

The engineer, Younes, had done his work well, and, armed with his report covering the company's vast, intricate organization of investments, interests, and operations, Nasser decided that Egypt deserved a far larger share of the gross income of nearly $100 million a year in canal tolls. As evidence that dividends to foreign shareholders were abnormally high, Younes could show that the company's modernization work was not nearly so extensive as it had been made to appear. Signal installations, for instance, were oil-burning, though electricity was readily available. Shortly before Christmas the Egyptian Minister of Commerce demanded that the company dispose of all its outside interests and invest its entire reserves in Egyptian undertakings; demanded that half the company's board of directors should be Egyptian, appointed by the government; and demanded further that the Egyptian government should appoint its own representatives to the *Comité de Direction*. These were not unreasonable demands from a nationalistic government, but they were anathema to the company spokesman who protested that he was being confronted in peremptory fashion with what amounted to nationalization. The substance of this critical development was passed to the British and French ambassadors, and Sir Humphrey Trevelyan reported to London: "The Egyptian government adopted new tactics of sapping at the company in order to increase Egyptian participation in management and operation to the greatest possible extent and to get as much money out of the company as possible." Typically, perhaps, a British official was interpreting natural nationalistic aspirations as greed.

In January 1956 the Egyptians made repeated attempts to force the company to lower the standards of the qualifications required for pilots, and when these failed entry visas were denied to a group of foreign pilots recruited by the company in Paris.

In the face of the company's refusal to even discuss these demands, the Egyptians requested that the talks be resumed on a different plane, and at the first meeting produced a new attack, this time on the legal standing of the company. It was, they claimed, completely subservient to Egyptian law.

Recognizing that any concession on this point would open the way for the Egyptians to order compliance with the earlier demands, the company negotiators hedged on the ground that a position of *régime special* had always existed and that any change in status should be regulated by mutual agreement. Deadlocked again, the discussions were temporarily suspended and both sides resorted to lengthy correspondence between legal advisers.

Throughout this extraordinarily important assault on the company's financial and operational structure, the British, French, and United States Ambassadors were kept fully informed, and presumably they in turn kept the Foreign Office, the Quai d'Orsay, and the State Department informed. All were aware that Nasser's régime was nationalistic and that the Suez Canal was Egypt's most important natural resource, even though it had been shaped artificially. It would be logical for Egypt to want the canal. Giving evidence before a Senate investigative committee after the event in February 1957, Ambassador Byroade said he thought Egypt would try to get hold of the canal operation prior to 1968.

The implications were not apparent to Sir Humphrey at the time, but he said later: "Looking back one might surmise that the Egyptians had in mind that getting control of the reserves, and Egyptianising the pilots' service was a desirable preliminary to nationalisation. But there was no reason at the time to assume that they had in mind more than the immediate aims of Egyptianising the character of the company and extracting foreign exchange."

M. Charles-Roux, president of the Canal Company in Cairo, was more suspicious of Egyptian motives than the British Ambassador. Alarmed by what appeared to him as a dangerous effort to undermine the company's legal authority, he saw the Foreign Minister, Dr. Fawzi. Few governments have been blessed with a representative so relentlessly determined to be noncommittal as Dr. Fawzi. Interviews in his office were protracted affairs, with all present seated in low chairs at an even lower table, while interminable cups of Turkish coffee were served. As the Minister spoke in a voice that was scarcely more than a whisper, his listeners were compelled to lower their heads and hunch forward to hear him. An unbriefed visitor would be convinced he had stumbled into a gathering of conspiratorial anarchists, when in fact, Fawzi might be reminiscing about the glories of the Pharaohs or declaring Egypt's wish to be friends with all and sundry. His position as a civilian in a military government was insecure to say the least, reason enough perhaps for him to talk ambiguously and almost inaudibly to the representatives of foreign governments. By far the most brilliant member of the Council of Ministers, he was also old enough to have served previous governments now considered corrupt. Nasser retained him because no army officer in the government had the knowledge, the skill, or the grace to handle day-to-day diplomacy, and Fawzi could be relied upon to do exactly what he was told.

Charles-Roux said the company was perturbed at the failure of the Egyptian government and the Suez Canal Company representatives to reach agreement in principle on the future of the canal administration after 1968, and asked what the government's intentions were.

Two hours later he returned to his headquarters convinced
that Fawzi had said with unexpected candour: "It is our intention
to seek an extension of the existing concession for such period
as will best serve the interests of the canal users."

Aware that so unambiguous a statement of intent from
Fawzi would not be credited in Paris, he saw the Foreign
Minister again a week later and politely requested reassurance
that what he believed had been said was actually what Fawzi
did say. The Foreign Minister replied smoothly that there was
no misunderstanding between them.

CHAPTER THREE

Divided Diplomacy

EL AUJA: a triangle of desert wasteland; a bleak, barren flash-point of war. Under the armistice agreements civilians were allowed inside the demilitarized zone; soldiers were forbidden. No civilians were there, just soldiers.

The Egyptian army garrisoned two major check posts astride a paved highway junction; the Israeli kibbutz settlement was manned by troops disguised as farmers and civilian police. Separated by a plain of rock, sand, and scrub, both sides were provocative, unimpressed by the constant urgings of General Burns and United Nations truce supervisors to "cease and desist." The Egyptians were truculent, the Israelis over-confident. Then the Soviet presence appeared.

Heavy Stalin tanks moved into the Sinai, fuelled and ammunitioned at arsenals and armament workshops mushrooming across the desert, and lumbered forward to the Egyptian advance positions. By the end of January a line of tanks faced through the El Auja swing door into Israel.

Concerned by reports from Burns that a bad situation could become infinitely worse if drastic measures were not quickly undertaken, Dag Hammarskjold interrupted a flight from New

York to South East Asia to see the Israeli and Egyptian leaders.

Nasser and Foreign Minister Fawzi entertained the Secretary General with warm Arab hospitality, and Hammarskjold reacted predictably to such suave and deferential treatment. He was charmed.

Nasser explained that his troops had been ordered into El Auja only after "the Jews put up fortifications in there." Hammarskjold suggested that if Ben-Gurion could be persuaded to "vacate these fortifications," they could be occupied by United Nations truce observers and Nasser could withdraw. Nasser replied to this naïve proposal with one of his own – that Hammarskjold should first speak with Ben-Gurion and then return to Cairo, when it might be possible for Egypt to reach an understanding "with the United Nations, you understand."

This interview was followed by a discussion with the Foreign Minister that occupied an entire afternoon. Fawzi's capacity for talking much and saying little and Hammarskjold's incisive brilliance when confronted by intricate intellectual exercises instilled in both men a sense of challenge. As soon as Hammarskjold made an unambiguous proposal, Fawzi sidled off into strange Arabian byways of thought, while the fascinated Hammarskjold followed intently, patiently waiting for the dead end in which the Foreign Minister would have to make a commitment. Heads low, voices subdued, the duel absorbed them both, and when it was over Hammarskjold returned to reality with an abiding sympathy for what he later described as "the struggle of these people toward a goal of peace and self-respect."

This birth of sympathy with the Arabs matured as the United Nations became increasingly involved in the intrigues of the Middle East. Hammarskjold visited potentates, prime ministers, and presidents, all of whom entertained him lavishly in magnificent surroundings, catering to his vanity with Oriental grace and skill.

It was different in Israel.

They sat facing each other across the enormous desk: Ben-

Gurion in open-necked shirt, and Hammarskjold immaculately blue-suited as always.

"If you withdraw your people, the Egyptians will go too. We'll take over from there."

"What makes you think Nasser will withdraw?" asked Ben-Gurion.

"I have his word."

Ben-Gurion said Israel was in the area because it suspected that the Egyptians would use the roads for an attack. It was all a question of controlling a strategic point along the Israeli-Egyptian border.

After considerable argument, Ben-Gurion asked what the United Nations would do if he agreed to withdraw. Hammarskjold replied that he would know that when he had spoken with General Burns and United Nations advisers in New York. "It will be for the Security Council to decide," he said. "At the moment it's a matter of reason. . . . "

"Reason!" Ben-Gurion broke in. "We have looked to the United Nations for reason for six years." He asked how Hammarskjold would care to sit in the Prime Minister's chair, responsible for a nation whose borders were lined with guns.

Hammarskjold had travelled too quickly from the insidious sensuality of Fawzi's subtle wit to the frank belligerence of a nation literally growing out of the earth. Although his relationship with Ben-Gurion developed subsequently into one of mutual respect tinged with grudging admiration, he retained the vague impression of one side being highly civilised, the other raw and unrefined.

After Hammarskjold subsequently left Cairo, the World Bank arrived, represented by its president, Eugene Black, who was accompanied by his engineering consultant, General R. A. W. Wheeler, lately of the United States army. Had the two groups overlapped, Wheeler would have met the Secretary General, who was to hire him ten months later to clear the Suez Canal.

The exploratory Anglo-American offer of a joint $70 million for the first year of construction for the Aswan Dam had no political strings attached, but it was dependent upon Nasser's compliance with the normal loan procedures of the Bank, which was considering Egypt's request for an advance of $200 million. Mr. Black's conditions were reasonable: evidence of ability to repay the loan over sixteen years, Wheeler's approval of the engineering plan, Egypt's undertaking to place the contracts open to international tender, and negotiated treaties with other riparian states interested in the Nile's headwaters.

But the climate of the deal was changing drastically. M. Solod, Soviet Ambassador to Cairo, had stated that if the West were to fail in providing financial assistance to Egypt, the Soviet Union would step in; and it was clear that despite Nasser's silence, the dam had become a test of strength in the economic struggle between East and West. For a week Wheeler studied plans of the dam project while Black patiently explained the sort of information he required before he could authorize a loan of such size. Nasser and Dr. Kaissouni brushed the conditions aside, demanding an outright lump-sum loan based not upon guarantees, but upon the faith of the World Bank in Egypt's future. The Egyptian press and radio, by contrived coincidence, broadcast news that the Soviet Union was not only willing to match the West's offer, but would supply the entire capital investment – $1,300 million. Black, however, was more perturbed by an official statement issued by the Sudanese government stating that it had not been approached by the Egyptian government and would not agree to the construction of a dam without prior agreement on the distribution of the Nile waters. Nor would he promise an outright loan; it would have to be spread over the period of construction, at the rate of about $15 million a year.

To Nasser this method of supplying money by instalments was deliberately designed to create the threat that payments might stop if he followed political policies contrary to the West's interests. He wanted the entire loan at once so that if the West didn't like what he did in the future, there would be no financial stick with which to beat him.

As the World Bank officials left Cairo, Nasser was quoted as saying that the West had undertaken to grant the loan, and he was considering the possibility of inviting the Soviet Union to participate to an equal extent. The only agreement as far as Black was concerned had been a decision to resume the talks in Washington when the Egyptian government felt able to comply with the safeguards he required.

Dulles and Eden, however, shared a growing distaste for being blackmailed into a project that promised little in return by way of future friendship or co-operation.

When testifying before the Senate foreign relations and armed forces committees in 1957, Byroade said: "I have heard the Secretary of State say that he felt getting into an agreement of this duration, which would place a tremendous burden on the Egyptian economy over fifteen years, because you see, three-fourths of the costs would have been borne by them, he felt that the austerity they would have to go through was probably such that there would be a tendency to blame others and particularly us for their troubles."

It was time for a reassessment of the West's relations with the Arab world, Egypt in particular. Temperatures in other areas of conflict having cooled down to a more normal state of inactive hostility, there was an opportunity to co-ordinate Anglo-American policies.

There were, as well, more personal reasons why Prime Minister Sir Anthony Eden and President Eisenhower should wish to meet. The President faced a summer and fall election campaign in which he wished to make peace the major issue; and Eden, after only nine months in office, looked as if he might not survive a further nine months.

II

—————

WHEN Eden moved to Downing Street, his earlier role in the British decision to abandon the Suez Canal Zone inspired some moderate Conservative newspapers to comment that he would make "the diplomacy and actions of his country cease to be objects of hatred and suspicion among Asians, Arabs, and Africans." But the extreme right wing of the party never forgave him for negotiating the withdrawal, and if they remained dutifully silent while he adjusted himself to his new responsibilities, the honeymoon was abruptly ended by Nasser's arms deal with the Soviet Union. The violent fiasco in Jordan brought their opposition into the open, and a barrage of bitter criticism was unleashed on the excuse that because of Eden's indecisiveness Britain was being maligned and insulted by an upstart Egyptian.

Eden was particularly sensitive to charges of appeasement. There was in the Conservative party cupboard a skeleton named Munich and no one felt its presence more anxiously than the Prime Minister. With all other Tories he was grimly resolved that should a future crisis ever resemble Munich, the Conservative party would seize the opportunity to erase the stigma of the past.

Britain entered 1956 not knowing quite where she stood in a world in which her good intentions were being battered as if everything she did were bad. Withdrawal from empire brought in its wake hate and insolence instead of gratitude; there was supposed to be a Commonwealth, but the behaviour of India and South Africa indicated the ties were flimsy. Eden had announced Britain would build H-bombs, but the British people were not quite sure why, because although politicians talked about the deterrent, it had yet to be explained in viable terms. Life had become extremely difficult under Sir Anthony Eden, and as a result his own party turned on him.

The London *Daily Telegraph* fired the opening broadside

with an editorial saying: "There is a favourite gesture of the Prime Minister's. . . . To emphasize a point he will clench one fist to smack the open palm of the other hand – but the smack is seldom heard. Most Conservatives, and almost certainly some of the wiser trade union leaders, are waiting to feel the smack of firm government."

Another Conservative newspaper said: "Too many events are wrapped up in uncertainty and indecisiveness. . . ." *The Times* complained that a "lost grip . . . had to be recovered."

Selwyn Lloyd had been the Minister of State at the Foreign Office who had helped Eden negotiate the withdrawal from Suez, so that now, as Foreign Secretary, he was coupled with Eden in the attack.

A rumour that Eden was about to resign drew a formal denial from Downing Street, an unprecedented step for a British Prime Minister so recently elected. Criticism broadened toward the end of the month, and one commentator wrote: "Conservative M.P.s will scarcely go on enduring with equanimity the surrender, one after the other, of all their cherished positions at home and abroad."

Sir Anthony was under siege. He could exchange his moderate foreign policy of friendly persuasion for a tough, Dulles-type approach to difficult opponents such as Nasser; he could also produce a defence policy showing that even under the shadow of the deterrent Britain still had a Big Power role to play; and then he could proclaim that there would be no further hasty retreats from overseas possessions. Or he could resign.

In this uncertain political climate, the Prime Minister and Foreign Secretary of Great Britain set sail for the United States, determined to return with a grand alignment of Anglo-American policies clearly stated in some sort of majestic manifesto expressing the might and nobility of their joint purpose. They needed above all else from President Eisenhower and Dulles an undertaking to demonstrate the credibility of the Tripartite Declaration by a show of force and resolution in the Middle East. Eden had convinced himself by then that to counter Soviet penetration effectively, to reduce the risk of an arms race, and to quiet Israeli fears would require forthright reaffirmation that the United States and Britain would intervene quickly and decisively should there be an outbreak of hostilities in the area.

To prepare the ground for the diplomatic achievements ahead, he sent an advance message to President Eisenhower that said: "I am not suggesting anything so grandiloquent as the Atlantic Charter, but something which shows . . . the West has its own message to give."

Eisenhower was fond of Eden. They had worked together almost continuously since 1942, and he referred to him as "my friend Anthony." In fundamental political thinking they were much in sympathy with each other, but in terms of national policies they were wide apart. Nowhere was the division between them more sharply defined than in their respective views of events in the Middle East.

The President liked Nasser's behaviour no more than did the Prime Minister, but he was wholeheartedly behind Dulles in the conviction that the United States should not stand in the path of emergent nationalisms, providing they were not artificially created by Communist subversion. He would countenance no display of Western strength nor approve any aggressively worded communiqué that might be construed as a threat to the Arabs. He was deeply influenced by what he called world opinion, which was really American opinion, and, as the British leaders arrived in Washington, American opinion was certainly not pro-Jewish, even if it was not obviously pro-Arab.

On the first day of their meetings at the White House, the four statesmen deadlocked. Using the dubious excuse of requiring the approval of Congress before he could deploy troops, the President killed Eden's proposal for a Tripartite show of force. Nor would he agree to a communiqué on this issue referring to anything stronger than "increased dangers." He would give no public undertaking that the United States would be prepared to act under the terms of the Tripartite Declaration, even in the event of an Arab-Israeli war.

Eden tried to persuade the President to act on an issue that Dulles had persistently avoided – the question of Saudi-Arabian financing of political agitation in Jordan and Iraq. Eisenhower merely agreed that the United States would do what it could to encourage King Saud to use his money to improve the living standards of his own people rather than distribute it among anarchists. Eden's message to the British cabinet, covering the discussions on Egypt, said: "We agreed that the future of our policy in the Middle East depended to a considerable extent on Nasser. If he showed himself willing to co-operate with us, we should reciprocate. The Americans thought that the present talks about the Aswan Dam with Mr. Black might indicate his state of mind."

When the relationship between foreign policies and nuclear weapons was discussed, Dulles reaffirmed his belief in massive retaliation, saying: "It stays good until they can hit us harder than we can hit them, and that's not going to happen in the proximate future."

The conference ended with the release of a declaration, which the two principals and their Secretaries of State flourished enthusiastically, but which in all probability the State Department and Foreign Office hoped would be quickly forgotten. It said that the two governments would "maintain human rights," defend them if they were imperilled, and "peacefully restore them" should they be temporarily lost. The declaration of Washington, upon which Sir Anthony Eden was counting to restore his own human right to rule Britain, was totally devoid of meaning.

On their return to London, Eden and Selwyn Lloyd were placed on the defensive during a Commons debate on foreign affairs as, in reference to the Washington declaration, one word was heard from both sides of the House with ominous frequency – fatuous.

Having waited so long to become Prime Minister, Eden had the misfortune to occupy the office at a time when Britain was weary of being the whipping boy for all the world's ills. The British people wanted to speak with the United States and the Soviet Union on equal terms and now, just as they had at last recovered from postwar apathy to reach a new height of confidence and strength, the advent of thermonuclear weapons threatened to relegate them back to a second-class status again.

Conservative newspapers joined in the general applause when Aneurin Bevan, speaking from the Socialist front benches in the House of Commons on Britain's weakness, said: "The ordinary man and woman is beginning spiritually to contract out of the quarrel." This was the malaise, a national sense of frustration and futility.

Powerful and persuasive pressures converged upon Eden. His initiative in taking Britain out of Suez now appeared as appeasement of Nasser, who was considered by the majority of the British press to be either a neo-Nazi or a crypto-Communist. Nasser was said to be working against British interests everywhere in the Middle East, yet Eden had so far declined to administer the fearsome, magisterial rebukes which British governments had always issued to control the lusts of petty tyrants. He blamed the United States for the lack of any effective counter to Soviet penetration of the area because he thought Dulles incapable of distinguishing Communism from pseudo-nationalism. Without United States support, he could not threaten, and even if he could he was uncertain of the sort of force he might commit himself to use. Military force as an instrument of national policy had become downright dangerous, and were he to attempt a reoccupation of the Canal Zone in strength, he could not rely upon Washington to protect him against a deluge of Soviet missiles with the umbrella of massive retaliation.

He had no convincing reply to the charge that, having decided to build nuclear weapons, he was still too weak to deter the Egyptian from stripping of their prestige the few Arab leaders remaining loyal to the West. His critics were already portraying him as the Prime Minister who accepted the role, declined by Churchill, of liquidating the British Empire.

Twenty years before, Eden had himself received a cruelly personal lesson in the cynical jobbery of international politics when, as a youthful foreign secretary, it had not occurred to him that any statesman with a shred of honour or decency would do business with Mussolini. The discovery that Prime Minister Chamberlain was actually treating with Mussolini behind his back, to the extent of sending a personal envoy to meet Italian diplomats in London taxis, proved a shattering experience. By naïvely underestimating the Italian, he had exposed himself to trickery; so he came to hate Mussolini.

By March he was beginning to think of Nasser in this context, wondering vaguely if he had been tricked again, whether Nasser's unexpected willingness to reach agreement on the Suez withdrawal had been inspired by the intent to clear the way for the entry of Communism and the march against Israel. If this were the case, as his opponents implied, then he had inexcusably underestimated another dictator whose word was meaningless. Hatred stirred again; and it was to harden as each and every blow to his confidence and pride fell in rapid succession.

The only effect of the declaration of Washington on Middle East leaders was to reveal the lack of unity among the Tripartite powers and to make dismally clear that there would be no display of Western strength. Propaganda broadcasts resumed, with Radio Cairo and Radio Damascus aiming their repeated incitements to riot and revolt at North Africa and Jordan, where the ex-Palestinian politicians and the "Society of Free Officers" were closing in around General Glubb and King Hussein.

III

THE propaganda attack on Glubb was malevolent and personal. For six weeks Cairo and Damascus broadcast non-stop radio programs charging that Glubb was the real ruler of Jordan, that his Arab Legion was there to stamp out freedom. In their eyes he represented the rule of the Pasha puppets and symbolized Arab domination by foreign masters. Hussein, whose ambivalent conduct in later years showed him to be capable of switching nationalism on and off when it suited his purpose, capitulated, choosing to preserve his throne on this occasion by joining the nationalists against Glubb. On March 1, the officer who had sustained Hussein's authority for seventeen years was summarily dismissed and given less than twenty-four hours to get out of Jordan. When the British Ambassador called at the palace for an explanation, Hussein waved a copy of a London magazine at him and shouted petulantly that the Englishman was trying to rule his people.

The next day, after Glubb flew from Amman to Cyprus, the leader of the "Free Officers" was revealed to be Hussein's personal aide-de-camp, Colonel Abu Nuwar, who insisted that he replace Glubb as commander of the Legion and be appointed Chief of Staff of the National Guard, a dual position which made him the military strong man of Jordan.

The repercussions of Glubb's dismissal reverberated through the Baghdad Pact capitals, through London, and eventually reached Washington. Nuri Birgi, Director General of the Turkish Foreign Office, told the British, French, and American ambassadors in Ankara that his government believed Nasser to be far too untrustworthy and ambitious to be shored up with economic assistance such as the West proposed with the Aswan Dam loan. He claimed that the evidence of Russian co-operation with Nasser was too overwhelming to be ignored, and quoted President Chamoun of Lebanon as saying: "Our time will come. The Russians and Egyptians are busy among the people. We will not be able to resist without strong support from the West."

At a council meeting of the Baghdad Pact members, the Pakistani delegate asked the United States observer if his government fully recognized the threat to the Middle East and received no reply; Iraq's Nuri es-Said, addressing his remarks in the same direction, suggested that the region could be politically stabilized if the United States government would exert pressure on Aramco to suspend the payment of royalties to King Saud for six months. Again there was no reply.

The dismissal of Glubb was unfortunately timed for Britain. Selwyn Lloyd had decided earlier to take the initiative by visiting Cairo for exploratory talks with the Egyptian dictator. Nasser had assured Sir Humphrey Trevelyan that the propaganda broadcasts against Glubb and Jordan would stop during the Foreign Secretary's stay in Egypt. When Lloyd arrived in Cairo the broadcasts were in full blast, their virulence accentuated rather than diminished.

As there could be no common ground between Nasser and Lloyd, there was no surprise on either side that the talks should prove fruitless. On March 1 they dined together at Abdin Palace for a last review of the unresolved issues before Lloyd left Cairo for Bahrein, a British-administered oil base on the Persian Gulf. Lloyd can be blunt, and over dinner he reiterated his view that the volume of hate propaganda being hurled at Glubb and Hussein in Jordan might bring a strong reaction from the British government. He pointedly remarked that in democracies public opinion could on occasion demand action, and he could assure his host that if driven too far, the British government would not shirk its duty.

Nasser replied that there was no reason for Britain to become incensed over matters that should be of no concern to anyone but Arabs. Glubb's position, and that of the Legion, occupied much of their discussion, and Lloyd suggested that

Nasser should not underestimate British influence in the Middle East as: "We still have Glubb and the Legion." Nasser apparently chose this moment to inform Lloyd that Glubb had been dismissed that afternoon and should be on his way out of Jordan.

Lloyd was too self-disciplined to allow the full extent of the shock he must have felt to show itself. It was a bitter moment for the Foreign Minister, only recently appointed to his office and as yet unfamiliar with the minor problems of a lingering empire. He returned to London and replied to a question asking what he thought of Nasser with one word: "Mussolini." He was the first British cabinet minister to make up his mind that Nasser presented as much of a threat to Britain as the dead German and Italian dictators had done, and that Britain would eventually have to choose between passive acceptance of a never-ending procession of provocations and indignities, and action designed to place Nasser in a straitjacket.

Eden, moving toward the same conclusion and already detesting the demagogue in Cairo, was jolted even more severely when Nasser followed up his victory over Glubb with an offer to replace the British subsidy to Jordan with $60 million a year to be provided by Egypt, Syria, and Saudi Arabia. As Egypt and Syria were economically incapable of sustaining this sort of annual burden, and the Saudis were unlikely to feel any obligation to support a Hashemite monarchy, Hussein recognized that his new-found nationalism was being tested, that there was no intention of giving him money. But someone else was waiting in the wings, ready and willing to hand out gold.

The Soviet Ambassador in Cairo called on the Jordanian Chargé d'Affaires to offer Jordan all the financial and military assistance it required "as a gesture of friendship."

The Soviet Union was not merely supplying arms to Egypt; it appeared in London that Soviet diplomats were collaborating with Nasser to subvert a weaker Arab state from Western connections. This was the first of three developments that combined to convince Eden beyond all reasonable doubt that Nasser was not simply a misguided nationalist, but an active, ambitious expansionist in partnership with Communism to further his own hegemony in the Middle East.

In all likelihood the second development affected Eden deeply, as it amounted to a palace revolt by the Foreign Office against his policies. A strongly worded analysis of British misfortunes in the Middle East said that if a link between Soviet subversion and Egyptian ambitions existed it had been brought about by the lack of Western leadership. After criticising American and British policies and saying that if weakness, division, and vacillation were to continue, the area could be expected to develop as Communist at worst, neutralist at best, it concluded: ". . . the division between the Arab states is widened by the conflict between policy originating in London and that which originates in Washington. . . . We have reached the position in which the United States actively supports one side, while Britain supports the other."

It would be the third development that would have had a decisive influence on Eden. An intelligence analysis of current Middle East developments said that since the arrival of Communist arms in the Middle East, Israel had been preparing for war. This was not unusual, the analysis said, as Israel was permanently prepared for an Arab attack and indeed might welcome one under different circumstances. However, the arrival of the Soviet arms had introduced the danger of Israel's fighting a preventive war – an accurate warning as, despite public statements to the contrary, Israeli leaders were then planning such a war.

The government was advised to consider that in the event of hostilities Egypt could respond to British intervention by closing the Suez Canal and denying oil supplies to Western Europe. The analysis warned that even a state of hostile peace could be prolonged to the point where Arab states might employ the threat of nationalisation of oil fields or of the Suez

Canal as political weapons against the West generally. On the other hand, any delay in hostilities would be to Britain's benefit, as there were indications that the United States was moving away from a pro-Egyptian policy, though not necessarily away from pro-Arabism.

Then came the shock. Washington and London had believed that Egypt had agreed to pay $150 million in cotton for Communist arms, and Syria $50 million. It was now confirmed that contracted payments were actually $450 million and $100 million respectively.

Nasser had been deliberately evasive when he announced the deal, so there was no question of deception. But Eden felt he had been somehow deceived, and when he exchanged messages with Eisenhower and Dulles, he thought they shared his misgivings.

The first sign that Eden had decided to instil a tough, no-more-retreat element into British policy came when Cyprus terrorists murdered British civilians. Two days later, he intervened personally to order the deportation of the Cypriot leader, Archbishop Makarios, to the Seychelles Islands in the Indian Ocean. For the first time since taking office, he was described by a majority of newspapers as being capable of strong, decisive action. Under what today appears to have been an obsessive compulsion to rid himself and the government of the lingering spectre of Munich and appeasement, confident that Dulles was becoming increasingly disenchanted with Egypt, and bitterly aware that the office he had coveted for so long might be lost before he had proved himself capable of holding it, he accepted wholly and without reservation Selwyn Lloyd's view that Nasser was another and more dangerous Mussolini or Hitler who would have to be "restricted and brought down by internal revolt if possible, by external action if necessary."

Makarios had been exiled, and it was time to come to grips with another troublemaker. Eden's determination was expressed on April 24 when, no longer suppliant, the Foreign

Office was instructed to inform the State Department and the Quai d'Orsay that "Her Majesty's government considers the restoration of political stability in the Middle East region to be of paramount importance and is resolved to make every effort in this direction."

IV

AT the end of January 1956, four men met in Paris at the office of the Foreign Minister: Pineau himself, Defence Minister Bourgès-Maunoury, and his *chef de cabinet*, Abel Thomas, another youthful ex-army officer who shared his Minister's determination to crush the Algerian rebels, and Shimon Peres, envoy extraordinary from the Holy Land.

Peres briefed the French leaders on Nasser's suspected strength and ambitions and on the relative military capability of the Israeli defence forces. Peres ranged over the political-military implications of the outbreaks of violence plaguing North Africa and the Middle East, linked them to the clandestine activities of the Egyptian government, and convincingly portrayed Nasser as the principal enemy of France and Israel.

He concluded with the warning that Israel might have to fight, but if so, and Nasser was defeated, then France would find a solution in Algeria easier to negotiate. For such a situation, France should provide the arms and Israel would do the shooting.

"What do you need?" asked Bourgès-Maunoury.

Peres handed him copies of a list and, while the two defence chiefs studied them, Pineau said: "You realize that we are bound by regulations governing the export of arms. We have also the machinery of the Tripartite Declaration and our contributions to NATO to consider."

Pineau remarked further that France, while sympathising with Israel and being prepared to help, would first make every effort to reach a settlement with Egypt by diplomatic means. There would be no objections, however, to military talks continuing in the meantime.

Peres was content, and after arrangements had been made for him to discuss detailed plans for arms deliveries with Abel Thomas, the conference ended. At a higher level, the fraternal brotherhood of international socialism was brought into play between Ben-Gurion and Guy Mollet, to give the embryonic alliance political purpose and respectability. When Ben-Gurion explained in one letter that Israel's cities were now vulnerable to Nasser's Soviet jet bombers, Mollet burst out to Pineau: "My God, whatever happens, we can't allow that" – a remark he was to repeat again and again with increasing vehemence.

Whatever doubts might have existed about the wisdom of France's becoming so involved with Israel's military preparations, they were quickly dispelled in March when events combined to convince Mollet and Pineau that Nasser would have to be brought to heel or overthrown.

A document said to prove that the Algerian rebels had set up headquarters in Cairo was found in the possession of a captured Arab leader; and in the propaganda furore that followed, Cairo Radio boasted that the Egyptian Army had made training facilities available to "our Arab brothers fighting the imperialists in Algeria."

On March 12 Mollet visited England, spent a day with Eden, and later announced that Britain and France would ask the United States to join them "so that we can present a common front to the problems of Colonel Nasser." Behind this oblique statement was one of those fortuitous moments in history when human frailty directs and dominates the events it creates.

Mollet informed Eden that France would seek a settlement in Algeria, providing it would not give the rebels the satisfaction of being able to say "they had kicked us out." The main obstacle to an honourable settlement, he said, was the constant active incitement of the rebels to violent refusal of anything but France's abject surrender. He expressed concern at the plight of Israel now that Egypt's military strength had been immeasurably increased, and then said, "They are in extreme danger. France would be failing in her duty if she did not extend all possible to help."

To Mollet's surprise, Eden not merely endorsed his policy but indicated that for the first time in twenty years there was little difference in the attitudes of their respective countries toward the Middle East. Eden's only reservation was to ask Mollet not to undertake any major action in North Africa or the Middle East without first attempting to persuade "our American allies to bring their policies into line with ours." It was important, he said, that the Arabs should be shown that the Western powers would not be trifled with "by an upstart like Nasser."

Mollet returned to Paris brimming with confidence. Pineau, attending a conference of South East Asia Treaty Organization foreign ministers in Karachi, had met Dulles and was anything but confident in the extent of United States support France might receive. After formal introduction at the conference itself, they had met privately late one evening at the French Embassy, and, as often happened on such occasions, Dulles delivered his standard sermon on anti-Communism. The sophisticated Pineau didn't agree at all and said so pungently.

"I think your policy is negative, and the results to date seem to prove it," said Pineau.

"For us Americans," replied Dulles, "there are only two things that count – Christianity and the free enterprise social system. We will fight to the death to defend our Christianity and to defend what we call economic liberty."

"I believe you would," said Pineau. "But we are in Karachi, for instance. The people at this conference are not Christians, but Mussulmans and Buddhists. Consequently, your Christian faith does not interest them. As for free enterprise" – and here the Socialist emerged – "it might work in a highly developed industrial country such as the United States, but it has no meaning whatsoever for underdeveloped countries."

"No," said Dulles. "Yours is the shortsighted viewpoint. In the long run these people can be made to respect Christianity and enjoy the benefits of a competitive society."

"You mean, they should have the freedom to do what we want them to do," said Pineau. "There are Christians, you know, who find it difficult to see the benefits of competitive poverty."

"We don't have poverty on any scale worth mentioning in America," said Dulles. "We have a saying that any man who's worth his salt can make a buck."

Pineau, mildly shocked, said: "The only valid arguments to these people, ones which might attract them away from the sham of Communism, are those of political liberty, individual liberty, and social security. We're not going to get anywhere in Africa and Asia by defending religions that don't interest them and capitalism, which is entirely unknown to them."

Pineau left Karachi for New Delhi, where he spent two days with Pandit Nehru discussing Algeria. He made it clear to Nehru that France wished for a peaceful solution but would not submit to revolt and violence aroused mostly from Egypt. He stressed the grave consequences of Egyptian intervention and asked Nehru for an opinion on Nasser and his aims. Nehru suggested he stop off in Cairo en route home to see the Egyptian personally, and offered to pave the way by recommending to Nasser that in the interests of peace he abandon active assistance to the Algerian rebels. Pineau agreed, and on March 14 arrived in Cairo for his first meeting with a man he half-suspected already of being a dictator in the same mould as Mussolini or Hitler.

They talked for most of a day, Nasser insisting that Egypt

was not helping the Algerian rebels while Pineau pointed out that Cairo Radio was inciting them to further sacrifice and violence every day, that there was evidence of rebel officers being trained in Egypt by the Egyptian Army, and that Egyptian arms were trickling into Algeria.

Since the overthrow of Farouk, Nasser had inculcated into the army's officer corps the notion that the most sacred of all oaths was "A soldier's word of honour." Now, as his talk with Pineau came to an end, he suddenly rose to his feet, walked across to his guest, and thrust out his hand, saying: "I give you my soldier's word of honour that the only aid I shall ever give to Algerians will be moral support. I cannot give less to my Arab brothers. No material aid of any sort, however, will be given either in Egypt or by Egypt. I count on France to seek a just solution."

Pineau also rose, with a barked comment. "I thank you for your word. Your actions, however, will mean much more in France."

He left Cairo in a mood of deep gloom, unimpressed by Nasser or his word, unenthusiastic about Nasser's personality, and unhappily certain that the most important results of his trip were that Nasser could not be trusted and that Dulles could not be counted upon as being sympathetic to French interests in the Algerian conflict.

Shadowy impressions, vague thoughts, began to take the form and substance of a course of action as he flew to Paris, and by the time he arrived at the Quai d'Orsay he could see sharply focused objectives.

In Pineau's estimation, Nasser's weakness was the Egyptian army, which, well-armed with Soviet equipment, might soon demand the right to erase the stigma of earlier defeats at the hands of the Israelis by seeking a sudden, vengeful victory. Nasser might find it hard to control his glory-hunting officers, and if so, the attack Shimon Peres had warned as inevitable in Israeli eyes might indeed be launched. If it were, and if it failed, what would be the consequences for Nasser? Pineau, thinking he knew the answer, arranged a meeting at the Prime Minister's office at the Hotel Matignon, which only he, Mollet, and Bourgès-Maunoury attended.

He proposed, and they agreed, that the Israeli military mission to Paris should discuss with French staff officers what was needed in terms of arms. This would result in an official list which could be approved at the NATO Council meeting due to be held the next month. At the same time, Peres and Thomas should compile a secret list on which all the items on the official list would be duplicated. Together the two lists would ensure that if Egypt attacked, Israel would have the means to resist.

The danger of this arrangement was that Israel might also feel strong enough to attack Egypt.

CHAPTER FOUR

Calculated Insult

EACH message from Cairo had the effect of a physical blow on Dulles. Communist arms, cash, technical aid, construction engineers, purchasing agents, missile scientists, cultural impresarios, military advisers – all were streaming into Egypt. Diplomatic representation from Communist-bloc countries grew in size as communities of their nationals blossomed down the Nile, the Soviet Embassy alone swelling from a staff of forty to more than a hundred and fifty. By the spring of 1956, up to two thousand specialists of one sort or another had arrived in Egypt from Communist countries. Under these circumstances Dulles became uncertain about the wisdom of the Aswan Dam loan.

This was the first major East-West encounter in the economic field, in which the weapons were cash, time-payment plans, and interest rates. Curiously, it was not the idea of buying alliances that appalled Dulles so much as the unbusinesslike methods of the opposition. If he had to go into battle as a banker, he felt at least the rules should include certain safeguards and a respectable rate of interest.

Nasser's word was the sole security for the loan. Egypt's

cotton crop was mortgaged for years ahead in the arms deal, and its economy was even unable to meet other commitments to the Communist bloc or anyone else. There was no guarantee that the money would be used for the dam and no visible means of repayment, yet if Washington turned down the loan, the Soviet Union might provide it. On the other hand, if the loan were made the uncommitted nations might quickly interpret Nasser's success as meaning the United States could be black-mailed, that guns from Russia could be paid for with cash from the United States.

Dulles dictated a letter to the World Bank saying the United States expected adequate assurances from Egypt that loans intended specifically for the Aswan project would "not be used for other unstated purposes," and then set off for the NATO Council meeting in Paris.

During the conference he discussed with Pineau and Selwyn Lloyd the problem of sustaining the validity of the Tripartite Declaration in the face of Communist arms pouring into Egypt and Syria. Typically, he declined to say either that the United States would refuse further Arab requests for arms or that it would attempt to maintain the balance of Middle East power by supplying arms to Israel.

When Pineau, using the sort of forthright language of which Dulles despaired, informed him curtly that France intended to supply arms to Israel, he merely asked to what extent. He surprised Pineau further by nodding vigorously with approval as he scanned quickly a summary of the "official" list specially prepared for the occasion.

After Pineau made formal announcement of a Franco-Israeli arms deal at the Council meeting next day, Dulles went a step further by informing Canada's Secretary of State for External Affairs, Lester Pearson, that he would not object if Canada sold Sabre jet interceptors to Israel. The astonished Pearson asked politely if he recalled that Canada had imposed an embargo on the sale of arms to Middle East countries at the request of the United States and Britain. Dulles replied offhandedly that circumstances had changed and he was sure it would do no harm if the few Sabres redundant to Canadian requirements were made available to Israel.

He generously "sold" other people's arms to Israel for the duration of the conference, then returned to Washington leaving behind the distinct impression that as far as the United States was concerned it was open season on Nasser. Later, when he had to deny publicly that the United States had switched to a pro-Israel and anti-Arab policy, he complained to Washington diplomats that "I didn't mean for people to go around implicating the United States in this arms business."

"Perhaps not," was the dry comment of Hans Engen, Norway's permanent delegate to the United Nations, "but you forgot to tell anyone."

While Dulles was indulging in oddly out-of-character activities in Paris, the Soviet leaders, Bulganin and Khrushchev, were on an official visit in Britain. Between the public antics, there were serious discussions at Downing Street in which the Middle East had priority. Eden's account says:

"I told the Russians that the uninterrupted supply of oil was literally vital to our economy. They showed an understanding of our interest and appeared to be willing to meet it. I said I thought I must be absolutely blunt about the oil, because we would fight for it . . . that we had no intention of being strangled to death. . . . Later events showed that the Russians heeded this warning and understood our position pretty well."

The combination of reports from Paris revealing that the Tripartite powers were agreed on supplying arms to Israel, and others from London indicating that British determination to maintain stability in the Middle East had deeply impressed the Russians, sparked off a violent reaction from Nasser. With what was obviously intended as a dramatic gesture of defiance, he withdrew Egyptian recognition of Nationalist China, recalled his diplomatic representatives from Formosa, and formally announced Egypt's recognition of Red China.

Dulles dismissed this move as "meaningless spite," but President Eisenhower felt it warranted a paternal warning. "We think Egypt is mistaken," he said, "but a single unwelcome act by another nation should not destroy friendship for that nation any more than spats within a family should lead to a divorce court."

Nasser expressed his contempt for this gentle homily with an announcement that he intended to make a state visit to Peking, that he had invited Chou En-Lai to Cairo, and that he would be sending Egyptian Defence Minister Amer to China for military conferences.

A few days later the government-owned newspaper, *Al Gomhouria*, published in Cairo the official reason for recognizing the Peking government. "In the Anglo-Soviet talks in London," it said, "Britain tried to tie a noose round the neck of the Arab states by attempting to persuade the Soviet Union to stop supplying Egypt with arms. Colonel Nasser has now put the noose round Eden's own neck. The People's Republic of China is the biggest producer of armaments outside the United Nations and can therefore supply us with all the arms we require without the restrictions and conditions of Western embargoes. Let the Americans and the British and the French supply Israel with arms, and Egypt will get two guns for every one sent to this colonist state of America."

Nasser, having spurned British friendship, having broken his "soldier's word" to France by allowing the Algerian rebels to set up headquarters in Cairo, was now alienating his most persevering friend in the West, the United States.

II

NASSER ranked abroad with such uncommitted statesmen as Nehru, Tito, and Sukarno. With powerful friends in Moscow, New Delhi, and Peking, he could afford to further indulge in the same bold, reckless gambles that had resulted in the arms deal.

Early in 1956 he introduced the term "Egyptianisation" and privately instructed his Council of Ministers to prepare for the Egyptianisation of foreign-owned companies. To avoid frightening away foreign investment, they were to let it be known that the process merely entailed an increase in the percentage of Egyptian staff employed by each individual company. The pressure on the Canal Company to hire more Egyptian pilots was part of this process.

Oil companies, the international shipping federation, and a dozen or so governments whose ships were principal users were concerned over the fact that traffic was increasing annually to such an extent that the canal would require extensive enlargement to handle it. Decisions could not wait for the concession to end, but the company would not pay an improvement cost estimated at $500 million if the canal was to be nationalised in 1968, and the Egyptian government had no right to undertake the work until 1968 even if it had the money.

Talks between the government and the company, aimed at reaching a decision on the canal's future, reached the stage where Egyptian insistence that the company should hire more Egyptian pilots and Egyptian engineers was taken by the company to mean that some sort of co-operative arrangement might emerge. It commissioned EBASCO (Electric Board and Share Company Services, Inc.), engineering consultants of New York, to undertake a traffic study and recommend the most feasible method of dealing with projected improvements, with the intention of submitting the report to the government as a basis for joint action.

But it seems possible that Nasser had by then already decided to take over the canal and build the improvements himself if he could persuade the World Bank to provide the funds.

When Eugene Black visited Cairo to discuss the Aswan Dam project, Finance Minister Kaissouni told him, "We have got to talk with you about the Suez Canal. We are going to need a lot of money to expand it."

"When will this be?" asked Black.

"Oh, some day," replied Kaissouni.

"Then let's stick to what you want now," said Black. "We are already talking about a little loan of $200 million. So we don't need to tackle more than one [loan] at a time."

The significance of this exchange, which Black subsequently reported to his directors, was that even while the Minister of Commerce was supposedly negotiating with the company toward a mutually advantageous arrangement for the future administration of the canal, and while Foreign Minister Fawzi was informing M. Charles-Roux that the company's concession would be extended, Finance Minister Kaissouni was sounding out the World Bank for a loan the government would need only if it intended to take over the canal.

It was the one mention of the canal made to Mr. Black during the Aswan negotiations, yet Fawzi used it as an excuse to summon the British, French, and American ambassadors to a conference on the canal's future.

"We have reached agreement with the oil companies on what should be done to enlarge the canal," he said. "We have also had encouraging talks with Mr. Black of the World Bank concerning the financing of these improvements. Egypt is confident that the enlarged canal as we see it will be the occasion for many more years of fruitful co-operation between our nations. This vast enterprise will forge another link between Egypt and the Western powers."

The diplomats could interpret this statement either as an expression of the government's intention to co-operate with the Canal Company in a joint expansion program, or as an indication that Egypt would take over management of the canal after 1968. They were unaware that Mr. Black had declined even to discuss the canal, and that the Egyptian government had neither sought the opinions of the oil companies nor been approached by them.

In May a British Foreign Office official said, "We are aware of the importance of making satisfactory arrangements for the future of the canal. Before then we shall certainly want to discuss the matter with the Egyptian government, but the first step is to obtain some idea of the physical and commercial nature of the problem which is likely to exist in 1968. The Suez Canal Company is now undertaking a careful study of this problem."

He was referring to the engineering study by EBASCO then in process, but it hardly satisfied some British members of Parliament, one of whom made a speech saying that as Nasser's conduct gave nobody grounds for confidence in him, the British government should act with France and the United States to ensure a satisfactory settlement of the canal's future.

A senior member of the military junta, Colonel Sadat, issued a statement saying that the canal was an integral part of Egypt, and "Egypt will not allow the canal to provide a gap threatening the sovereignty and independence of the country. Britain should keep her nose out of Egyptian affairs."

Further discussion in the House of Commons inspired Nasser to react with a statement to American correspondents saying: "The Suez Canal will eventually become Egyptian property. Britain is trying to prevent this happening."

This was the first hard indication of Egyptian intentions, and it was followed by a letter from Burhan Said, Egypt's representative on the Canal Company's board of management, to the board's chairman saying: "Egypt intends to take action concerning the future of the canal some time during June."

At the beginning of that month the Ministry of Commerce abruptly ended a meeting with the company by proposing to exempt it from the Exchange Control Law for the remainder of the concession, in return for a company undertaking to invest $60 million in Egyptian government bonds.

The company gave way, an agreement was signed, and, although richer by $60 million, the government proceeded to attempt to extract more money by a confidential proposal that Britain should conspire with the Egyptian government to get round the agreement by arranging for the dues of British ships to be paid in Egypt into a blocked account and then used only for payment of imports from the United Kingdom. This suggestion was politely turned down in London, while Cairo prepared for a celebration.

The last British troops would be leaving the Canal Zone on June 18. Shepilov, now Soviet Foreign Minister, arrived with a flock of aides and his twenty-year-old daughter. Six hundred political prisoners were freed, and massed bands were ready at Port Said to give the troops a derisive send-off. The British army decided otherwise. Several days previously the senior British officer remaining in the Canal Zone handed over the keys to the canal base to a junior Egyptian officer and embarked his troops aboard a freighter. By the time Nasser's celebrations took place, Egypt had been free of foreign troops for nearly a week.

Shepilov's previous visit had resulted in the Czech arms deal. This time he came to offer Nasser the loan of $1,300 million, the full price of the Aswan Dam project, to be repaid over sixty years at two per cent.

Dulles, angered by such ruthless exploitation of Egypt's desperate economic plight, decided to contract out of his one-sided courtship of Nasser. He did not believe the Soviet Union had the financial resources to back the Aswan Dam 100 per cent, therefore the offer was cynical sham which he would expose as such – expose so forcibly that any Soviet economic offer in the future would be suspect. The offers of the United States, Britain, and the World Bank had been waiting for Nasser to pick up on reasonable conditions; as far as the United States was concerned, the option had expired. It was too late for Nasser to change his mind, because Dulles had finally made up his. The United States would allow the Soviet Union the privilege of financing Nasser's pyramid, and Dulles was convinced the Russians would renege.

III

IT is sadly evident in retrospect that Eden's desire for peace and his fear of dictators were conflicting with his urge to lead a strong Britain into the future. His determination to contain Nasser's spreading influence in the Middle East, by use of force if necessary, was matched by the conviction that another world war had to be avoided at all costs. His somewhat erratic conduct in relation to Egypt contrasted strangely with a more typically responsible attitude toward larger issues.

Ten Commonwealth prime ministers met in London at the end of June to discuss together the impact of the H-bomb on the business of international diplomacy. Thermonuclear power had preoccupied the United States and the Soviet Union for the previous eighteen months; now, at last, the six hundred million people represented at this conference were to have it introduced into their affairs.

Eden informed the prime ministers that Britain would begin testing H-bombs within six months, that he thought France cherished ambitions in the same direction, and that he also felt world security depended upon limiting the number of nuclear powers. Britain's own security, however, depended upon possession of H-bombs and the means to deliver them.

In reply to a comment from Nehru that possession implied intent to use, he sharply stated that in his view no nation would ever use its own nuclear power voluntarily, that possession was necessary to deter potential enemies and to compensate for the imbalance of manpower between East and West.

Reporting on his discussion with Bulganin and Khrushchev in April, he said, in effect, "The Soviet leaders appear to have understood that strategic changes have been created by the advent of nuclear weapons. They are applying the new lessons to their diplomacy. We must do the same. War means mutual destruction; therefore we must avoid it. It is our duty to keep clear of confrontations in areas where major conflict might result. There is no room left for provocation."

IV

NASSER was being made uncomfortably aware that he might soon have to produce the Soviet offer of economic assistance which he had publicly claimed to "have in my pocket."

Dulles was making his feelings clearly evident. Nasser's personal friend, Ambassador Byroade, received a curt notice terminating his appointment to Cairo, and George Allen was removed from responsibility for Near Eastern Affairs at the State Department. Ahmed Hussein, Nasser's ambassador in Washington, had returned to Cairo to report personally on the anti-Egyptian mood of Congress and to urge that the loan offers be accepted in spite of the conditions. Nasser himself, about to leave for Belgrade to attend neutralist "summit" talks with Tito and Nehru at the Yugoslav dictator's summer resi-

dence on the island of Brioni, suddenly ended months of pre-
varication, delays, and evasion by deciding that if it was not
already too late he would accept the World Bank's conditions
without reservation.

The decision was made at a late night conference in Cairo
early in July.

While Nasser listened, Ambassador Hussein described how
widespread antipathy toward Egypt had taken root and blossomed in the United States to the extent that it was touch and
go as to whether the Administration would proceed with the
loan.

Nasser then admitted that he had already made up his mind
on a course of action. "I do not believe," he is reported to have
said, "that the West intends to proceed with their offers of loans
for the Aswan Dam. They will reject us, and when they do I
shall nationalise the Suez Canal Company. I shall change my
mind only if I am proved wrong about the West's intentions
regarding the loans."

Three weeks later, when Ambassador Byroade was about
to leave Cairo for the United States, Colonel Nasser described
this meeting to him. The meeting had apparently concluded
with Nasser turning to the disturbed, anxious Ambassador
Hussein and saying, "You must not worry so much, my friend.
Keep your nerve, and it will turn out all right."

Much has been made by commentators and historians of
Nasser's sense of shock and bewilderment when he learned that
the United States and Britain had declined to make the Aswan
loans, and that he seized the canal in the manner of a dictator
lashing out in a tantrum.

The only shock was the calculated insult delivered by
Dulles.

In mid-July Selwyn Lloyd summoned the United States
Ambassador in London, Winthrop Aldrich, to the Foreign
Office and informed him that Britain considered it unwise to
advance the Aswan loans for the present. Three days later the

State Department received a message from Cairo, saying that Ambassador Hussein was en route to the United States with formal authority to accept the Aswan loans on the conditions laid down by the World Bank. An early interview with the Secretary of State was requested.

Presented with an unexpected opportunity to execute his decision to counter Soviet successes in the economic conflict and teach Nasser a lesson that would be clearly understood by all uncommitted nations, the Secretary of State proceeded to deliver a devastating diplomatic riposte to the Soviet Union.

Whatever brilliance there might have been in the Dulles character, it generally lay passive and submerged under a thick overlay of learned professional ordinariness. On this occasion it broke through to the surface to burn off the tentacles of Russian expansionism in the Middle East.

Ahmed Hussein landed in New York on July 17 and immediately told reporters that Egypt had decided to accept the West's offers of loans for the Aswan Dam.

"I shall have an early meeting with Mr. Dulles to speed up the details of the transaction," he said. "We wish now to take all further economic assistance from the West, and it is now up to London and Washington. We are progressing with negotiations with the Sudan for an equitable distribution of the Nile waters and we want a settlement with the West so that work can begin as soon as the agreement with the Sudan is signed."

For two days Dulles was unavailable. The Egyptian Embassy called the State Department at regular intervals seeking an appointment for Ambassador Hussein, without success. At 3:00 p.m. on the 19th Hussein was summoned to the office of the Secretary of State for a meeting that lasted ninety minutes. Dulles greeted the Egyptian Ambassador with a perfunctory handshake, listened to his prepared address of acceptance for the loans, then picked up a sheet of paper which lay on his desk. With brief reference to the arms deal he read on: two hundred tons of small arms from Red China . . . seventy-two shiploads of arms from Soviet-bloc countries so far . . . mine-sweepers from Poland . . . torpedo boats from Yugoslavia . . . five hundred Egyptian naval officers being trained in Poland . . . Czechoslovakia building rubber and cement factories in Egypt . . . Hungary contracting to build six bridges across the Nile . . . East Germany building a shipyard, sugar refinery, automobile plant, and chemical laboratories designed to produce rocket fuels . . . Bulgaria contracting to build a food-preservation factory and an oil-processing plant.

When Dulles finished speaking, he handed a second slip of paper to the Egyptian, who read it and then left the office without uttering a word of protest at his treatment.

The note he had been given said: "It is no longer feasible for the United States to participate in the project of the High Aswan Dam. . . . In the seven months since the original offer was made, the situation has changed . . . the adequacy of Egypt's resources to assure success are more uncertain than at any time since the offer was made."

When Ambassador Hussein reached his Embassy, he learned that the State Department had released the contents of the note to Washington correspondents while he was still with Dulles. Nasser would not be spared the humiliation of a damning public insult.

At approximately the same time in London, the Foreign Office announced with terse finality: "We have concluded that in present circumstances it would not be feasible for Her Majesty's Government to participate in the project." The Egyptian Ambassador in London had to wait another three hours before he was officially informed.

Dulles and Eden were under no illusions about the importance of the Aswan Dam to Nasser as a symbol of revolutionary purpose and achievement, nor about the risks he would be prepared to take to achieve his aim. His obvious course would be to cut oil supplies to Western Europe by seizing the Suez

Canal, and the prospect of some such response had been considered in both London and Washington. If, in his search for an adequate weapon with which to strike back, Nasser grabbed the canal, Dulles would not be unduly concerned. No matter what difficulties arose, he was confident that American know-how and ingenuity would overcome them. Eden hoped that dissident elements inside Egypt and anti-Nasser Arabs in other countries would revolt and overthrow Nasser before he had time to resort to drastic countermeasures. If not, and Britain's oil lifeline was threatened, Eden would be justified in sending troops back into the Canal Zone, and Nasser's fate would be the same.

That evening of the 19th, on the Adriatic island of Brioni, Nasser was unaware of the diplomatic tumult in Cairo. By all accounts is was a gay evening, and at the end of it Nasser invited Nehru to accompany him when he left for Cairo at noon on Friday, the following day. Shown foreign press reports of the West's action the next morning, he postponed departure for three hours while Cairo confirmed the news by radio, and when he eventually boarded the aircraft with Nehru, he was smiling, giving little outward sign of anxiety.

At this stage he knew only that the loans had been cancelled, nothing of the enormity of the rebuff administered by Dulles. The discussions of the two leaders during the flight were devoted to the advisability of nationalising the canal as an immediate gesture of defiance, of allowing a cooling-off period in which the West might be persuaded to retract the withdrawal, or of reaching a *modus vivendi* with the Canal Company.

At Cairo, Nehru was driven to the Indian Embassy while Nasser summoned an immediate Cabinet meeting, read the dispatches of his ambassadors in Washington and London, and the commentaries in British, American, and French newspapers.

On Saturday morning the two leaders met for talks which lasted four hours and, before leaving to continue his journey to New Delhi, the Indian leader issued a statement harshly condemnatory of Britain and the United States.

The myth has arisen that Nehru knew nothing of Nasser's intentions before leaving Cairo. The Indians naturally wish to believe that Nasser could hardly have had it in mind before July 21, the date of Nehru's departure, since they are loath to contemplate that he was implicitly deceiving Nehru during the talks at Brioni and subsequently in Cairo.

Nasser himself told those ambassadors who inquired that he made up his mind to take over the canal late on Saturday, the 21st, after Nehru had left. There is evidence that this was not quite the case. He made up his mind during the morning talks with Nehru, who, possibly realizing the widespread consequences certain to follow, is now believed by many diplomats to have made it appear as if he were ignorant of the decision.

Sir Humphrey Trevelyan reported: "I have myself little doubt that the decision was effectively taken before Nehru left Cairo. At the airport at the time of his departure, the Minister of the Interior told me that they were not so worried at the withdrawal of the offers, as they would find other means to finance the dam. It was the manner of the withdrawal which upset them, since it appeared to conceal some other purpose directed at them."

In all probability, then, Nehru knew. Yet he remained silent.

Of all the Western statesmen in those tense, critical hours which stretched at an agonising crawl into days, Dulles alone kept his eyes firmly upon Moscow. He waited for Shepilov to produce a cheque book or back down.

That Saturday evening in Moscow, Shepilov attended a party at the Belgian Embassy and held an informal press conference to answer questions about his intentions now that the Western powers had backed away from the Egyptian loans.

"The question is not a live one," he said. "The problem is not put here in such acute form as the United States cares to think it is. I had the impression when I visited Egypt last month that there are more vitally important problems in industrialisation, although I would not minimise the importance of the Aswan Dam. If the Egyptians ask for our help in developing their industry, we will give sympathetic consideration to their requests."

Next day, Cairo Radio managed to twist this unambiguous statement to read: "If the Egyptian government asks us for economic aid for the High Dam project, we will give it favourable and friendly consideration."

On Monday, the 23rd, Cairo newspapers reported the new Soviet Ambassador to Egypt, M. Kisselev, as saying that the Soviet Union would definitely supply all the money required for the project. They said further that two Soviet engineers had attended meetings of the National Production Council to begin preliminary planning. That same evening Kisselev issued a formal denial of the remarks attributed to him, saying: "I merely repeated Mr. Shepilov's recent statements on economic aid without reference to the High Dam."

On the 24th Nasser attended the opening of a new oil pipeline on the edge of Cairo and made his first major speech since returning from the Adriatic. After an hour of inflammatory statements about Western imperialism, he leaned forward toward a battery of microphones and shouted hoarsely: "I look at Americans and I say – Americans, may you choke on your fury."

After the speech, Ambassador Kisselev was again questioned by foreign correspondents, and this time he reversed himself again. "We are now ready to finance the dam if Egypt wishes it," he said.

Later that evening Kisselev emerged from a meeting with Nasser and announced he was leaving for Moscow to discuss the High Dam "and other projects" with the Soviet government. Early next morning the press attaché at the Soviet Embassy issued a curt statement: "Ambassador Kisselev did not make any statement about the High Dam yesterday."

Dulles read the reports of these conflicting statements and relaxed, confident that he had been right. The Soviet Union might covet the Egyptian body, but the price was too high. The first round of the economic war was his, and, without any further thought of what else dangled from the chain of events he had manufactured, he set off for Peru to enjoy the drowsy beauty of Lima and to attend the inauguration of a new president.

V

THURSDAY, July 26, was the third anniversary of the Egyptian revolution. Tens of thousands thronged Liberation Square after nightfall and spilled out into the side streets under powerful arc lights blazing down from rooftops. Nasser stood before the microphones under a huge emblem of three concentric circles. It was the classic scene of a leader appearing before his mob, reminiscent of the infamous Nuremberg rallies of the 'thirties. Cairo Radio's propaganda chief stood just below the dais, arm upraised, a stop watch in his hand, counting away the last minutes of hushed expectancy with the rhythmic ticking of a time bomb.

In London a dinner party was being held at No. 10 Downing Street in honour of King Feisal of Iraq and Nuri es-Said, who were on a state visit to Britain. Other guests included Selwyn Lloyd and the Minister for Commonwealth Relations, Lord Home. Outside, in one of the offices adjoining the cabinet room, a private secretary waited by a telephone connected by open line to the BBC monitoring service.

At the State Department in Washington a teleprinter link with London was open and ready for transmission of the

monitored text of the Egyptian's speech. A memorandum from
Dulles instructed that he should be called at Lima when the
text was complete.

Mahmoud Younes, the former army engineer who had
planned for this night seven months ago, sat in his car parked
close to the Canal Company's administrative offices in a Cairo
suburb. Beside him was an army communications jeep in radio
contact with Army Headquarters, which was in turn connected
by radio to strategic points along the entire length of the canal.
Behind Younes's car were trucks filled with armed soldiers.
Similar groups waited near the operating headquarters of the
company at Port Said, Ismailia, and Suez, making a total
strength of about a battalion in support of the dozen or so engineers personally selected by Younes to supervise this particular
operation. Speed was vital if even the briefest interruption of
the functioning of the canal was to be avoided.

Younes listened to his car radio as the announcer introduced the President of Egypt, and Nasser began to speak,
vehement from the outset. The first reference in the speech to
the builder of the canal, Ferdinand de Lesseps, was the pre-
arranged authorization for Younes to act.

It came when Nasser portrayed Eugene Black of the
World Bank as another grasping Ferdinand de Lesseps. Younes
started his car and moved forward, the trucks following. At
the company's buildings no orders were necessary, the troops
simply rushing along corridors, into offices, and covering the
startled, often terrified staff with their sub-machine guns.
Younes relayed orders and received reports through Army
Headquarters as the other groups occupied every inch of the
company's property.

While Nasser was still speaking, the Suez Canal was nationalised and literally grabbed at gunpoint – a brilliant, brutal
theft.

At Downing Street, Eden's private secretary interrupted
the dinner party to hand him a message. The Prime Minister

read it aloud to his guests, and took his leave with Lloyd and Lord Home to preside over an emergency Cabinet meeting.

Until early morning on Friday, the 27th, a glittering assembly surrounded Eden in the cabinet room: his Ministers, the Chiefs of Staff, the diplomatic representatives of the United States and France.

Speaking to Andrew Foster, United States chargé d'affaires, Eden said, "The Egyptian has his thumb on our windpipe. Tell Mr. Dulles I cannot allow that." The right arm swung, clenched fist smacked into open palm, and the sound was mightily reassuring.

When the meeting at Downing Street broke up, Eden spoke on the telephone for an hour with Pineau in Paris, a curious conversation in retrospect, as neither knew that the other was grimly relieved that Nasser had at last provided an opportunity for decisive action.

The French arms conspiracy with the Israelis had developed through the persuasive efforts of Shimon Peres and the eager enthusiasm of Bourgès-Maunoury and Abel Thomas into what amounted to a secret military arrangement for occupation of the Sinai and the Gaza Strip. If Eden could be persuaded to reoccupy the Canal Zone quickly, Nasser's downfall would be assured without a desert war. Not too much persuasion was necessary. Eden was within reach of a moral right to react strongly and he wanted as much support for it as he could muster. Hs suggested to Pineau that they should ask the United States to join them in preparing the ground for a conference of those countries whose ships made up the bulk of the canal's traffic. He envisaged a situation in which twenty or more countries would demand that the canal be placed under international supervision, and if, as was likely, Nasser rejected the proposal, Britain and France could then go in with force to "protect the canal in the name of the nations represented."

Pineau replied that such a course would take too long and probably become entangled in a mesh of conflicting views. He advocated immediate diplomatic circulation of such countries to achieve the same end, but eventually gave way to Eden's comment that action should be "publicly seen to be the wish of the user nations." They agreed to begin talks with the United States and to take immediate military precautions as a screen for joint preparations for the military occupation of the Canal Zone.

Later that morning, a message to Lima informed Dulles that the British and French proposed that he, Lloyd, and Pineau should meet in London by Monday at the latest to concert policies in the face of "a grave danger to world peace."

Not knowing of the Eden-Lloyd determination to encourage the downfall of Nasser by all possible means, nor of the French-Israeli secret agreement to achieve the same objective, and being so absorbed by his enemies that he had no time to beware of his friends, Dulles declined to admit that the danger was so grave he should cut short his stay in Peru. Robert Murphy, Assistant Under Secretary of State, was instructed to represent the United States at a meeting not designed to decide between peace and war, but just when the war should start.

Next morning, messages informing the Commonwealth prime ministers of the British intention to summon a conference of maritime nations went out from Downing Street, the last sentence of which said: "I know I can count on your joining us in expressions of concern and indignation."

Prime Minister Louis St. Laurent received this message in Ottawa on Saturday morning. Lester Pearson happened to walk into his office while he was reading it and he tossed it across the desk with the dry comment: "See what he wants? Canada should express indignation because Nasser has grabbed the Suez. What do you think?"

"We will certainly have to take a hard look at that," said Pearson, who was really more concerned over another sentence which filled him with a chilling sense of crisis. It said: "We believe that we should seize this opportunity of putting the canal under proper international control in permanent arrangement."

CHAPTER FIVE

Shifting Sands

DEFENCE chiefs in Paris and London were given until Saturday evening to produce reviews of their respective resources in men and materials for what their political directives described as "joint intervention in Egypt aimed at occupation of the Suez Canal Zone for an indefinite period."

Mollet and Pineau, determined to persuade Britain and the United States into immediate action, expected French forces to be redeployed and ready within a matter of days at the most. Bourgès-Maunoury quickly dispelled their hopes.

He reported that France, despite the wars in Indo-China and North Africa, could muster a formidable force given the time and facilities. Several short-range Mystère fighter squadrons were available but useless, because they needed bases almost on Egypt's borders. Three long-range squadrons were in Germany and could be moved at short notice, but they required a base no further from Egypt than Cyprus.

Two reserve paratroop groups were standing by in Algeria, but they consisted principally of untrained conscripts, and eight battalions of infantry were in southern France with nowhere to go because there were no landing craft to move them. Bourgès-

Maunoury was confident, however, that Britain would have sufficient landing craft for the sort of joint operation envisaged. If France acted alone, the armed forces would require about a month; if they were to operate with the British, the process of integration between the two forces would require at least six weeks.

Britain, with an annual defence budget of $4.5 billion, was revealed to be in an appalling state of unreadiness. The ministers in charge of the Army, Navy, and Air Force reported through their political overlord, Minister of Defence Sir Walter Monckton, that since there were no training-parachutes in Cyprus the three paratroop battalions stationed there would have to be flown back to England for retraining. There were eight infantry battalions in Cyprus but no landing craft; the nearest supporting artillery units were in Germany assigned to NATO; and an armoured division based by treaty agreement in Libya was immobilised by lack of tank transporters.

The Mediterranean Fleet was ready, but its carrier-borne aircraft were obsolete compared with Egypt's MIGs, and, despite the decision two years before to turn Cyprus into a strategic base, no natural harbour existed and no attempt had been made to build one.

General Challe of the French General Staff and Admiral Nomy, Chief of the French Naval Staff, flew to London in the first few hours of the crisis to urge upon Eden that the military operation should be speedily prepared and swiftly executed. The British Chiefs of Staff demurred on the pretext that more haste might in fact result in an ill-conceived plan.

No matter how eager Mollet and Eden were to end Nasser's career, they would not be able to use force for the time being. They enjoyed the popular support of their respective countries, and, had their armed forces been in a position to act at a few days' notice, they could have occupied the Canal Zone with little more than transitory protests from the United States, the United Nations, and the Commonwealth. The opportunity was lost primarily through British unreadiness to enter into a hurriedly planned operation in which France would be the predominant partner by virtue of superiority in arms.

British and French military leaders began, however, to improvise with assiduous, surprising efficiency, directed primarily by Britain's Minister of War, Antony Head, who, as a wartime brigadier at Combined Operations Headquarters, had helped to plan such adventures as the raids on St. Nazaire and Dieppe. Under his guidance, something approximating the ponderous D-Day organization took shape in London, Paris, and Cyprus. British land, sea, and air commanders were provided with French deputies under the supreme command of General Sir Charles Keightley, British senior officer in the Middle East, an Anglo-French planning team was buried in the catacombs beneath Whitehall, secure from the curious eyes of NATO, and in the best traditions of Combined Operations an Outline Plan was born.

It called for preliminary air strikes against Egyptian airfields followed by paratroop drops and sea-borne landings. Britain would supply fifty thousand troops, France thirty thousand; Canberra jet bombers would be covered by British naval aircraft and the French Air Force; an Anglo-French combined fleet would protect the landings and provide the sea bombardment. The entire force would gather, rehearsed and equipped, at Malta and Cyprus by September 15.

The objective was occupation of the Suez Canal Zone; the Outline Plan, approved by Mollet, Pineau, and Bourgès-Maunoury for France, and Eden, Lloyd, and Head for Britain, took a strangely unmilitary route. Instead of aiming directly at the canal, the force was to be landed at Alexandria and then head south down the desert road *straight to Cairo*.

While these military preparations assumed a semblance of order and liaison officers in civilian clothes travelled daily between Paris and London, the meeting of the Tripartite powers began at the Foreign Office: Robert Murphy for the United States, Pineau for France, and Lloyd for the United Kingdom.

The context of their talks was the Anglo-French position that Nasser could not be allowed to seize the canal in contravention of international agreements, that the threat to Western Europe's oil supplies was too great to permit legal quibbling, that if political pressures failed to persuade Nasser to undo his act of nationalisation, then the two countries reserved the right to resort to force.

Murphy, playing for time in the hope that when Dulles returned to Washington late on Monday he would fly on to London, regarded his part as a holding operation against the bellicose mood of his British and French colleagues.

Little has been revealed about this conference, yet it was one of the pivots around which the future swirled opaquely until each event in turn took form and appeared in focus. It established the courses each of the participants was to follow, and from which none was to deviate appreciably.

The United States, said Murphy, wished to base discussions on international rights to free and unrestricted use of the canal as opposed to the right of Egypt to nationalise it. The two were separate issues, and he thought that if Egypt operated the canal efficiently in the interests of nations using it, then legal objections to nationalisation would be difficult to argue.

When the question arose of what should happen if the meeting of maritime nations failed, Murphy proposed that the whole matter should be referred to the United Nations. Pineau and Lloyd reacted against this proposal, the British Foreign Secretary saying with quiet finality: "The United Nations does not fit into this picture anywhere."

By Monday evening Murphy was convinced that Britain and France were so dangerously united in purpose that, unless Dulles exerted the prestige and authority of his office by attending the talks himself, there was a chance that Egypt would be attacked before serious negotiations began.

He sent a cable to Washington saying that "the United Kingdom and France are deadly serious in their intent to resort to force." He could not guarantee that he had been successful in persuading them to first exhaust all other means of reaching a settlement with Egypt. "They do not trust Nasser and they feel that the crisis in their affairs matches in historic significance the Nazi occupation of the Rhineland and annexation of Czechoslovakia," he said. He concluded that in the interest of world peace "your presence here is vital and urgent."

Dulles flew to London on Tuesday, at last nervously aware that his one bold counterstroke against Communist expansionism had created a major international crisis, and bewildered by it. Like the President, he viewed the issue as "a business dispute over the control of an international public utility."

Murphy's later report underlined the gravity of the situation. He said: "I found that the intentions of the United Kingdom and France were not the result of panic. Their attitudes were relaxed, confident, and determined, as if their course had been well thought through and found to be the only one open to them. After the Secretary of State took over as head of our delegation, we met the Prime Minister at Downing Street and he told me: 'If Nasser is permitted to get away with this criminal act of theft, the United Kingdom will be regarded in world affairs as just another Netherlands. We are not prepared to accept this situation.' "

Pineau, impatient of diplomatic niceties and legal argument, was disturbed by the United States approach. Public opinion in France, already translating the canal theft as a victory for Arab nationalism in general and the Algerian rebels in particular, clamoured for action. He was worried from the beginning by "Murphy's extraordinary reserve on this matter," which he eventually decided was really "a reflection of the reserve of the United States government." He felt instinctively that despite an outward appearance of sympathy none actually existed, and this surprised him as, in his opinion, the United States was to a large extent responsible for the Anglo-French predicament and had no right to pose as a disinterested spectator.

"When Dulles arrived to continue the talks I felt even more keenly that the Americans were refusing to accept the fact that the crisis was a logical consequence of their own actions and were trying to minimise the importance of it," he has said.

In spite of the reservations Pineau and Lloyd held on the extent of United States support, it was Dulles who contrived to bring about agreement through his unique facility for declining to be specific. He believed that Nasser had acted petulantly, if drastically, and should be treated like some devious business tycoon who had stolen his clients' property through shady dealings. He was not even sure of his clients' rights to ownership, but being a good lawyer he would defend their interests by seeking a mutually acceptable settlement.

He had no way of knowing that Eden and Lloyd, Mollet and Pineau, informed by then of the considered opinions of their respective ambassadors in Cairo that Nasser had decided two months earlier to nationalise the canal if the Aswan loans were withdrawn, looked upon the crisis as yet another stage in a carefully calculated program of revilement, insult, and castigation aimed at destroying their rights in the area, destroying their friends, and eventually culminating in an attempt to strangle their economic lives by depriving them of oil.

It was hardly likely that Dulles, who had once written a thesis implying that Britain and France were causing a drift toward war by standing in the way of the forces of change – Germany and Italy – would be impressed now by talk of Munich, Hitler, and Mussolini. But by repeatedly asserting that Nasser should be made to "disgorge" the canal, and by condemning the Egyptian in harsh language for his arrogance, he managed to evoke the impression that should the proposed conference fail to reach a settlement with Egypt, he would give moral support to further action.

Over lunch on Wednesday Dulles said to Pineau: "I had no

idea I would run into such strong emotions here. I just can't understand why you people are willing to risk so much for the sake of this damn canal."

"What surprises me," said the ironic Pineau, "is that you did not expect precisely this emotion, because it seems perfectly natural to me."

By the time the talks ended with agreement to convene a canal users' conference, Pineau was convinced that Dulles had decided to employ as many delaying tactics as possible in the hope that time itself would erode the strength of the Anglo-French determination.

When the United States delegation returned to Washington on August 4, it became quickly apparent through Canadian diplomatic channels that Lester Pearson's earlier feeling that Eden's note had indicated a crisis of greater magnitude than a dispute over the Suez Canal was justified. Dulles immediately saw Prime Minister Menzies of Australia, who had arrived from Ottawa that morning, and told him that the crisis was "already the gravest international incident since World War II." The British and the French had agreed to a conference, he said, "but they're in no mood to let Nasser get away with a favourable settlement. My worry now is that Nasser might reject whatever comes out of the conference. If he does, then I'm afraid they'll launch their military."

"Do you think they've weighed the risks carefully?" asked Menzies.

"I asked Eden the same thing," said Dulles. "He said – and Lloyd repeated it often – they'd rather risk a world war than sink to the level of a third-rate power with a depleted economy."

Menzies had attended the conference of Commonwealth prime ministers only five weeks earlier at which Eden, assessing the impact of the H-bomb on international affairs, had said that all nations had a duty to avoid acts provocative of war.

Less than an hour later Dulles was reporting in the same vein to Canada's Ambassador Arnold Heeney. He said Eden, Lloyd, and Macmillan had reached "the calm and deliberate decision that they cannot accept having Britain at the mercy of a man like Nasser . . . even though the calculated risk of their decision is nuclear war."

Then it was Murphy's turn, the same evening, to call on Heeney at the Canadian Embassy.

"The British and the French mean business," he said. "Regardless of the legal position of the canal, they are determined to get it back and place it under international control. Nasser will resist, and God knows where the mess will end. Perhaps you people in Canada can do something to urge caution on them."

It was the first time that the diplomatic bridge Pearson had striven for some ten years to build between North America and Europe as the key structure of Canadian foreign policy was formally used by the United States for a specific purpose. Murphy's appeal to Heeney amounted to invoking Canada's special relationships with Britain and France on one side, and the United States on the other.

II

AFTER agreement that Canada's reply to Eden's message should ignore the British request for an expression of Canadian "indignation," St. Laurent proposed that, in view of the urgent and spreading nature of the crisis, Pearson should assume responsibility for the Canadian role in the crisis with the full confidence of the Cabinet.

During his unspectacular years of international service with a dying League of Nations and a newly born United Nations, Pearson had acquired a vast reservoir of experience, knowledge, and diplomatic skill which would, in more normal circumstances, have remained hidden while he himself passed into honourable retirement. It needed a severe, personally testing cataclysm to reveal the qualities lying dormant within him.

While powerful external forces were building up to just such a cataclysmic moment in world affairs, his failure to express unqualified support for Britain was being bitterly condemned in Canada. The Member of Parliament for Prince Albert, J. G. Diefenbaker, said: "Canada should not be a mere tail on the American kite but should, as a senior member of the Commonwealth, give to the government of the United Kingdom moral support and encouragement." The letter that follows shows precisely what Pearson's intentions were on August 6, only ten days after Nasser took control of the Suez Canal, when most politicians were still stunned and floundering. Addressed to the Canadian High Commissioner in London, Norman Robertson, it might, in retrospect, be described as a brilliant analysis of what lay ahead. At the time, however, it merely reflected intelligent, educated guesswork, coupled with a genuine personal impulse to do whatever might be possible to help Britain and France. It said:

"Our feeling here of relief and satisfaction that the Tripartite meeting resulted in an agreed communiqué which provided for an international conference is qualified by anxiety as to what will happen at that conference and subsequently. Our main worry is that the United Kingdom and the French have gone too far in committing themselves to the use of force if the forthcoming conference does not produce a result satisfactory to them.

"I assume that the British position is based on the hope that an agreement for international control of the canal . . . can be reached at this conference. . . . I find it difficult to share the hope that Egypt will accept such an agreement.

"I hope I am wrong, but if not, where do we go then? Presumably the British and the French and the others who support them at the conference will try to impose the arrangement by political pressure on a resisting Egypt. . . . Among other things, this will split the Commonwealth . . . and may break up the Baghdad Pact. . . . Furthermore, is there any assurance that the United States will co-operate . . . ? The Egyptians know that American interest in this matter is not as immediate or as strong as that of the United Kingdom and France, and they will try to . . . exploit this difference.

"If the Americans do not, in fact, back the British . . . there is bound to be grave disappointment and even bitter criticism, and this will impose strains on the Atlantic Alliance; especially as the United States government's hesitation will be related, no doubt with some justice, to the current domestic political situation of a pending presidential election.

"If political pressure fails, then the British and the French seem committed to the use of force for which they might have little legal justification. . . . But here I think they will be entirely on their own. . . . As the use of force would probably extend beyond the Suez area into Egypt itself, the consequences would be far-reaching for the Commonwealth, for Anglo-American co-operation, and for peace in the Middle East generally. In these circumstances, it seems almost inevitable that Egypt would appeal to the United Nations, which would be a very strange result indeed from the developments of last week and one which should, I think, be most embarrassing for the United Kingdom, and hardly less so for her friends. . . . I take it that there is no possibility of the United Nations being brought into the matter at this stage, and I assume also that there is no possibility of extending any proposed international régime for the Suez to other international waters, like Panama.

"It is clear that every possible effort must be made to prevent a chain of developments which would result in Anglo-French military force being exerted against Egypt in a way which would split the Commonwealth, weaken the Anglo-American alliance, and have general consequences which would benefit nobody but Moscow."

It was a remarkable document. The situations he envisaged did, in fact, unfold in faithful and dreadful conformity to his worst fears. He could not bring himself to believe then that the threat of force was anything more than a diplomatic bluff, a means of exerting pressure upon Egypt, of encouraging dissident elements within the Egyptian government or army to revolt, and of inspiring uncertainty about Nasser's wisdom among the Arab states. He could believe that France was serious, if only because it was already fighting the Arabs and had nothing much to lose, but he found it difficult to believe the same of the British, who had more to lose than France and less to gain.

III

DURING the first two weeks of August world opinion swerved, switched, and otherwise adjusted itself into alignments that were overwhelmingly against the Anglo-French threat to resort to force. Scandinavia and West Germany took the United States–Canadian view that Nasser's tactics were unforgivable, that some form of international administration of the canal would be the best solution, and that his legal right to take over the canal should not be, at this stage, the major preoccupation. Of the Commonwealth countries, only Australia and New Zealand openly supported Britain, and in both there were vociferous critics.

Nehru, whose foreknowledge of Nasser's intentions was at least probable, accused Britain of "proceeding from one blunder to another"; King Hussein of Jordan, who owed his throne to Britain, talked of the need for "Arab resistance to imperial-ist exploitation"; and the government of Iraq's Nuri es-Said, Eden's personal friend and Nasser's avowed enemy, was among the first to announce support of Egypt.

In Britain itself, the erosive effect of inaction was mounting opposition to further talk of force. France, however, remained firmly behind Mollet and Pineau. Pineau repeatedly asserted that he was prepared to go *jusqu'au bout*, and it was evident that if the pending London conference resulted in failure to reach a settlement with Egypt, there would be a widespread demand for the government to go a step further. The canal issue had come to be regarded as a test of national strength, and the sudden awakening to a community of views with Britain provided a fortuitous opportunity in French minds for a demonstration of national will to act with power and deter-mination. If the inclination to see the destruction of Nasser as a solution to the Algerian problem was based on emotion rather than on fact, it was conversely true that an Egyptian success on the canal issue would, in fact, so weaken France's prestige as to make a solution in Algeria almost impossible to achieve.

Unlike Eden, the French leaders were not required to en-courage a national psychological adjustment to the probability of war. The use of force against Egypt would appear to most Frenchmen as a mere extension of the operations in North Africa.

In the third week, representatives of twenty-two maritime nations met in London to rubber-stamp the prepared Anglo-American-French proposal that Egypt should co-operate with the users by allowing an international authority to operate the canal. Egypt declined to attend, but its interests were safe-guarded competently by Shepilov, and incompetently by India's Defence Minister, Krishna Menon, who was so pathologically anti-American and anti-British that even the Russian delega-tion thought he must have been once "hit on the head by a London bus conductor."

Krishna Menon saw in Nasser's quarrel with the West an opportunity for a spectacular diplomatic *coup*, one which might elevate him to the stature of statesman, but his constant attempts to occupy the centre of the political stage in London led him to so bungle his objections to the West's proposals that India was placed squarely alongside the Soviet Union, a position Nehru could hardly equate with consistent neutrality.

After a week of quibbling, the conference appointed Prime Minister Menzies of Australia to head a delegation that would place the proposal for an international operating authority before Nasser. While Menzies was in Egypt, President Eisenhower held a press conference in Washington in which he said that "the United States cannot, in any circumstances, support the use of force." This had the effect of condemning the Menzies mission to failure. Nasser rejected the proposals of the maritime conference outright, and the mission returned to London having achieved precisely nothing.

Menzies interrupted his journey home to Australia in Washington to tell Dulles and senior State Department officials of the disastrous effect of Eisenhower's statement.

He said: "I had been making some impression upon Nasser by keeping him guessing as to whether the United Kingdom and France would actually resort to force. Then came newspaper reports of Eisenhower's statements. That did it. The pass was sold as far as I was concerned. Nasser became cool, confident, and impossible to deal with."

Worried by the nervous sense of crisis, now approaching a peak, Norman Robertson called on Lord Home, the British Secretary of State for Commonwealth Relations, and said: "Are you really going to work for the best international agreement you can get, or is your intention to proceed with an attempt to humiliate and replace Nasser?"

Robertson was privately worried that even if there were a good deal to be said for both objectives, the way things were working out the British might find themselves with the worst of both worlds – no agreement, and Nasser in supreme control of the canal.

"The last possibility can't be washed out," replied Home. "You have to understand that we are a nation at arms." Then he asked a question of his own. "If we have to use force, would we have the approval of Canada?"

"In my opinion, no," said Robertson.

Canada had crossed the diplomatic bridge to deliver a North American reply to a European question, and British officials responded with a powerful, persuasive appeal for Canadian support which, if successful, might have led to pressure being exerted on Washington from Ottawa.

Within hours of seeing Lord Home, Robertson was called to the Foreign Office for a private talk with Sir Ivone Kirkpatrick, Under-Secretary of State.

Kirkpatrick saw the whole tragic situation in terms of the 'thirties, and piled parallel upon parallel to make his point. At one moment Nasser's expropriation of the Suez Canal Company was Hitler reoccupying the Rhineland, as a test and try-on, probing the weaknesses and divisions of the countries that stood in the way of his ambitions.

"We know now," he said, "that if we had acted resolutely together in 1934, Hitler could have been stopped quickly and cheaply. And at that stage the Nazi régime would probably have collapsed in the face of a resounding and spectacular failure."

At another point Nasser was Mussolini, originally at one with the West in trying to curb German expansionism; then, losing faith in the determination of his Western associates, his vanity snubbed, and his own ambitions checkmated, he swung right over into the opposite camp and made common cause with the Nazis.

Nasser had also come to power with pro-Western orientations, said Kirkpatrick, as the talk lengthened along a bleak, darkling plane. But his ambitions were much too grandiose for him to realize in British company. He had been checked and snubbed, and had now thrown in his lot with the Soviet Union. His hostility to the West, to Britain and France in particular, was now settled and firmly entrenched. Kirkpatrick thought that if the West had bothered to study Nasser's *The Philosophy of a Revolution* as seriously as it had failed to study Hitler's *Mein Kampf*, "we would have a better measure of the man and of the menace he represents to the whole world of the Middle East."

While Robertson stirred uneasily, deeply affected by the sincerity and brilliance of the analysis, yet skeptical of it and fully alert to the sound of guns behind the solemn fateful words, Kirkpatrick prophesied that the next step would be the confiscation of foreign assets in Egypt. Nasser was, according to Foreign Office intelligence, already plotting to overthrow other Arab régimes – Saudi-Arabia, Libya, Syria, and ultimately Iraq – by inspiring "Young Officer" revolutions. One timetable, he said, allowed four years for this process to work itself out in Iraq.

Once the process of *gleichshaltung* was under way, the oil leases and pipeline franchises in the Middle East would be repudiated. With Nasser in effective control, probably in alliance with the Soviet Union, of the oil lands and of the Suez Canal, the position of Western Europe would be absolutely intolerable.

When Robertson inquired whether Britain would react favourably to a United Nations guarantee of freedom of transit through the canal, providing Egypt could be persuaded to accept some form of United Nations supervision over the canal's operations, Kirkpatrick replied that Egyptian undertakings *per se* had been proved worthless, and that any United Nations guarantee would itself be subject to the caprices of a Soviet veto and of a volatile and irresponsible Assembly majority.

The sort of situation he expressly feared, as he constantly

reiterated during this conversation, was not any general stoppage of canal traffic by Egypt, but selective and discriminatory
interference with the traffic of particular countries with which
Egypt might find herself at odds. He could see British and
Egyptian interests conflicting on at least a score of issues in
one area or another, and expressed concern that the temptation
to use his *de facto* power over canal traffic to blackmail Britain
into a settlement of such issues in his favour by stopping its
ships might be irresistible to Nasser. Nor would Britain have
any effective remedy. Other countries not affected by the disputes would find sufficient reason – as all had done in the case
of Israel – to condone an interference in which they were not
directly concerned.

"If anybody can show me a satisfactory way of overcoming
this situation," he said, "then I would be much more prepared
than I am now to consider a negotiated settlement as a tolerable
alternative to the action we feel is imposed upon us."

Understanding now that these ominous prospects were
firmly implanted in minds already hagridden with memories of
missed chances of stopping Hitler in the years before the war,
Robertson could see why a note of desperation had begun to
creep into British policy. While he listened, he could envisage
a British Cabinet so fearful of vital oil supplies being arbitrarily
stopped by Egypt, with disastrous results to the civil economies
and defensive alliances of Western Europe, that some ministers
had reached the point where they felt it their duty, regardless
of consequences, to take any steps within their power to prevent
such a situation coming about.

"I can tell you," continued Kirkpatrick, "that a very senior
and respected member of the Cabinet has already said that if
the country flinches from its first readiness to back the government in the use of force, then the Prime Minister should resign
and let the Opposition take responsibility for a policy of appeasement – and for the five million unemployed any stoppage
of oil supplies would create in this country very quickly."

Fascinated and entirely absorbed, Robertson wondered aloud if the British government had considered the wider implications of a resort to force – for instance, the danger to international security and the frightful consequences of a world war in which H-bombs might be the weapons.

While Bulganin and Khrushchev were in London during April, said Kirkpatrick, they had been told that interference with British oil supplies from the Middle East would mean certain strangulation for Britain, and that if threatened by strangulation, Britain would fight. The Soviet leaders admitted they recognized the logic of this position, and Britain now relied upon that exchange of views as an assurance that Russia would not intervene.

The British soul had been bared; Robertson could do nothing less than outline the Canadian attitude with equal frankness.

"No appreciable amount of Canadian shipping or cargo passes through the canal," he said. "But we have an interest as a trading nation in the efficient and non-discriminatory operation of the waterway. Our concern over the implications of the Egyptian action was stated at the outset in Ottawa and in Mr. St. Laurent's messages to Sir Anthony Eden. The basis of our policy in this matter remains the same. We support the announced objectives of the London conference of maritime powers and the principle of international use of the canal."

The Canadian government had considerable apprehensions about British and French references to the possible use of force, as any such resort would, in its view, likely result in an appeal to the United Nations by Egypt. In this event the United Kingdom would be in the unenviable position of having to defend itself on a charge of aggression. Canada wished to avoid that happening.

"We are also worried about the severe strains upon the Western alliance, the Commonwealth, and the United Nations itself, which must inevitably result if the United Kingdom and

France do resort to force," said Robertson. "We sympathize with your predicament; we even support your concern that the canal operations should be insulated against the political whims of any one nation. But we cannot support, nor even approve, any resort to force."

At last, after more than two hours, the meeting ended, and Robertson left the quiet corridors of the Foreign Office to walk along Whitehall, disturbed and pensive after so frank and lengthy a confession of British fears and motives.

Kirkpatrick was, first and foremost, a German expert who had held high diplomatic appointments in Germany before and after the war. During the war he had been the Foreign Office liaison officer with the British Broadcasting Corporation and with various allied organizations concerned with psychological warfare. His parallels and analogies were apt and ingenious, but not always viable.

The evoked echo of 1938 was misleading. By then Hitler had broken international treaties four times; Nasser had so far broken none. Hitler destroyed established democratic government, enforced vicious racial theories, ruled by terror and concentration camps; Nasser's military government was more concerned with eradicating corruption. Nasser's behaviour was shocking; he blustered and abused, but his excesses were as yet confined to home-grown nationalism, not very much different from that which flourished in Canada.

Moreover, in 1938 the League of Nations was expiring, whereas now the United Nations was growing. It needed the strength of international morality which might be denied if Britain and France resorted to the use of force.

However, Kirkpatrick was the senior permanent diplomat at the Foreign Office, a confidant of Eden and Lloyd, and a man who could influence British policy. The bridge was working for both sides of the Atlantic. Murphy had spoken to Ambassador Heeney for the ears of Lloyd and Pineau; Kirkpatrick had spoken to Robertson for the ears of Pearson and Dulles.

IV

———

DURING the Indo-China crisis in 1954, when Britain had declined a United States invitation to the brink, Dulles had taken Eden's rebuff as a personal affront. Now the United States was being invited to join an Anglo-French excursion to another brink, and Dulles, compromised by his own responsibility for precipitating the affair, was unable to return the rebuff as bluntly as it had been given. He circumvented the issue instead, setting in motion a series of diplomatic manœuvres designed to preserve the appearance of transatlantic unity while holding Britain and France in check.

Unfortunately, he persisted in keeping his ideas to himself, so that even President Eisenhower was much in the dark about what his Secretary of State was doing. With typical self-contradiction, Dulles proclaimed in London that force might be permissible if all other avenues of settlement were first exhausted, and then stated in Washington that force was not permissible under any circumstances.

During the initial Tripartite meetings with Pineau, Lloyd, and Eden, their intransigence had forced him to improvise. He had agreed to a three-power blockage of Egyptian assets on condition that Britain and France agreed to the draft "statement of views" he intended to put before the conference of maritime powers. When eighteen of these nations supported a mildly diluted version and sent Menzies to Cairo to meet Nasser, he felt he had bought both time and room for further manœuvring.

He had not expected a demand for international control of the canal to be accepted by Nasser, because he had drafted it to be acceptable to Britain and France. Moreover, he had insured himself against the unexpected by personally briefing Eisenhower for the remarks which had later proved so embarrassing to Menzies and by commenting further himself that "the

Suez Canal is not of primary concern to the United States."

By this means he had contrived to keep his allies guessing and could congratulate himself on having warded off disaster for six weeks – a formidable display of statesmanship made possible by his own unique admixture of sophistication and inarticulacy.

Eden and Pineau had been compelled to endure his charades because they were militarily incapable of acting decisively, because they were angling for the approval of the United States for the course upon which they were ultimately set, and because they hoped in the meantime to pick up by the wayside a considerable balance of European sympathy.

By the fifth week of the crisis, early in September, there was an impressive amount of evidence to show that Dulles was reaching the limit of his ingenuity and capacity for evasiveness, while his allies were recovering from a momentary flagging of spirits and might be even stronger in their determination to act against Egypt than before. Moreover, there was a State Department analysis of intelligence and diplomatic reports which complained of military movements indicative of something far more than mere precautionary measures, and not much less than general mobilisation for outright war.

And when Khrushchev warned that "if there is an attack on Egypt there will be volunteers," Dulles began to give ponderous consideration to the probability of war, to its effects on the presidential election campaign, and consequently on his own future, and to what could be done to avert it. He might have thought more quickly and clearly if there had not been so many divergent intrusions.

M. Georges-Picot, Director General of the Suez Canal Company in Paris, had circulated a private report showing that if the British and French pilots quit their jobs, Egypt would be unable to operate the canal. These pilots, comprising about half of the two hundred-odd employed by the company, wanted to leave Egypt but had been persuaded, in the interests of keeping the traffic moving, to remain at their posts. The company had decided not to terminate their contracts until mid-September, by which time it was hoped a solution might be imposed, either by international pressure or by force.

The Norwegian delegation to the London conference, unconvinced and suspicious that the company had carefully fostered the myth that only their own élite corps of pilots could navigate the narrow ribbon of water stretching for a hundred miles from Port Said on the Mediterranean to Suez on the Red Sea, had the masters of some two dozen Norwegian ships then docked in London summoned to the Norwegian Embassy. By chance it happened that all had been through the canal regularly, and it was their unanimous opinion that they could take their own ships through without the help of pilots. As a result, Norway, the second largest canal user, treated the conference with something close to indifference.

Though the sympathy they had sought was conspicuously absent, Britain and France continued to promulgate the fiction that Nasser was operating the canal only because the company had refrained from withdrawing non-Egyptian pilots. When the conference ended, Dulles had taken back to the United States the suspicion that when the pilots were eventually to be withdrawn in mid-September, canal operations might indeed break down and provide his allies with just the excuse they wanted for military action.

The Canal Company was actually preparing for precisely such an event. Pilots on home leave were held on call with full pay and allowances for an emergency situation.

At the same time cheques were sent privately to newspaper editors in Paris with covering letters thanking them for upholding the company's legal and moral rights to ownership of the canal. Unhappily for the company, one cheque for $300 turned up at the offices of the Communist *Liberation*, which had been consistently pro-Nasser. Facsimiles of cheque and letters appeared on its front page, forcing other Paris newspapers to admit that they too had received and rejected similar cheques.

While London, Paris, and Washington teemed with activity, Nasser remained in Cairo, supremely aloof and eminently reasonable. The canal functioned, British and French residents were unmolested, their property untouched, and the only indications of uncertainty, even fear, lurking behind the confident façade were advertisements appearing in European, American, and Canadian newspapers for qualified navigators to train as canal pilots. When Britain and France instructed their shipping companies to pay canal tolls in London or Paris, he wisely refrained from being provoked into making passage through the canal dependent upon payment of tolls to his new Suez Canal Authority. The contrast with his earlier behaviour, marked as it had been by provocative immaturity, implied that he was receiving shrewd advice from an outside influence, which presumably was Nehru.

Shortly before Menzies left Egypt, the British and French governments coupled an announcement that reservists were being called up, with another revealing that French armed forces had been granted temporary base facilities in Cyprus. Nasser complained to the Indian Ambassador in Cairo that "with all this beating of tom-toms I feel like an English public schoolboy being caned before the whole school."

He countered the Menzies mission with an embarrassingly tempting proposal that, in return for their agreement to pay tolls to Egypt, the canal users would have their rights embodied in a treaty to replace the old 1888 Convention guaranteeing unrestricted passage through the canal for all nations. The new agreement would provide the same guarantees and be lodged with the United Nations, which would act as arbitrator in the event of a dispute.

The offer was quickly quashed by the Foreign Office in London, where an official dismissed it with the offhand remark that "Nasser's word is meaningless, the Security Council is at the mercy of the Soviet veto, and the Assembly is too capricious to be the custodian of Britain's future." Nevertheless, the United Nations was being brought into the dispute by the need for Britain and France to parade before this forum of world opinion as peace-loving nations who, provoked beyond endurance, had been forced into an abhorrent military adventure.

The joint intent to overthrow Nasser by an immediate military response being frustrated by common unreadiness, two factors combined to enable it to be translated into a plan of action: a report from General Sir Charles Keightley, British Commander-in-Chief in the Middle East, that "our enterprise will be ready for September 15," and the Georges-Picot announcement that pilots would be withdrawn in mid-September. By correlation, therefore, September 15 became for London and Paris a day of decision.

Once British and French pilots left Egypt the canal traffic would begin to slow down dangerously, and at that stage the dispute could be placed before the Security Council on the ground that Egypt was in breach of the Convention guaranteeing freedom of movement.

The Soviet Union could be counted upon to veto any motion condemning Egypt, but the British and French governments would be seen to have made every effort to seek a just and peaceful solution. They would be able then to occupy the Canal Zone by force as the last means at their disposal to uphold the convention. Reference to the United Nations was envisaged, in fact, as a necessary ruse to cloak the actual military attack on Egypt with the cape of pious self-righteousness.

Sea- and air-troop transports arrived in Malta and Cyprus from bases in England, France, and North Africa daily, until by September 10 there were in the region of eighty thousand men encamped and waiting for the order to move out. At NATO headquarters in Paris the Supreme Allied Commander, General Gruenther, received a puzzling report saying that three squadrons of French Mystères had been moved and might be in southern France designated for operations in North Africa.

They were not in southern France. NATO had "lost" three entire squadrons of long-range jet interceptors.

V

THE NATO Council met in early September to discuss the crisis in private session. Lloyd's report adhered closely to the official British position that the canal had been unlawfully and arbitrarily nationalised, that an early, decisive response was vital if this particular dictatorship was to be stopped before plunging humanity into disaster, and that Britain and France had already shown their desire for a peaceful settlement by joining with the United States in summoning the London conference.

He said: "We have reached no decision yet on subsequent steps. I think it is understandable that we should make certain military arrangements, because after all there are thirteen thousand British residents in Egypt who expect protection. The Council can be assured that any recourse to force is abhorrent to us and will be taken only as a last resort." The British residents about whom he was being so solicitous needed no protection then. And when the attack was eventually made, they were not given any prior warning by the British government to leave Egypt.

Then it was Pineau's turn and, in far more emotionally anti-Nasser tone, he portrayed events in Egypt as a reflection of a new Arab-Asian nationalism contemptuous of international engagements. After referring to the loyalty of the canal company pilots, he said, "We cannot rule out, however, that through negligence or by some action of Colonel Nasser's the canal service might be interrupted. We could not tolerate such a situation. There is a limit beyond which it is not wise for free nations to go in acquiescence."

The United States Ambassador was expected to conclude with a report on his government's intentions; instead he remained seated and silent, while Pearson rose to warn against use of force before the United Nations had been given an opportunity to seek a settlement.

"Though Canada is geographically remote from the Suez," he said, "we cannot escape the consequences of failure to find a satisfactory solution through peaceful means. We don't underestimate the seriousness of the problem, especially for countries like the United Kingdom and France, for whom it is of vital importance. We have heard a lot about the issue in terms of nationalism, internationalism, colonialism, imperialism, et cetera, but the problem is the concrete one of ensuring the efficient, impartial, and non-political operation of the canal in the interests of all who use it.

". . . But we must rule out force except as a last resort and use it only in accordance with the principles we have accepted in the NATO pact and in the United Nations charter.

"I feel that if the problem comes before the Security Council, the majority of opinion there – even if it is vetoed – might be an important and valuable support for subsequent negotiations or action."

The invitation was obvious. If Britain and France wanted Canadian support for military action, they stood a better chance of securing it by making a genuine attempt to seek a solution through the United Nations. The clamour in Canada for unqualified backing of Anglo-French action was matched by an equally vociferous demand that the government dissociate itself from any action designed to impose a solution by force. Pearson felt instinctively that, unless some reference to the United Nations was made quickly, the Commonwealth relationship as far as Canada was concerned could be severely strained.

After the meeting, Pineau angrily challenged United States Ambassador Perkins to explain his silence, and, receiving an equivocal reply, coldly retorted, "At this moment, when we have a unique occasion to affirm our solidarity, we take contrary positions. If the world knew, we would be exposed in disorderly disunity. No one would believe that if threatened we would ever do anything serious in common."

Perkins confessed ruefully to Pearson that he was silent on instructions from Dulles, who was worried that the meeting might be interpreted as a rallying of the Council to an Anglo-French policy of firmness, even as an endorsement of their military preparations. By not participating in the discussions, he said, the United States hoped to avoid creating the impression that the Tripartite powers were "ganging up" on the rest.

There was no question of "ganging up." Lloyd and Pineau simply placed their positions before the Council and made no attempt to solicit sympathy or approval for them. Throughout, they studiously refrained from implicating NATO, though Pineau was always of the opinion that the crisis was more of a NATO affair than one for the United Nations.

Two days later, however, Selwyn Lloyd expressed to Pearson his perplexity at Canada's anxiety about the military preparations. "The chances are ten to one against us using force," he said, "but if Nasser just feels that the chances are ten to one that we will, he might be more reasonable." Then, referring to Pearson's demand that the issue be placed before the Security Council, he continued: "We will probably go to the Security Council because, as you say, even if our resolution condemning Egypt is vetoed by the Russians, we'll probably get a majority vote, one that should give us a firm United Nations basis for further action."

His omission of the operative condition that they should go to the United Nations with a genuine intent to seek a solution, and the indication that Britain and France would be more interested in "a firm United Nations basis" for whatever they planned to do next, compelled Pearson to say that neither Canada nor the United States would stand for the United Nations being employed as a cover for war.

Changing the subject, Lloyd said, "If things drag on like this, you know, Israel might take advantage of the situation to move against Egypt. Frankly, I wouldn't mind if it happened. They'd probably win, Nasser would go, and most of our troubles would be solved for us."

"Ingenious idea, but it won't work," said Pearson. "A few Arab leaders are sitting tight on the fence right now. An Israeli attack would unite them all behind Nasser. I hope you won't do any urging in that direction. The repercussions would be deplorable."

Disconcerted by what he later described as "the lack of skill being shown by the United Kingdom in the handling of the problem" and depressed by a nagging worry that so little "sureness of touch" would expose a wide rift in the Atlantic alliance, Pearson's next step unwittingly contributed to it.

On September 5 Ambassador Heeney in Washington was instructed to find out how the State Department would regard an Anglo-French resolution to the Security Council which "might invite automatic use of the veto by the Soviet Union, but also serve to provide them with the excuse of having the support of the majority vote for whatever is to follow."

Pearson's intent was to use the information as the basis for a forceful, impartial appraisal of probable United States reaction should Selwyn Lloyd and Pineau canvass the idea of confronting the Security Council with a resolution branding Egypt as the instigator of an aggressive threat to world peace. He hoped that by moderating their approach while urging Washington to be "a little firmer and less ambiguous," Britain, France, and the United States could at least be made to appear before the United Nations with unity of purpose.

But by then the presidential election campaign, in which Eisenhower wished to appear as the President of Peace, was making a powerful impact upon foreign policy. Senator William Knowland, a member of the Senate foreign relations committee, had stormed into the State Department to tell Dulles, "Now don't you get us mixed up in another of those European wars, Foster. You do, and Congress will have your hide." Eisenhower had added the warning that the administration needed to parade "a positive gain toward peaceful solution."

The pressures on Dulles were formidable and complex. When he heard of Ambassador Heeney's inquiries, his sensibilities were deeply offended. He accused the British of "trying to impose your will on Egypt in order to get new rights to the Suez Canal, and what's more, you're attempting to push the Security Council into the position of appearing to support you." Speaking to an official of the British Embassy, he said, "You can inform Mr. Lloyd that we are finding it increasingly difficult to go along with the whole operation in its present form."

Pearson's diplomatic manœuvre brought the rift into the open. Selwyn Lloyd's reply to Dulles said that Britain and the United States "are drifting further apart . . . than at any time since the beginning of this crisis." He argued that the canal issue could not be isolated from the general Egyptian threat to Western European oil supplies and to other Arab states "friendly to our Western purpose," and in that context the Secretary of State should make himself unmistakably clear, as at present "we cannot make out where the government of the United States stands."

In the swift, angry exchanges that followed, Lloyd insisted that "as the United States government appears unable to clarify its attitudes," a letter should be sent to the President of the Security Council informing him that a threat to peace existed and that the signatories reserved the right to consult the Council at an appropriate time in the future. Dulles described this idea as "cockeyed" and declined to sign the letter, which was eventually deposited undated and signed by Pineau and Lloyd only.

This device of preparing the Council in advance aroused the curiosity of United Nations delegates to the extent that the permanent British representative, Sir Pierson Dixon, felt compelled to give some explanation to other Commonwealth missions.

The Security Council, he said, had not been requested to do anything, and there was no intention of summoning a meeting. The British and French governments had simply warned the President that they might find it appropriate to refer the matter of the "Suez theft" to the United Nations in the near future.

The problem of Council consideration was further complicated, he said, "because the Secretary General is desperately worried about the mounting tension in Palestine." It appeared that, despite public statements to the contrary, Hammarskjold was "bitterly angry because the Israelis did not co-operate with him during his last mission to the Middle East." As he intended to make a strongly worded report to the Security Council complaining of Israel's attitude, Hammarskjold did not want the Council to be seized of the canal issue at the same time. Dixon said he shared the Secretary General's concern that the Palestine question should be kept separate from the canal issue, and for that reason Britain and France had decided to rely upon the "considerable moral effect" of bringing the crisis to the attention of the United Nations by means of the deposited letter.

Dixon was far too astute a diplomat to believe his own words. The "considerable moral effect" was not evident to his listeners, nor did it ever materialize. His unenviable task was to reflect as convincingly as possible the delusions of London.

In this climate of rising temperatures and cooling personal relationships, the crisis unexpectedly ceased to move and hovered instead over Washington, Paris, London, and Cairo.

VI

SHIPS and landing craft were congregated in a vast armada at Malta; fleets of bombers and jet fighters were dispersed over Cyprus; and reservists were becoming restless, impatient to throw off uniforms and return to their civilian jobs. Diplomacy had so far failed, the British and French Suez pilots were about to quit, and a breakdown in the flow of canal traffic appeared imminent.

Mollet and Pineau were ready to act; Dulles was making it increasingly evident that America's benevolent neutrality would not be forthcoming in the event of war; and Eden, confronted by the imperative need for a momentous decision, recoiled from it.

His Cabinet was hopelessly divided. R. A. Butler, Leader of the House of Commons, approved the gathering of forces as a precautionary measure, but vehemently opposed use of them. So did the Minister of Defence, Sir Walter Monckton. In consequence Eden formed a more comforting, less critical inner cabinet consisting of himself, Selwyn Lloyd, Macmillan, Antony Head, Lord Home, and Lord Salisbury, Lord President of the Council.

Apart from calculated leaks, security about the movements of troops and equipment was tighter than any allied officer then in London or Paris could remember since the days immediately preceding the invasion of Normandy. Explicit directives to both French and British planners, issued over the signatures of Prime Ministers Mollet and Eden, forbade any military information of any kind being given to anybody who had no direct and demonstrable need to know. These orders effectively dried up all ordinary channels of information, on which NATO, friendly military missions, and service attachés usually relied for day-to-day intelligence; and in consequence diplomats grew increasingly worried and anxious as they hurried from one government department to another, from one embassy to another, to conjecture and speculate for the benefit of their respective governments.

Canada, as yet uncommitted but conscious of Commonwealth responsibilities, was particularly concerned, to the extent that a visiting British diplomat was asked in Ottawa to shed some light on the mystery. He replied, "All I can say is that these precautions are regarded in London as a military operation, and security measures are as tight as they were on June 6, 1944." But diplomats and military observers were not totally idle or blind. A Suez Canal Company statement in Paris that British and French pilots would be withdrawn from canal service on September 14 was quickly coupled with persistent rumours that an Anglo-French invasion force was due to sail on the 15th. The Canadian Joint Staff in London reported to Defence Headquarters in Ottawa that September 15 could be D-Day; Norman Robertson informed External Affairs that it might more correctly be described as the day when Anglo-French preparations would be completed.

Precisely the same information reached the State Department, where Dulles was busy with a vast staff of political and legal advisers trying to put down on paper the details of his latest manœuvre in the long procession of delaying tactics. When he was, as he later told Canada's Ambassador Heeney, "assured that the United Kingdom and France were prepared to act on September 15," his staff were given until the 9th to produce a plan that might have at least the appearance of feasibility.

The 9th was forty-eight hours away; in a week there might be war.

Neither the President nor Dulles was reassured by an inspired leak from London that the Prime Minister had told a select group of influential British friends that "the volume and tempo of military preparations is at all times under effective ministerial control"; there was no question or risk of them acquiring their own momentum so that the government might be compelled to take a drastic political decision on purely military grounds.

Antony Head, an efficient military planner turned politician, was responsible to Eden alone, and, despite French protests that the Egyptians were untrained Arabs, not highly professional Germans, he and his War Office staff were plodding grimly toward completion of a monumental operational plan based upon the premise that though your enemy be an ant, treat him as if he were an elephant. The Egyptians would have been flattered had they known; and knowing, the French commanders were disgusted.

Paradoxically, Selwyn Lloyd was reputed to be the least belligerent of the inner cabinet. He served Eden loyally, and never appeared to be wholly convinced either that force was the only way to rid the Middle East of Nasser, or that it was the right way. If he intended to divert this great Anglo-French enterprise from its course, however, there were no means by which he could do so.

But Dulles was ready with the plan he hoped would stop it in its tracks – an unsparing, ruthlessly conceived betrayal of Eden. Though the Secretary of State's motive may have been the simple, honourable, and sincere one of stooping low, even to duplicity, on the eve of war, to prevent its happening, other considerations made the plan easier for him to rationalise and influenced the manner of its execution.

There are those who worked under or with both of these vain and powerful men who thought they could sense that Eden, feeling himself the superior in intellect and experience, was resentful in the presence of Dulles that his country's decline from greatness should deprive him of the right to appear as the decisive presence in world affairs; and that Dulles, representing a new and greater power, was given to tactlessly reminding Eden on occasion that despite the authority he had once enjoyed he now played a lesser role.

Accurate or perhaps not wholly so, only a judgement such as this can explain the abrasive Eden-Dulles relationship which reached its nadir on this occasion and provided a plausible reason for Eden's lapse from polite restraint in his memoirs to write with bitter brevity: "Such cynicism towards allies destroys true partnership. It leaves only the choice of parting, or a master and vassal relationship. . . ."

The betrayal, when it came, demonstrated so forcibly who was master and who was vassal that even the most jaded diplomatic sophisticates still relish the classical simplicity of it, the devastating effects of it.

CHAPTER SIX

Last Resort

MOLLET and Pineau arrived in London on Monday, September 10, to persuade the British that military action was imperative. They had no love for the ponderous military plan that had been devised, their own General Staff favouring direct paratroop action aimed at occupation of the Canal Zone. Pineau said: "We get the canal; Nasser goes. Why waste time on a protracted campaign to capture Alexandria and Cairo first?"

Eden, surprisingly, agreed, but for different reasons. He believed the political climate had changed so drastically that a military attack directed at Cairo, and transparently intended to overthrow the Nasser régime, would not be condoned by world opinion. A direct attack on the canal would be more desirable, subject to the professional advice of the soldiers who would have to undertake it.

They agreed to draft a new political directive to the joint Anglo-French command, and during these discussions, at approximately 9:30 P.M., Dulles telephoned from Washington to describe the subtle twist that might transform a diplomatic deadlock into a dramatic victory. The Tripartite powers, all rifts healed and once more in harmony, could stab their way into the canal, each with a hand on the hilt of a weapon called the Suez Canal Users' Association (SCUA).

The vision of three good companions marching in step again to smash down the ramparts of yet another despotic dictator shone with dazzling intensity at Downing Street. Eden, elated and convinced of the durability of the Anglo-American alliance, grasped at this remarkable new weapon proffered by Dulles and brandished it triumphantly in front of his skeptical French colleagues. Three days later its total lack of authority was revealed with cruel and humiliating speed.

The SCUA had no point.

Dulles had known from the dispatches of Ambassador Byroade, long before taking his Aswan Dam decision, that the canal was vulnerable to "Egyptianisation" and had gambled on American organisational genius to overcome any difficulties that might have arisen should it happen. In his view, it was the depth of Anglo-French feeling and their joint obduracy that was causing all the backfires. He regarded the crisis as being essentially one of keeping his allies in check, traffic moving through the canal, and oil flowing from the Middle East. At the end of August, Byroade, then awaiting replacement in Cairo, reassured him about the canal.

"Even though pilots may be severed in fairly large numbers," said the Ambassador, "I believe that with some delay and considerable rerouting of traffic the canal can be kept in operation. Global recruiting of new pilots is producing more applicants than the anticipated vacancies, and training is being rushed so as to be completed in three months rather than the usual six months."

Subsequently Dulles received from Arthur Flemming, director of the Office of Defence Mobilisation and co-ordinator of the committees studying the redistribution of Middle East oil in the event of a canal stoppage, a report that rerouting was a feasible proposition.

If the canal closed but pipelines to the Mediterranean remained open, Western Europe's consumption of 800,000 barrels a day could be met by bringing 350,000 barrels a day round South Africa, by supplying another 350,000 barrels from increased United States production, and by an extra 50,000 barrels a day each from Canada and Venezuela. If pipelines were shut down as well as the canal, small coastal tankers could be pressed into service with the large ocean fleets to bring more than a million barrels a day round the Cape. In either event the price tag would be in the region of $600 million a year, which could be underwritten by United States loans, two-thirds of which would be accounted for by British requirements alone.

Dulles was at once captivated by the implication that as Western Europe need not be totally dependent upon the canal for oil supplies, the Anglo-French argument that they could not permit their economic survival to be at the mercy of Nasser was no longer a valid excuse for war. He knew, however, that they would never accept the Cape route alternative if doing so might be interpreted as surrender to Nasser – unless the idea could be attractively disguised. He had it gift-wrapped with such glittering prospects that Eden would have certainly seen through them had he not been so anxious to have American support.

The SCUA scheme involved forming an association of users to hire its own pilots, collect tolls from its members, make payments to Egypt for technical co-operation, and run its own convoys through the canal. Pilots and "convoy administrators" would live aboard headquarters ships stationed at either end of the canal to avoid physical contact with Egyptian soil.

Dulles argued that the 1888 Convention guaranteeing un-molested passage for all users clearly implied that if this right should be threatened they could act together to safeguard their

interests. SCUA was simply a means by which users could effectively apply this legal intent of the Convention. Legal experts
and naval authorities would demolish so specious a proposal
quickly, but Dulles knew that nothing could shake Eden from
a political conviction, the most significant at present being his
preoccupation with Anglo-American unity.

He invited Eden to take the initiative, adding that any
interference with an association convoy would be a breach of
the Convention calling for appropriate action. By this Dulles
privately meant the alternative Cape route; to Eden it was an
invitation to force a way through the canal if Nasser tried to
interfere.

At Downing Street that night Eden emphasised to his
French guests the necessity of accepting the United States as a
partner in a venture that would render the Egyptian helpless
and impotent. If Nasser acted rashly, then the three major
Allies, not just two of them, would demonstrate their unity of
purpose and will to act for the common good.

Pineau, never an enthusiastic believer in the sincerity of
American co-operation, was astounded. "I think this is just
another Dulles bluff," he said. "We've left a visiting card with
the Security Council, and he's determined that we won't
actually make the visit. Trying to unravel this latest scheme
will get us all so involved that by the time we find the whole
affair is impracticable, everyone will be bored to death by our
threats."

For the next forty-eight hours telegrams flowed in full
spate between Paris, London, and Washington; telephone lines
were kept open, and emergency technical committees were
formed to study the proposal in detail. Eden explained to
Dulles that he intended to summon a conference of the eighteen maritime powers which had supported the Tripartite
"statement of views" taken by Menzies to Cairo, in the hope
that all would become members "of the club." Dulles promised
United States support, added that "Egypt is going to like this

less than our earlier proposals, but having refused those, they can hardly expect to get as good a deal the second time around."

Some appealing advantages began to appear which not even Dulles had expected. The scheme provided a means of a general withholding of canal tolls from Egypt, thereby denying Nasser his objective of using them to help build the Aswan Dam. It also provided Dulles with an opportunity to suggest that if Nasser interfered in any way with SCUA convoys, or if the SCUA scheme itself ran into insurmountable obstacles, there was always the alternative of massing tanker resources and carrying oil round the Cape. Eden reacted strongly on the ground that the Cape route would involve additional financial burdens he was unwilling to accept.

On the afternoon of the 11th, President Eisenhower was asked at a press conference if the United States would back Britain and France if they resorted to use of force. He replied:

"I don't know exactly what you mean by backing them. . . . This country will not go to war ever while I am occupying my present post unless the Congress is called into session and Congress declares such a war. . . . We established the United Nations to abolish aggression and I am not going to be party to aggression. . . ."

For the first time the Anglo-French position was branded by the United States as potentially aggressive; implicitly, therefore, Eisenhower rejected their claim that Egypt had become an aggressor by grabbing the canal.

The ominous first light of what Eden has since described as a "disastrous chapter of delusion" was seen only by Pineau. Before he left London with Mollet that evening, he warned Eden: "I promise you we will regret what we have done today. It would be better if our forces were already at sea."

Eden, in no mood to pay much attention to such gloomy predictions, began drafting the speech he would make the next day at the opening of an emergency session of the British

Parliament. But Pineau had made an impression on Selwyn Lloyd, who went home to face a night of sleepless anxiety. Lloyd's attitude to the use of force was ambivalent. One day he would appear as a strong advocate, and back away on the next, indicating he may have been personally averse to it while yielding to the Cabinet in their powerful advocacy in favour of it.

Next morning Dulles and Mollet agreed to the precise wording of an announcement Eden would make later in the day to the House of Commons. Mollet would repeat it in the Paris Assembly, and Dulles would issue a similarly worded statement to the press in Washington.

II

DRAMA was inevitable. At 6:00 P.M. Washington time on September 11, the Suez Canal Company in Paris formally announced that as all contracts expired at midnight on the 14th, the company would arrange for withdrawal of British and French pilots the next day. No one doubted that chaos would follow. Lloyd's of London slapped a 15 per cent surcharge on the insurance premiums of ships intending to continue using the canal, deliberately forcing the larger shipping companies to balance the risk and extra cost of using the canal against the time factor involved in taking the Cape route.

This action not only indicated the extent of opposition to war that prevailed in the financial circles of the City of London, but also served to give Dulles unexpected help. While government supporters read it as a sign of lack of confidence in Egypt's ability to maintain unrestricted passage through the canal, it had, by decreasing traffic, the actual effect of easing the pressure on the pilots who would remain. Within a week the daily traffic rate dropped by 20 per cent.

Talk of war pervaded European capitals. The Italian Foreign Minister, Signore Martino, still in Paris after the recent NATO Council meetings, called at the Quai d'Orsay in evident distress, demanded to see Pineau, and said bluntly: "You people are planning on war at any moment. Don't count on Italy's support"; the French Ambassador in Luxembourg let it be known that Nasser's day was nearly over; Marshal Bulganin wrote formally to Eden and Mollet accusing them of intending to attack Egypt and violate its territorial sovereignty; and Nehru dispatched two appeals to Eden within twenty-four hours, and sent his indefatigable envoy, Krishna Menon, to Cairo. From the beginning Nehru had guided Nasser's words and deeds. Krishna Menon, his personal representative throughout, had flown constantly between Cairo and London in vain efforts to sell the West proposals he had previously arranged with Nasser. On arrival in Cairo he called on the Canadian Ambassador, Herbert Norman, to say that Nehru hoped Pearson would use his private influence with Eden to persuade him to use the utmost discretion in dealing with the canal situation. If Eden could be persuaded to give India enough rope and trust it, he could almost certainly guarantee that Nasser would agree to a satisfactory settlement.

Reporting this conversation to Pearson, Norman said, "What Menon really means is that he hopes you will influence Eden into agreeing to India, meaning himself, working out a solution with Nasser."

That evening Nasser issued a memorandum suggesting that if the canal users were willing to recognise Egypt's right to own and operate the canal and were prepared to pay "just and equitable tolls" to the Egyptian government, he was willing to reassert their rights to freedom of passage at all times without regard to political relations.

Krishna Menon arrived at the Canadian Embassy for a

second time in a state of nervous agitation. He brandished a copy of the memorandum in front of Norman, saying he had to go to London, as Nehru believed England would soon attack Egypt. He had sent another appeal to Eden, but believed that, as the government of Canada had expressly stated that a real settlement could not be reached without the consent of both parties, Pearson should press hard to secure appointments for Krishna Menon with Eden and Lloyd.

Pearson, however, remembering vividly how lack of collective action at the League of Nations had allowed a drift toward world war, was more concerned that somehow the affair should be brought before the United Nations. He might have replied politely to Krishna Menon and thought no more of it, but for the international uproar that followed Eden's speech to the British Parliament on September 12.

III

EDEN rose to speak in the House of Commons against the backdrop of an imminent collapse in canal operations, increasing Russian arms supplies to Egypt, a rising crescendo of anti-West vituperation from Cairo Radio, the likelihood of tiny Jordan breaking apart under the stresses imposed by violent pro-Nasser rioting, and rumours that Anglo-French forces in the Mediterranean were poised for the attack on Egypt.

Labour members watched him, ready to jeer the first mention of force, although their leader, Hugh Gaitskell, had advocated it at the outset of the crisis; the extreme right wing of the Conservatives – the "Suez Rebels" led by Captain Waterhouse – sat impassively behind him ready to cheer a declaration of war.

The preamble of his speech described the conception of a Suez Canal Users' Association and led to the prepared announcement in which he said, "I must make it clear that if the Egyptian government should seek to interfere with the operations of the association, or refuse to extend to it the essential minimum co-operation, then that government will once more be in breach of the Convention of 1888. In that event, Her Majesty's government and others concerned will be free to take such further steps as seem to be required, either through the United Nations or by other means, for the assertion of their rights."

The "Suez Rebels" cheered; the Labour party rallied to unanimous condemnation; moderate Conservatives sat stunned and incredulous. Britain, it seemed, was now committed to action. As Nasser would oppose such an outrageous scheme that would virtually take the operation of the canal out of his hands, the unmistakable inference was that Britain and France would shoot their way through.

If war had seemed probable before Eden spoke, it now appeared certain. Mollet's corresponding statement in Paris confirmed what the world assumed to be the real intention: to place a battleship at the head of a convoy and sail it into the canal with orders to shoot up anything that got in its way.

In Washington, the White House and State Department were placed under siege by correspondents who were told that neither the President nor the Secretary of State was available for comment. In Ottawa, Pearson reconsidered Krishna Menon's request for help and sent a message to London urging that before irrevocable decisions were made the British leaders should at least hear what Krishna Menon might have to say. But Krishna Menon was by then glued to Cairo, passing Nehru's advice to a Nasser who, according to diplomats then in Cairo, was for the first time showing serious concern.

India was playing a role hard to define, even in retrospect. Nehru undoubtedly approved of what Nasser had done and was doing, without necessarily liking the means by which he was doing it. The Indian leader encouraged non-alignment among newly independent states and lent his authority on their behalf when they exercised their rights to deal with East or West as they felt inclined. He attempted to explain provocative acts as being the natural outcome of political immaturity and felt that older nations should show understanding, patience, and tolerance.

India's sympathy for Nasser's aims could be taken for granted, but it appears probable that Krishna Menon's personal proclivities influenced his interpretation of the instructions he was receiving from Delhi.

The effect of the West's failure to make good the threats of weeks before, and the obvious indecision of London and Paris, had provided Nasser with an opportunity to recover his foothold on the summit of power. But were he to be pushed too hard he might still topple, and the probable humiliation of failing to stop a SCUA convoy escorted by warships could be the fatal push.

He wanted to place European canal pilots under guard to prevent them quitting, but Krishna Menon deflected the intent on the ground that such an act would cost Nasser the sympathy of those countries which had not taken sides. According to Krishna Menon's later account, Nehru insisted that no attempt of any kind should be made to interfere with the liberty of the pilots. He apparently confided to Krishna Menon at this stage that Dulles, in a recent exchange of views, had assured him that the United States would react strongly against the use of force "even to the extent of risking a showdown with Britain and France, with whom he was impatient and exasperated."

September 13 was the day Dulles chose to expose his deception, regardless of the political havoc it would create.

That morning Ambassador Hussein called on him to say that Egypt would regard any move by the proposed users' association to force a way through the canal as a deliberate act of

aggression. He added, "You had better understand that we are
serious in our intention to fight, even if it means national
martyrdom."

Dulles made the scua announcement at a press conference
later the same day. He read from a text similar to those used by
Eden and Mollet, and his actual statement conformed to their
agreement. No one could doubt that the United States was
acting in full partnership with its allies, even to the extent of
warning Egypt that interference with the legal rights of the
association would bring about drastic consequences.

Then came question time, and the Secretary of State
pushed his official papers aside to become a relaxed and composed trial lawyer, ready to prosecute a defendant.

Asked if the United States would join Britain and France
in forcing an scua convoy through the canal, he replied: "I
know nothing about a plan to shoot a way through. . . . We
certainly have no intention of doing so. It may be that we have
the right to do it, but we don't intend to do it as far as the
United States is concerned. We don't intend to boycott the
canal, either. If force is interposed by Egypt, I do not call it a
boycott to avoid this use of force in order to shoot a way
through. If we are met by force, we shall advise our ships to
avoid it, that's all. I do not call this a boycott. The alternative
for the United States is to send our vessels round the Cape. . . .
I want to say right now that it is fantastic that anyone should
wish to impose some undesirable régime on Egypt and we
won't do it, certainly not as far as the United States is
concerned.

"The association is not intended to guarantee anything to anybody. I think that each nation has to decide for itself what action
it will have to take to defend and if possible realize its rights
which it believes it has as a matter of treaty. I do not recall just
exactly what Sir Anthony Eden said on this point. I did not get
the impression there was any undertaking or pledge given by
him to shoot their way through the canal."

The door was closing on more than a century of Anglo-American-French friendship and co-operation. When asked if he thought smaller nations could afford to send ships round the Cape, Dulles said, "We shall help them with loans. It will not be financially catastrophic or beyond our capacity to deal with." And when it was suggested that he had "virtually handed all the trump cards to Nasser," he replied with chilling self-esteem: "That's just not so, particularly from a moral standpoint. I do not feel adequate appreciation has been given to the fact that great powers with vital interests at stake, possessors of over-whelming . . . military power, have exercised . . . a very great measure of self-restraint. . . . History will judge it that the exercise of that self-restraint in deference to the obligations taken under the United Nations Charter adds more from a moral standpoint. . . ."

There was jubilation in Cairo. Nasser had been told he could have the canal, that he could reject the users' association plan, use force if he wished to stop its ships, and, as far as the United States was concerned, operate the canal without censure and with impunity. In Paris momentary confusion was quickly countered by Pineau, who said: "The Secretary of State speaks for his own country, not France."

In London there was political chaos. A bewildered, desperate Eden faced an emergency meeting of the full Cabinet, at which Butler, Monckton, and the anti-military group acidly demanded explanations for his commitment to scua without the support of the United States. When Lloyd attempted to defend the Prime Minister by saying that all Eden had done was to accept a Dulles idea and act, as he thought, in concert with the United States, he was reminded that "Mr. Dulles can be relied upon only if he puts down in writing what he thinks and is asked to sign it."

In the House of Commons the entire Conservative side sat in angry silence while Socialist after Socialist rose in vain attempts to extract explanations from the government of what had happened and what they intended to do about it. Eden was absent; no one else could answer.

Later in the evening Eden took his place in the House, looking, as the gallery correspondents were to write, "pale and grim, his features sagging and obviously in a raging temper." For an hour he parried demands for an unequivocal promise to abandon SCUA and refer the affair to the United Nations, then finally announced that in an emergency he would consider reference to the Security Council.

The rupture in the Atlantic Alliance was starkly bared; after seven weeks of convergence and divergence, Washington, Moscow, New Delhi, and Cairo were aligned against London and Paris. Yet Vice President Nixon was able to appear on television at a later stage to describe this policy as a "bold declaration of American independence," an extravagant phrase written into his speech by none other than Dulles himself.

The second blow fell on the 15th. Taking advantage of the repatriation arrangements made by the Canal Company, and expecting to be rehired by the users' association when it had been formed, French and British pilots left their jobs *en masse.* Nasser permitted their evacuation by air, then played a trump of his own by passing forty ships through the canal that day, four more than the daily average. With his own Egyptian pilots reinforced by more than a hundred newly recruited and only meagrely trained pilots from Russia, Yugoslavia, Greece, Germany, Scandinavia, and the United States, he exposed the emptiness of the Canal Company's claims that without the élite corps of pilots, traffic would be paralysed, and demonstrated that Egypt could keep the canal open in conformity with the 1888 Convention.

At an informal discussion in Paris between the foreign ministers of Canada, Norway, the Netherlands, Italy, and Turkey, M. Beyen of the Netherlands stated flatly: "This new association thing won't work, obviously because it is not intended to work." And Norway's Halvarde Lange reported that during lunch with Mollet the previous day he had been told that France was determined, regardless of the clash between Eden and Dulles, to "see this matter through even if, as a last resort, force has to be used."

"We want international control of the Suez, of course," Mollet had said. "But more important, we think it desirable that a defeat should be inflicted upon Nasser which will result in his disappearance so that other Arab states will have a chance of withdrawing from Egyptian hegemony." According to Lange, the French Premier then said, "We'll not flinch from sending a warship through the canal ahead of a merchant vessel. If the Egyptians interfere, they'd better look out."

The melancholy masquerade of scua was played out to an ignoble demise, Dulles delivering the fatal blow with a statement saying: "I can't understand this talk of the United States pulling the teeth out of the users' association. There never were any teeth in it as far as I am aware."

Little more than a week later, Lloyd's of London withdrew premium surcharge on ships using the canal, an expression of faith that Egypt could operate it efficiently; and if Britain and France were now ready and able to fight, the canal was no longer an issue worth fighting about.

Deserted finally by Dulles, who had never really been with him, Eden decided to go to the Security Council. He sent a message to Washington urging that the formal approach should be made on a three-power basis, but the Secretary of State turned his back upon this appeal, and when the official reference was actually made toward the end of September, it bore the signatures of Britain and France, but not of the United States.

The dent in the nato shield had become a hole. Politically, the three major members were widely separated; militarily, France was in the process of diverting a wide range of military equipment from its nato supplies to Israel.

Apart from the Mystère jets supplied under the "official" and "secret" lists, United States mobile artillery and anti-tank weapons, delivered under NATO off-shore arrangements for use by the French army, were shipped to Tel Aviv.

While the lengthy Security Council procedure involved in placing the Anglo-French complaint on its agenda was set in motion, the initiative at this low ebb gradually passed from Downing Street to the Quai d'Orsay, where Christian Pineau had not, and would not, waver from the objective he had set himself at the beginning: an honourable settlement in Algeria, even if it first entailed the downfall of Nasser.

IV

THE motives that inspired Dulles to treat Eden so harshly were the indisputably decent ones of restraining his allies from an action he suspected would have disastrous consequences, of providing them with honourable alternatives and of maintaining under severe stress the façade of Atlantic unity.

Whether by design or accident, he achieved a remarkably paradoxical success by involving Eden to such an extent that British policy seemed to lack direction, while his own appeared firm and consistent. His was the practical concept of SCUA; Eden was blamed for confused interpretation of it.

Though communication between the Western leaders was becoming increasingly difficult, Dulles dined in London on September 20 with Eden and Lloyd at Downing Street. During the dinner he advised that at all costs Britain and France should avoid reference to the United Nations until a plan had crystallized with clear objectives, one which the United States could readily support. Selwyn Lloyd appeared eager to get the matter before the Security Council at the earliest possible moment, but the Prime Minister assured his guest that they would proceed with caution.

Eden and Lloyd had, in fact, taken the decision to go to the United Nations before Dulles came to dinner. Thirty-six hours later, when Dulles arrived in Washington convinced he had successfully postponed the showdown again, he learned that at Anglo-French request the Security Council was already seized of the crisis.

Dulles, whose turn it was to rage at the perfidy of allies, admitted to the Australian Ambassador in Washington that he was "considerably put out" by this double cross. He confided in evident exasperation that he had no "idea where Britain and France expect to end up, because perhaps they didn't know themselves; and if they did, they probably wouldn't let me into their confidence."

A typical example of his bland ability to contradict himself followed.

"I've told the French I would find it very difficult to oppose a resolution at the United Nations containing an injunction against use of force," he said.

The Australian drew his attention to a remark by Prime Minister Menzies that to believe force could never be used other than in self-defence or in pursuit of a United Nations decision was a "suicidal doctrine."

"I agree," said Dulles – who was the author of the "doctrine."

Though the crisis centre was shifting, superficially, to New York, beneath the surface of the storm, governments seethed with activity, as would-be mediators canvassed support, and those who enjoyed fringe benefits from the canal no matter who owned or operated it tried to dissuade their bellicose friends from folly.

A senior Foreign Ministry official in New Delhi gave formal warning that if Great Britain "throws away her great moral position in the world India will find it difficult to remain in the

Commonwealth." And in Paris the Canadian Ambassador was summoned to the Quai d'Orsay to be told privately that "the infliction of a defeat on Nasser is not necessarily an immediate objective; therefore there is an opportunity for Canada to use its influence with Dulles to see that NATO is not disunited by his refusal to see things the way we do."

On September 17 Nehru received a letter from President Eisenhower, which said: "I give you my personal assurance that the United States government has no intention of using force over the Suez question. We ruled out the use of force at the beginning. . . ."

And on the same day, in Cairo, Nasser saw the Indian Ambassador and said: "I prefer the United Kingdom and French attitudes of open hostility, which I can understand, to the Americans who are always blowing hot and cold and complicating the situation."

Two days later, in Paris, the British Defence Minister, Sir Walter Monckton, confessed to Pearson during a NATO dinner that he admired Canada's "sensible urgings upon us in London and elsewhere" and that he shared Pearson's "anxieties about the possible use of force." Referring to press reports of a Cabinet split with himself and Butler leading the opposition to Eden, Macmillan, Lord Salisbury, and Head, he surprisingly portrayed Selwyn Lloyd as being "only intermittently for strong action." He described the reports as "embarrassingly accurate" and added: "It is very difficult for a Cabinet member holding a minority view to admit the existence of considerations which do not fit neatly into pictures which the majority have made for themselves. Nobody in government seems to feel it his duty to bring forward bad news – a grave dereliction, I think, among our advisers."

In London, the Foreign Office agreed with Pearson that there could be no harm in talking to Krishna Menon, who had been putting in so much overtime in Cairo that when he finally left for England the scene had moved to New York. Krishna

Menon complained bitterly that Nasser had kept him kicking his feet idly for too long, then energetically set about arranging to move himself to the United Nations.

To the dismay of those who hoped that economic sanctions and denial of canal tolls would damage Egypt's economy, it was discovered that between July and September Egypt had been collecting 45 per cent of all tolls – 10 per cent more than in 1955, when they could be paid in London, Paris, or Cairo. On the other hand, the maintenance of military forces at readiness in the Mediterranean was costing Britain $3.5 million a week.

Allen Dulles, head of United States Central Intelligence Agency, visited New Delhi at President Eisenhower's request and was told by Nehru that his brother's "heartless treatment of Egypt on the Aswan Dam business is unforgivable." Dulles replied that the United States Congress was against the loan and that in any event he felt that Nasser's "intemperate language against us was inexcusable."

"His language was intemperate," agreed Nehru, "but you should allow for his youth and inexperience in these matters. He is liable to be affected by mob psychosis. Eden was also intemperate, and he is experienced."

Near the end of September, Norman Robertson in London was reassured by the Minister of State at the Foreign Office, Anthony Nutting, that the prospect of war was fading rapidly. "The Cabinet," he said, "is now looking toward a solution by negotiation. The Prime Minister and Foreign Secretary are persuading the French government to agree that this is the best approach. Unfortunately, until they do we cannot give our delegations in New York adequate and coherent briefings."

At last, after two brittle months of crisis, the harsh sounds of war were being softened, passions were subsiding, and tension was perceptibly slackening. The crisis was where most governments, and their peoples, wanted it to be – with the United Nations. Eden and Lloyd were in Paris, as far as Nutting knew, to cajole Mollet and Pineau into the quieter waters of reflective mediation. Nutting could not know that something quite different was happening; and when he did eventually learn the truth, he was to express his distaste for it so forcibly at Downing Street that when he left, he also left the government.

V

REFERENCE to the United Nations was the break in the crisis Canadian, Scandinavian, and other friends of Britain and France had been waiting for patiently, almost despairingly. They believed that if the principle of international control of the canal, to which London and Paris had obstinately clung since the first London conference, was to be made acceptable to Egypt, only a United Nations solution with the backing of majority opinion could do it. Until now the cold war had denied the organisation an opportunity to "peace-keep" in a credible sense, and no one expected the freak circumstances in which the Korean intervention was made possible—the absence of the Russian delegate to the Security Council during a crucial debate—to be repeated. Suez promised to be a classic issue that would decide if "United Nations diplomacy" could be applied effectively, which was one reason why Pearson had so carefully avoided committing Canada during the initial convulsions of the crisis. The United Nations was the primary pillar of his foreign policy, and the respect he enjoyed in New York was largely due to the obvious independence of Canada where friends and enemies alike were concerned. Throughout the crisis Canada's motives were never suspect, never challenged.

Pearson's prestige and the esteem in which he was held made it inevitable that the Canadian representatives should take the initiative in preparing the ground for a possible Assembly debate.

The head of the Canadian permanent mission, Robert A. Mackay, had little hope that the British and French would reach an equitable compromise. He reported to Ottawa: "We are less hopeful now that the Western powers can win a favourable response from the Afro-Asians . . . who have been driven closer to Nasser. The United Kingdom and France have maintained the threat of force even though the United States and other members of the users groups are opposed to force. . . . In a United Nations context the Latin Americans too might be expected to react unfavourably to any form of coercion.

"Nasser's 'heroic' stand against powerful 'white imperialists' is hand-made for the applause of Asia and Africa. On the other hand, the advantage of having the question discussed in a United Nations forum is that the real issues and difficulties can be exposed."

He envisaged Canadian effort being directed toward persuading Britain and France to back away from international control to international supervision, with advisory and consultative responsibilities rather than managerial.

"This is probably going to be unpalatable to those who have been thinking in terms of an imposed solution," he said. "The Western powers must get rid of the idea Egypt should be hauled into court. There has been too much provocation . . . too much appearance that might is right."

On September 26, the counsellor of the mission, Geoffrey Murray, at thirty-eight one of the most capable of the younger Canadian diplomats and already a skilled United Nations tactician, questioned the British and French delegations about their intentions. He discovered they were adamantly determined to accept nothing less than international control, information that caused considerable despondency when it circulated throughout the United Nations. On the other hand, the Australian delegation, which expected to support the Anglo-French proposals without reservation, were engagingly cheerful, one member informing Murray that "when the Council meets we're

going to have a bashing session with Egypt as the victim."
Referring to the British representative, Sir Pierson Dixon, he
said: "He's given us pep talks to go in there with flags flying
and give the gypo a real bashing." Murray's report said: "These
tactics imply a disappointing use of United Nations machinery."

   If Britain and France were carrying through a strong theme
of insistence upon removal of the canal from the control of
Egypt or any other one power, Dulles was being consistent in
his search for a more flexible formula. He believed the Anglo-
French condemnation of Egypt was more of an ultimatum
than a negotiable position, that the United Nations had been
brought into the affair as a matter of procedure rather than of
policy. He sent messages to London and Paris and to Hammarskjold, and as foreign ministers and delegates gathered for the
first Council session on October 5, it was learned that the real
discussions would be held between Lloyd, Pineau, and Fawzi
in the privacy of Hammarskjold's office on the thirty-eighth
floor. Suddenly and unaccountably, a sense of fragile, dangerous uncertainty pervaded the corridors of diplomacy, as if all
were warned that finally the last resort had been reached.

   Fewer than two dozen men in the world were aware that
the real decision-making was taking place, not in New York,
but in Paris, where Israel was arranging for survival through
conquest.

FROM AN ACCOUNT BY CHRISTIAN PINEAU: *We arrived at the
middle of September without anything useful having been done
about Nasser. We were at a dead halt. Peaceful negotiations
had failed. Dulles was an interesting personality in every sense,
evidently motivated by preoccupations completely different
from ours. They were of an order more metaphysical than
political. I recall the words of someone who was quite unkind
on this subject. He said: "Dulles is indeed an average American, but he has his eyes turned to the sky and his feet planted
in oil."*

I will admit that on a personal level his users' club was utterly disagreeable to me. It convinced some members of the French government that we were operating on a private plan in the interests of the old Suez Canal Company and its share-holders – of whom there were more than two hundred thou-sand in France. This was not the case. While one cannot ignore entirely the element of justice in respect of suitable indemnity for shareholders, this was not the factor that led me to insist so forcibly on common action.

I felt that if we did not do something we would put our-selves in an inferior position in Algeria, that we would give the FLN rebels a major trump. Also, we would discourage every kind of aid to underdeveloped countries by allowing a manifest violation of international law. I saw no other course but com-mon action, and by that I mean action by NATO, not users of the canal. I insist strongly therefore today, as I did then, that in the mind of the French government it was really a question of great principles, and a question of providing for the future by making it clear that international agreements should be binding, and that nations with greedy and ambitious objectives would not be permitted to get away with criminal action.

We had always been overshadowed by memories of 1936, when Hitler and Mussolini started to annex Europe and parts of Africa. I am convinced that if the French government of the day had acted against Hitler then, the League of Nations and the entire world would have treated us as aggressors. Yet such action would have prevented a second world war and the death of twenty-five million or more people.

On the British side the problem was more complicated. The English were incontestably humiliated by the Suez affair, coming as it did after the difficulties they had had with Egypt. They were wondering what was the best means of preventing Nasser from arriving at his ends in the Middle East. I have always been greatly struck by the fact that Jordan has always

been the key to the Middle East, and on many occasions dur-
ing this period I heard Selwyn Lloyd advance the argument
that Jordan had to be held together. Perhaps he underestimated
the power of Great Britain in this region of the world and the
importance of taking action quickly and firmly. The oil factor
influenced the British considerably, as it did us in Paris.

But I thought at this time – and on this point there was
disagreement between us – that as far as the Arab countries
were concerned, they would be much more influenced by ener-
getic, even brutal, action by NATO members and canal users
than by any show of weakness. History shows that those people
who run hardest after the victor would turn most quickly
against us if we showed ourselves to be weaker.

NATO was the key to my thinking, not the United Nations.
I did not believe this was an affair for the United Nations, as
the Soviet Union could veto any proposal we made. Deci-
sion could have been taken within the framework of NATO,
but instead those who tried to diminish our force eventually
extended the framework so much that Atlantic solidarity was
weakened and we were persuaded to put the matter to canal
users and then to the United Nations, which was not capable
of solving anything.

Having reached this impasse, there was time to give more
attention to the situation in Israel, which was becoming in-
creasingly tense. Mr. Peres was able to show us that the Egyp-
tians were preparing themselves for war with weapons and
aircraft hidden at huge bases built in the remote wilderness of
the Sinai Desert. We were impressed because although tension
had existed between the Israelis and the Arabs since 1949,
Israel had now strong fears that an attack was imminent.

Our discussion had first begun at the level of the secret
services and the military, as is usually done, in order to explore
the field of possible co-operation. Later, at the beginning of
October, Mr. Peres returned to Paris accompanied by other
Israeli military and political officials to give us a warning. . . .

CHAPTER SEVEN

The Conspiracy

THE small, artificial kingdom of Jordan, riddled with intrigue, facing an election on October 21, but already in the clench of pro-Nasser military and political cliques, was crumbling under the steady hammering of Cairo Radio. A British outpost in the Middle East might soon become a puppet of Egypt.

The "Society of Free Officers" attempted to stir the dormant war against Israel into a key election issue by setting up fedayeen bases at frontier police posts. Raids from Jordan were even more violent than those from the Gaza Strip, and Israel retaliated with heavy counterattacks.

This increased military activity was matched by a toughening of political attitudes. Moshe Sharett was replaced at the Foreign Ministry by Mrs. Golda Meir, whose militant patriotism and obsessive love of the Negev matched Ben-Gurion's.

After she took office, the government began denying any and all involvement in border incidents. When General Burns asked for facilities to investigate Jordanian complaints about Israeli attacks, Mrs. Meir peremptorily informed him that "none of our forces are involved, so what is there for you to investigate?"

Burns later reported to New York that the situation was worse than at any time in the last two years, that he feared outright war was imminent. He could not possibly have known at the time how amply his fears were justified.

Through the collaboration of Shimon Peres with Bourgès-Maunoury and Abel Thomas in Paris, Israeli air force pilots were being brought to France in civilian clothes and trained to fly and fight Mystère jets; their ground crews, also in civilian clothes, were receiving instructions in aircraft maintenance; French instructors, in civilian clothes, were in Israel to show Israeli army engineers how to extract maximum performance from a variety of military equipment.

Officially supplied tanks were landed in Israel by day and lined up on jetties for all to see; at night extra tanks were unloaded and hidden in warehouses. The French army and air force drew an immense store of spare parts from NATO and shipped them to Israeli repair shops.

FROM AN ACCOUNT BY ABEL THOMAS, CHEF DE CABINET OF THE FRENCH DEFENCE MINISTRY: *Our role was decided by formal agreement between governments. Mollet, Pineau, and Bourgès-Maunoury have kept the secret of it because they agreed to, but the truth is far more favourable than what has been said internationally as well as in France. We have not said the whole truth until now – and the truth does not frighten us. I was the principal liaison between the military authorities in France and Israel, and there was also an Israeli liaison officer in Paris who translated messages into Hebrew. General Dayan came to Paris from Tel Aviv to discuss with us what assistance he needed and to explain the objectives his government wished to achieve. But the serious visits of Mr. Peres began in January and continued on until the actual attack.*

We could not supply everything ourselves, so we asked the Americans for material supplies. In fact, the Americans were constantly informed of all we were doing on the military side.

The American officer with whom I was in closest contact was at the right hand of Eisenhower, and I do not feel at liberty to disclose his name. All our secret flights to either London or Tel Aviv were made in French military aircraft from the base at Villa Coublay, near Paris. Indeed, on one occasion when I was returning from a visit to Downing Street the military control people at Villa Coublay were so uncertain about the identity of our plane that as soon as we landed I was placed under arrest by my own security guards.

As a result of these activities the unofficial list of arms supplied to Israel greatly exceeded the official list, though we originally intended to have the items on one duplicated on the other. But when the day of the attack drew close, our main problem always was to speed up the pace of British preparations and to accelerate the attack timetable. The main obstacle was the British political objection to making any move before the Israeli attack began, so as to avoid later charges of collusion.

There can be no doubt that we helped the Jewish people save their country, and they expressed their appreciation afterwards by printing a medal bearing our names.

Thomas's medal came with a brief letter from Ben-Gurion, which said: "The modest souvenir joined to this letter is to express our deep and boundless gratitude. . . . I hope that you will accept this medal as a gauge of my true sympathy."

It is bronze, much too big and heavy to be worn, yet there can be little doubt of Thomas's right to wear it. He organised in total secrecy a crash program of arms supply that gave Israel military superiority over every Arab state but Egypt.

The problem for Britain and France, once the storm centre had crossed the Atlantic to New York, was how and when to launch their joint venture, if indeed they were to launch it at all.

II

FRANCE, disillusioned and frustrated by lack of action, demanded that Nasser be checked, and it didn't really matter how it was done – by negotiation or by force. "Whatever the tactic adopted," said *Le Monde*, "the Western powers should now know that, if it is a grave matter to go to Munich, it is still more grave to go there after having sworn a hundred times to the contrary."

Maurice Schumann, then in opposition in the Assembly, openly charged that in reality the SCUA concept hid "*la dégradation de l'énergie Britannique et peut-être l'usure de la volonté Française.*" Other political leaders joined him in calling for "*des actes précis*" which, if not forthcoming quickly, would be taken against the government.

Responding to this angry mood, Mollet said he had discovered with "bitterness and anxiety that the free nations have not taken conscience of the danger as we have, and that our determination is not matched by sufficient unity among our friends and allies."

Mollet's resignation would be merely a matter of time unless he could appear resolutely purposeful when there was no clear purpose to be resolute about.

On September 23 Peres returned to Paris again, accompanied this time by the chiefs of Israeli military intelligence and members of Dayan's staff, who brought impressive evidence of an alarming Soviet penetration into the Middle East and a clear invitation to France to help Israel fight a defensive war.

Pineau, believing it to provide an excellent opportunity to force Eden's hand, flew to London and met briefly with Eden and Lloyd at Downing Street.

The upshot of their talk was Eden's agreement that, as Israel had come to Paris and Pineau had come to London,

Pineau should act as an unofficial intermediary with Israel on behalf of the British and French governments.

Pineau recalls: "It was the first time I had brought up the possibility of Israeli collaboration with Eden and Lloyd. Their reaction was, at first, very subtle. Eden showed a great deal of interest, Lloyd a great deal of reticence. Mr. Lloyd's preoccupations seemed to be above all not to compromise Britain with regard to the Arab countries, and not to run the risk of involving Britain's treaty obligations with Jordan. Nevertheless, I was able to persuade them to give me a kind of *carte blanche* to undertake further negotiations with the Israelis and keep them up to date on developments."

When he returned to Paris it was decided that too many envoys flying backwards and forwards between France and Israel was an unnecessary risk, particularly for Peres and Thomas, who were by then travelling regularly either between Paris and London or between Paris and Tel Aviv. Bourgès-Maunoury offered General de Gaulle's personal aircraft, a DC-4 that had been a gift from President Truman. De Gaulle, then in official retirement but active behind the scenes, had given it to the army for the use of members of the government and the General Staff on condition that it would always be available for his own use should he need it. The War Minister, who thought it likely that de Gaulle could be persuaded not to need it for a few weeks, undertook to provide a specially selected crew. When Peres and his companions left Paris early on September 25, it was the first of more than twelve clandestine flights between Tel Aviv, Paris, and occasionally London, within the next four weeks.

The new plan, decided upon some two weeks earlier at Downing Street, to attack through Port Said into the Canal Zone, was ready by September 26, the day on which Eden and Lloyd arrived in Paris as Mollet's guests, officially to discuss a proposal by Mollet that Britain should join France and other continental countries in a European free trade area, and to set a suitable date for the Queen to make a state visit to France.

During the afternoon the British leaders met members of the Cabinet and later attended an official dinner at the Hotel Matignon. Then they adjourned with Mollet and Pineau to the Premier's personal quarters for a private meeting.

They began, according to a French version, by discussing their joint approach to the United Nations, Eden hoping that it might be possible to concede a little from their stand on international control of the canal, "if Egypt is willing to co-operate and offer firm guarantees." Pineau was adamantly opposed to any concessions.

Mollet brought up the Anglo-French military plan, saying that his advisers strongly recommended a surprise paratroop drop into the Canal Zone rather than a sea-borne invasion. They felt that the bulk of the land forces could be landed by sea after the canal was captured. The British leaders thought differently, saying that since the plan had already been changed, it should not be tampered with yet again. Pineau reminded them caustically that this was the Suez Canal, not the Kiel Canal; that they were to be opposed by Egyptians, not Germans. And when Eden declined to be persuaded, he suddenly introduced the possibility of an Anglo-French action being concerted with that of Israel.

Selwyn Lloyd apparently thought they could not under any circumstances enter into an agreement, military or political, with Israel, because if they did so, the entire Arab world would be hostile.

The French leaders could understand British concern for Arab feelings generally, and for Jordan's future in particular, but were becoming exasperated by it. Discussion ranged loosely around Nuri es-Said's warnings to Eden that Jordan would become an Egyptian puppet unless something was done to counter a certain pro-Nasser victory at the polls. He had urged that Britain should accept the necessity of Iraqi troops being stationed in Jordan on some valid pretext to maintain law and order.

Since the pattern of border raids had shown signs of switching from Egypt to the Israeli-Jordanian frontier, it would not be too remarkable if Israel's reprisals assumed major military proportions. If the threat of war were to become demonstrably serious, Eden could warn Israel that Britain would honour treaty obligations to defend Jordan, should Jordan be attacked. This would serve to separate Britain from Israel publicly and remove any suspicion of covert association.

At the end, it seems they agreed rather inconclusively that Pineau should continue to negotiate with Israel through Peres and that British and French government spokesmen and diplomats should meanwhile begin stressing the extent of Communist penetration of the Middle East.

Next day an official communiqué announced that Britain would consult with Commonwealth governments on the proposed European Economic Community, that the Queen would visit France in April 1957, and that both governments were agreed on a common course of action at the United Nations on the canal issue. "The primary purpose of the meeting," it said, ". . . was to strengthen French and British solidarity in every respect. This result was fully achieved."

A British diplomat who had been with Eden and Lloyd during the "official" talks dined that evening in Paris with two Commonwealth ambassadors and said: "The Prime Minister was in excellent spirits. He warmed to Mollet, but apparently still regards Pineau with some suspicion. On one occasion he mentioned in an aside that Pineau was much too clever for his own good. Funny thing, but Selwyn Lloyd didn't really participate at all. He seemed so preoccupied he hardly said a word the whole time he was here."

There was nothing dreadful or sinister about these preliminary moves. Nasser had asserted often enough that he was at war with Israel and had built up a formidable army, by Middle East standards, to perform the task of extermination. Israel had canvassed for help, found it, and now thought in terms of preventive war. France and Britain made no secret of their intention to use force as a last resort in the canal crisis. But the ground was dangerous; quicksand was everywhere.

On September 29 Peres returned to Paris. With him were Moshe Dayan and four senior Israeli staff officers who would stay behind in Paris to co-ordinate Israel's military planning with that of France and Britain, should the secret discussions decide upon a three-power attack on Egypt. Dayan spent four days of talks with Bourgès-Maunoury and Thomas, arranging for an increase in the rate of supplies to Israel and for closer co-operation in Israeli-French operational planning.

During this visit Peres delivered Ben-Gurion's assurance to Pineau that, while Israel had no intention of attacking Jordan, heavy reprisal raids would serve to create the impression that it might. Then Peres gave the information that merged France's parallel partnerships with Britain on the one hand and Israel on the other into a single three-power conspiracy for war – the timing of Israel's attack on Egypt.

As it was France's turn to be president of the Security Council, Pineau was flying to New York on October 3, expecting to be absent from Paris for at least ten days. He arranged for his deputy and personal friend, Albert Gazier, to handle the negotiations with Peres while he was away, and telephoned Downing Street to suggest that he interrupt his flight in London "to convey information of utmost importance." Eden agreed, reluctantly, Pineau thought, and it is indeed quite likely that the conspiracy would have expired from the sheer exhaustion of interminable discussions, but for the unwitting intervention of Dulles in Washington.

In a letter to Eisenhower on October 1, Eden said: "You can be sure that we are fully alive to the wider dangers of the Middle East situation. They can be summed up in one word – Russia.... There is no doubt in our minds that Nasser, whether he likes it or not, is now effectively in Russian hands, just as Mussolini was in Hitler's. It would be as ineffective to show weakness now to Nasser in order to placate him as it was to show weakness to Mussolini. The only result was and would be to bring them together. . . ."

It was Eden's first attempt to lift the Communist "bogey" from the undercurrent of the crisis into a tangible and apparent menace demanding counteraction. If he thought it would arouse fighting instincts in Washington, he was soon disillusioned – the next day, in fact – by Dulles, who issued what Eden called a "damaging statement . . . likely to make Nasser believe that if he held fast, the United States would fall apart from Britain and France."

"The United States," said the Secretary of State, "cannot be expected to identify itself 100 per cent with the colonial powers or with the powers uniquely concerned with the problem of getting independence as rapidly and as fully as possible. There are, I admit, differences of approach by the three nations [United States, France, and Britain] to the Suez dispute, which perhaps arise from fundamental concepts. . . ."

So chilly a response to his letter hardened Eden's resolve, and when Pineau arrived on the afternoon of October 3, the Prime Minister was ready to abandon further consultation with Washington. They were alone in the privacy of Eden's study for a meeting, which can be recognized in retrospect as the hinge of the crisis. Use of force had been virtually talked to death by frequent and prolonged delays; now it was reborn and established so firmly as Anglo-French policy that the excited activity and hopes at the United Nations were actually of no consequence at all.

Israel was at last ready for war. The attack would begin at sunset on any day between October 29 and November 5. France was under an obligation to provide sea and air protection for the Israeli homeland, while Jewish land forces struck across the Sinai toward Ismailia and on to Cairo. This intelligence hovered portentously between Pineau and Eden as they examined their common predicament. The Israeli decision

called for an Anglo-French decision; no time was left for
further political manœuvring.

The pressures which crowd in on those in high office cannot always be properly understood by others who have no
wish to share their experience. Immense responsibilities sap at
strengths of will and intellect to a degree unknown in other
fields of endeavour. Men who deal in issues of war and peace,
who are in the business of saving lives while furthering national
ambitions, constantly look ahead to the verdict of history.
Each day in office is another day in the dock where the morality
and ethics of their behaviour and the sincerity of their motives
are mercilessly exposed to the jury of nations.

Ben-Gurion's ruthless exploitation of France's suffering in
Algeria in order to win an ally for his struggle against Egypt
was a bid for a favourable verdict. Pineau, who enjoyed the
support and confidence of Mollet, was tenaciously pursuing
peace in Algeria by removing what he thought to be the most
serious obstacle in the way of reaching it.

Eden was bidding for high acclaim with no such over-
ridingly powerful motives to explain his actions. He was attempting to be as bold as a Churchill at a time when Churchill
himself would probably have given way to the cautious advice
of an Eden.

When the talks at Downing Street ended that evening, there
was agreement in principle between Pineau and Eden that their
two countries should act jointly in concert with Israel against
Egypt; and further, that Eden and Lloyd should go to Paris on
October 18, after the formality of taking the crisis to the United
Nations had been completed, to discuss the next steps in detail.

As Pineau presided over the opening session of the Security
Council in New York two days later, Eden lay in a hospital bed
in London assailed by a mysterious fever, with a temperature
of 104 degrees.

III

—————

THE United Nations had not since its founding seen such a galaxy of statesmen. Recharged by the simmering passions of Afro-Asian nationalisms, the crisis assumed forbidding proportions as the Security Council, attended by seven foreign ministers, became formally seized of it. The chamber itself was filled by delegations and by the press, to the exclusion of all but a handful of public spectators. If the pattern of earlier speeches in London, Paris, and Cairo continued, Lloyd, Pineau, Shepilov, and Fawzi could be expected to revile, insult, and condemn each other without restraint.

Instead, Lloyd was mellow and overwhelmingly reasonable; Pineau was sharp, subtle, and witty; Fawzi was quiet, suave, and vague; and Shepilov reserved his right to speak until later. The Council adjourned into closed session for three days and then adjourned itself totally to allow for Lloyd, Pineau, and Fawzi to meet privately in the office of the Secretary General for direct uninhibited talks. The three ministers agreed that Hammarskjold should be present, not as a mediator, not as a referee, not as a rapporteur, but as an onlooker only.

No records were kept, but Hammarskjold dictated a résumé from memory several days later. It reveals a curious divergence between Lloyd and Pineau, the former seeming to want an agreement with Fawzi at the beginning, while Pineau, knowing the real decisions were being made in Paris and London, considered the whole procedure a waste of time. Lloyd and Fawzi were so mutually accommodating, in fact, that the mere mention of force appeared incongruously unreasonable. The principal exchanges were these:

OCTOBER 10

LLOYD   What is Egypt's basis for negotiation?

FAWZI   Egypt will set aside an agreed percentage of reve-
         nues for canal development; accept an agreement on
         tolls for a fixed number of years; recognize an asso-
         ciation of users; accept a system of combined meet-
         ings of the association and Egyptian board; accept
         an arbitration tribunal to settle disputes consisting
         of one user, one Egyptian and a United Nations
         chairman.

PINEAU   Will the users' association employ its own pilots?

FAWZI   It is not impossible to come to some arrangement on
         this. The Egyptian board will have to be satisfied as
         to the technical competence of the pilots.

LLOYD   Will Egypt accept the principle of insulating the
         canal from the politics of any one country?

FAWZI   Yes, of course.

OCTOBER 11

Hammarskjold produced a piece of paper containing his impressions of what had been said the
previous day. It caused such prolonged, acrimonious
argument that he was instructed to tear it up.

LLOYD   Vague promises from Dr. Fawzi are not enough.
         Will Egypt give reality to insulation of the canal
         from the politics of any one country?

FAWZI   I have said so yesterday. Egypt accepts this principle
         without qualification.

PINEAU   Will Egypt guarantee free and open transit through
         the canal to all users?

FAWZI   Yes. We will propose a new treaty to replace the
         1888 Convention.

LLOYD   Will Egypt accept the users' association as already
         being formed?

FAWZI   The users can organize themselves as they wish.
         Does this association of yours exist, or was it still-
         born?

LLOYD   It will live. There must be a collateral agreement regarding tolls, as these will be applicable to all users of the canal, not merely to those who join the association.

PINEAU   Will you persist in refusing passage to ships wearing the flag of Israel?

FAWZI   Israel will have the same rights it had under the 1888 Convention.

OCTOBER 12

Lloyd described the main areas of accommodation while the Secretary General made notes. Hammarskjold produced from these the six principles which later convinced delegates that the Middle East was at long last teetering on the brink of peace. The principles were:

1. There should be free and open transit through the canal without discrimination, overt or covert;
2. The sovereignty of Egypt should be respected;
3. The operation of the canal should be insulated from the politics of any one country;
4. The manner of fixing tolls and charges should be decided by agreement between Egypt and the users;
5. A fair proportion of the dues should be allotted to development;
6. In case of disputes, unresolved questions between the Suez Canal Company and the Egyptian government should be settled by arbitration, with suitable terms of reference and suitable provisions for the payment of sums found to be due.

In Hammarskjold's view these principles reflected the major areas of the discussions in which agreement seemed possible to negotiate, and in retrospect they appear so eminently reasonable that it is difficult to understand how they were permitted to become submerged by events.

Fawzi avoided any mention of how Egypt proposed to implement these principles and declined to give any guarantees that they could be implemented. Lloyd described them as "a good-natured preamble to a missing treaty." Pineau's telegram to Mollet in Paris said: "Nothing has happened to bring us nearer to a solution of the main issue. Lloyd now behaving better since last private meeting."

The formal Council session ended on the 14th with a Soviet veto on the Anglo-French resolution demanding international control, and with unanimous approval for the six principles. The next move, it seemed, should be for direct negotiation among the three countries to continue either in New York or Geneva. Tension subsided into a relaxed, confident atmosphere as delegates began referring to Suez as a crisis that had passed, and President Eisenhower gave a public sigh of relief by saying "the crisis is now behind us."

When Lloyd and Pineau left the United Nations building on the last evening, they were stopped beside their car by Hans Engen, Norway's permanent delegate, who asked: "When will you next see Fawzi?" They replied they thought further meetings might be possible later in the month, but nothing had been decided. According to Pineau there was no definite intention of seeing Fawzi again or of returning to New York. Yet the rumour grew that the next meeting would take place in Geneva on the 29th, a date that the Egyptians were later said to have inspired to create an impression of being willing to continue direct negotiations.

Testifying before the Senate Foreign Relations Committee early the following year, Dulles said: "It was my belief that direct negotiation would continue on October 29 in New York or in Geneva, but the British and the French just used this as a smokescreen. . . ."

Anglo-French distrust of Egypt was not entirely without foundation. While Pineau and Lloyd were indulging in rather outrageous subterfuge in New York, Nasser was giving evidence of his own duplicity to the Indian Ambassador in Cairo. When the Ambassador expressed surprise at Fawzi's agreement that the canal should be insulated from the politics of any one country, Nasser replied, "I have no intention of removing the canal from Egyptian policies. We have used a conciliatory tactic in New York, that's all. What we shall do is to remove the canal from international politics so that Western powers will stop interfering."

Before leaving New York, Lloyd entertained Commonwealth ambassadors and delegates to lunch, but said little while the Indian, Pakistani, and Ceylonese representatives, members of the Afro-Asian bloc, were present. Tactfully, they left early, and he was able to unburden himself to a small, more reliable audience.

Asked what the next move might be, he said, somewhat facetiously, "Fawzi might come back with a practical offer in the near future, but meanwhile it's all a question of for whom the canal tolls." He coyly confessed to being the author of the six principles and expressed concern that if they were not liked in Britain he might be called an appeaser.

Lloyd was also concerned about the reaction of the French Parliament, which might criticize Pineau so harshly for "giving way" that the Mollet government would find it difficult to remain in office. If this should happen, Lloyd said, it would "almost certainly stiffen" the British position against Egypt.

When questioned about disunity in the British Cabinet, he admitted that a split existed, that he had felt its effect during the talks in New York. "They've been blowing hot and cold throughout the proceedings," he said, and revealed himself more than a little shaken by Eden's reported statement to a Conservative party meeting in England to the effect that "Britain means business . . . and the government will not flinch from its duty. . . ."

"I would not be surprised," he said, "if I were handed an

umbrella when I get back to London, perhaps a bowler hat too."

Lloyd had every reason then to be anxious about his future. Eden, recovering from his sudden attack of fever, and heading toward unreserved commitment to overthrow Nasser by force, was likely to be angry indeed once he heard that the six principles which appeared so reasonable were the work of his Foreign Secretary.

IV

ISRAELI reprisal raids against Jordan were sharp, as Peres had predicted they would be: four progressively heavier attacks during early October, culminating on the night of the 10th-11th in a major assault on a border police post being used as a fedayeen base.

On October 12, the British Chargé d'Affaires called on Mrs. Golda Meir in Jerusalem to deliver a formal counter-warning that if Israel attacked, the British government would feel compelled to honour treaty obligations by giving military assistance to Jordan. Israel repeated that it would do whatever might be necessary to protect itself, and the government of France, reflecting Pineau's cutting sense of humour, issued a protest at Britain's continued insistence that Israel should remain in political quarantine.

As Jordan had no air force and relied upon the British for air protection, the Middle East was suddenly faced with the weird prospect of RAF squadrons already in Jordan fighting alongside Egyptian MIGs against French Mystères while an Anglo-French invasion force gathered in the area to attack Egypt.

The world was spared so bizarre a spectacle only because another, infinitely more harrowing, was being fashioned in Paris.

French military leaders were becoming alarmed by an apparent lack of any sense of urgency on the part of their British colleagues. Israel was committed to an attack timetable; French planners were deploying naval and air forces to fit into it; but the British persisted in abiding by their own planning schedule regardless of changing political circumstances.

On October 15 Bourgès-Maunoury sent General Challe to Downing Street for another conference with Eden, Antony Head, and Lloyd, who had returned that day from New York. The purpose was to persuade the British that instead of waiting until Israel had attacked to sail the invasion fleet from Malta, which would mean a minimum of six days' delay in the actual landings, it should be sailed at least three days ahead of Israeli action to shorten the delay in landing. If Eden persisted in the view that no ship should sail until the Israeli attack began, the war might be over before the fleet arrived, having sailed approximately nine hundred miles at the speed of the slowest ship.

Bourgès-Maunoury's version of what transpired includes the curious statement attributed to Selwyn Lloyd that, when the Israelis reached the canal, the Anglo-French naval forces could shell their positions as well as those of the Egyptians, thereby sustaining the fiction of strict impartiality.

Challe succeeded in impressing the British leaders with the need to establish an Anglo-French timetable, and Eden agreed that he and Lloyd should fly to Paris the next day, instead of waiting until October 18, as previously arranged with Pineau. Accordingly, a statement was issued from Downing Street saying that because the Prime Minister intended to open the British Motor Show in London on the 18th, his official visit to Paris would be advanced by two days.

Within twenty-four hours of supporting the six principles

for peace in the Security Council, Britain and France were abandoning them.

FROM AN ACCOUNT BY MAURICE BOURGÈS-MAUNOURY: *The first meetings between myself and Mr. Peres took place more than a year before the war, in the autumn of 1955, when I was Minister of the Interior. But they developed seriously in January 1956 when I became Defence Minister in M. Mollet's government. We reached complete understanding on Franco-Israeli co-operation in the struggle against the Arabs during March and April. After the nationalisation of the Suez Canal, Britain came into the picture, and it was our policy not to undertake any form of military operation without British partnership.*

It has not been made public before, but British planning was so long and slow that I had to send General Challe of our General Staff to see Prime Minister Eden to hurry things up. Mr. Eden had assumed complete charge of British planning, but it was only later, when Mr. Head became Defence Minister, that we began to shorten the time required for the operation. The principal British reason for caution was that they had played a large part in training the Egyptian army and they believed it was a good army when, in fact, it was not good at all. There was also the difficulty that the British were pro-Arab and anti-Israel, whereas we were anti-Arab and pro-Israel.

Once our own preparations were under way and the Israelis decided when to attack, our assistance programme was speeded up and I had to consult with the Americans to get spare parts and items of equipment we lacked. The Americans knew just about everything that was going on in Paris. I saw Ambassador Dillon about once every two weeks to request further supplies from the United States, and in my opinion he was quite aware that they were destined for Cyprus, from where a proportion was sent on to Israel.

It was Ambassador Dillon who told me that the British

*were also asking United States Ambassador Aldrich in London
for equipment and supplies from the United States. In total,
we asked for and received ninety different items of arms equipment, and the British received a hundred and sixty-seven different types. It is quite pointless for the Americans to continue
to say they were kept in the dark about our plans. Certainly
Mr. Dillon was a clever man, and not likely to be deceived. In
fact, on one occasion I asked him why, in view of the readiness
with which the United States met our requests for arms and
supplies, it was being politically so anti-French and anti-British,
particularly in New York. He replied that Washington was
exerting heavy pressure on the English in the hope that they
would stop the French. If that was the case, Ambassador
Aldrich must have been lacking powers of persuasion in his
dealings with Whitehall.*

*I also kept General de Gaulle informed of what we were
doing and we did, in fact, use his personal aircraft for some of
the secret flights between Villa Coublay and Croydon in England, because it was comfortable and equipped for keeping in
touch with both capitals by telephone. General de Gaulle was
always in favour of our plans except that he objected to us
allowing the British to occupy the chief military commands
and thereby take control of the operation. Because of his fears
I instructed General Ely, the Chief of our General Staff, to
make sure that if the British advance during the operation
slowed down or looked like stopping, French units would go
on to reach their objectives.*

*The United States military were also kept informed through
the Chief of Staff in Washington, with whom I sometimes had
to be in touch to iron out delivery schedules, and through the
Central Intelligence Agency. It is sometimes customary in
such circumstances to allow information to pass through secret
channels rather than formally through normal diplomatic exchanges. Of course, there is always the possibility that President*

Eisenhower, facing an election, was not informed until it was too late.

When Eden and Lloyd arrived in Paris on October 16 for four hours of fateful talks at the Hotel Matignon with Mollet and Pineau, only thirteen days of peace remained. Pineau began preparing for the future in the afternoon with a speech in the National Assembly, in which he reflected bitterly upon the concept of an Atlantic alliance in which there was neither unity nor partnership, only division and American dictate. There was, however, Anglo-French solidarity, and in this context he said: *"Une alliance est un tout; on ne peut pas la diviser en petits morceaux dont on accepte les uns et dont on refuse les autres."*

V

THE four statesmen sat facing each other amid the ornate splendour of the Hotel Matignon, once the home of the Monagasque princes and Talleyrand, and now the official residence of the prime ministers of France. The wall behind a grimly determined Eden and Lloyd was covered by a magnificent tapestry showing Don Quixote tilting at his windmill; behind Mollet and Pineau was a portrait of the arch-conspirator, Cardinal Richelieu, who gazed down upon this intimate gathering – austere and sardonic.

The future of the Suez Canal was not so important for the French leaders as the future of Algeria; there was nothing so important for the British as the canal, recovery of lost prestige and influence in the Arab world, and satisfaction for the humiliations heaped upon them by the transgressions of Egypt.

The obstacle in their way was Nasser. The French, at least, openly and energetically proclaimed it.

If there were once any lingering doubts about the wisdom of proceeding further without the United States, they had been abruptly banished that morning when a message from Dulles to Selwyn Lloyd accused Britain of being more concerned with punitive measures against Egypt than with peaceful solutions.

After nearly three months of patient procrastination, the spectre of Munich was vividly real on both sides of the English Channel. To finally acquiesce without making even a feeble attempt to retaliate would bring a cackle of triumph from Cairo, and the modern label of contempt – appeasement.

Once again, according to a French version of what transpired, Mollet emphasized that this was a decisive conference in which he expected to resolve the manner of co-operation with Israel and a schedule for occupation of the Canal Zone. Eden replied that, though he had agreed to the principle of collaboration with France, there would be no question of British forces fighting alongside those of Israel. France, throughout, would be Britain's ally, and both, he insisted, should appear to be "reacting" to an Israeli-Egyptian war, as opposed to being part of it.

"There is no reason for France to hide its friendship with Israel," said Pineau. "We are told now that Nasser is planning a military alliance with Syria and Jordan, once a puppet régime is elected there. The Israelis expect the three armies to be integrated under an Egyptian supreme commander, so naturally they wish to prevent such integration crushing them. What is so disagreeable about helping a free, democratic country to protect itself from a unified, encircling army?"

The plan that eventually emerged assumed that if Israel attacked on November 1 it would take four days at least for advance columns to cross the Sinai and reach the canal. By November 5 they could reasonably expect that the canal would itself be a no man's land separating the opposing armies. Firing across the canal would halt traffic, and justification for joint intervention would exist to push both sides far enough back on either side of the canal that traffic could be resumed in comparative safety. In fact, that would mean occupying the Canal Zone.

They agreed that the timetable should be adjusted to avoid American intervention should anything go wrong. As election day in the United States was November 6, it would be desirable for the Anglo-French landings to take place no earlier than dawn on the 5th, no later than dawn on the 6th.

The success of the plan depended upon the Israelis being near the canal before Britain and France issued an ultimatum calling on both sides to withdraw from it. The question of an agreed wording for the ultimatum arose and the French leaders expressed the view that, because of the serious nature of such a document, Ben-Gurion would probably need a signed agreement or treaty binding the three governments to their undertakings. It was probably the first time the British had given a thought to the possibility of having to commit themselves on paper, and they tended to shy away from the prospect.

Next day the mechanics of the plot evolved at speed. Cable lines hummed between Paris and Israel; French troops in southern France were issued with special currency stamped "Occupation of Egypt" and embarked in their transport ships; British bombers were flown out to Malta and Cyprus; Ben-Gurion surprised Jews and Arabs alike, all of whom thought Jordan was the principal cause of his anxiety, with a major policy speech saying that Egypt represented the primary threat to Israel's security; and an impenetrable barrier of diplomatic silence shut off London and Paris from Washington. Senior Foreign Office and Quai d'Orsay officials, who were intimately involved in Middle Eastern affairs and accustomed to working in close contact with their opposite numbers at the State Department, were struck off route slips for important, confidential documents, some being suddenly ordered to take unexpected

leave. Eden went so far as having the centre of official diplomatic exchange between London and Paris moved from the
Foreign Office to Downing Street. United States military, naval,
and air attachés in the British, French, and Israeli capitals
reported a drying up of normal channels of information and
total loss of contact with their French and British colleagues.

Israeli ambassadors in London, Paris, Moscow, and Washington were summoned home for urgent talks with Mrs. Golda
Meir; German, Dutch, and British salvage firms that had signed
contracts with the Royal Navy for canal clearance sailed tugs
and equipment from Malta to Cyprus; and Nasser, called a
"Fascist despot" by Ben-Gurion, an "apprentice dictator" by
Mollet, and a "congenital liar" by Pineau, retorted to American
newspapermen that "I am not a dictator because the majority
of the people support me." As he had outlawed all opposition
parties, there was no way of knowing if the people really did.

On October 18, Eden met with his inner "war" cabinet,
gave them a general outline of what was planned, and implemented a change he had known would be necessary once he
agreed to collaborate. Sir Walter Monckton, Minister of Defence, was shifted "for health reasons" to another ministry and
replaced by his political junior, Antony Head.

The French navy captured the private yacht *Athos* off the
North African coast, claimed that it was carrying arms from
Alexandria to the rebels in Algeria, and the government, having
fortuitously provided itself with "proof" of direct Egyptian
involvement in the Algerian drama, recalled its ambassador
from Cairo, and sent a formal protest to the Security Council
in New York.

On October 21 the expected pro-Nasser victory in the
Jordanian elections was triumphantly announced in Amman;
Nuri es-Said abandoned his intention of moving Iraqi troops;
and Nasser issued a statement saying that Egypt would give aid
to Hussein "any time he asks for it."

Next day the most politically important meetings of the

tortuous Suez tragedy began at a secret rendezvous "somewhere in France."

VI

FROM AN ACCOUNT BY GUY MOLLET: *I did not know a lot about Israel. I had met its leaders first as members of the Socialist International. Ben-Gurion was Secretary General of the Socialist party there, as I am here in France. The only thing I knew was that a democratic country, in some way trying to find a socialist solution to its problems, was in danger.*

One day I received a visit from their leaders, who explained to me quite clearly that they were condemned to disappear, that they would be attacked very soon. They had information that Nasser had received Soviet MIGs and bombers, so naturally when they asked for help, I gave it to them by having French arms sent to Israel.

My reasons were that when a free country is menaced, all the free countries of the world must protect it. I do not mean we should make war on the régimes of Hungary and Poland to bring liberty to their peoples. You cannot bring freedom with arms to a state that is not free. But when a country is free, you cannot allow dictators anywhere to make this country disappear. I gave a great deal of help to Israel, because this was my purpose. Then other questions came up, problems of oil supplies, the Suez Canal, and Algeria. My British allies in this did not have the same purpose. They did not think so much about the freedom of Israel as they did about the canal.

It is not finished. A lot of people have never read Nasser's book [Philosophy of a Revolution] *in which he explains frankly and freely what he aims to be: leader of the Moslem world, leader of the Arab world, and leader of the African world. It should be read. He describes the three circles of which Nasser is the centre, the centre of each of these worlds he aspires to dominate. He forgets that there are forty million Arabs, four hundred million Moslems.*

I am in favour of Arab unity, but I am against the sort of treachery that enabled Hitler to use national socialism to achieve pan-Germanism, and Stalin to use Communism to reach pan-Slavism and a Greater Russia. I do not object to Nasser building a world for Egypt, but I object for many reasons – oil, the canal, etc. – that he should wish to lead the Arab world. I tried to stop him. But we have not finished. He will try again, because Israel is trying to do something new and worthwhile, and that is a danger to him.

It began at Suez when there were common discussions with the British to settle the canal crisis, and on my part with Israel to help save its life. Then, some weeks before the attack, they came to France. . . .

They came shortly before dawn on October 22, when a large passenger aircraft wearing Israeli markings touched down in the damp morning mist on a little used airstrip at Villa Coublay, southwest of Paris. Louis Mangin, the famed Resistance son of a French general and a personal friend of Bourgès-Maunoury, drove across the field in his own car, while another with a French officer at the wheel followed. Mangin's position in the Defence Ministry was obscure, but he ranked with Thomas as one of Bourgès-Maunoury's principal assistants and was responsible for security at the meetings about to take place.

A group of men left the plane and quickly ducked into the waiting cars, the last one short, broad-shouldered, with long, white, unruly hair escaping from beneath his hat, and were driven away from the airfield through the darkness to nearby Sèvres, a quiet suburb of Paris where Mangin had arranged for them to stay at a small villa set well back from view in its own grounds.

Bourgès-Maunoury recalls: "The villa belonged to private friends of mine who were in no way involved in government business. I asked them for the loan of it and they agreed without knowing the purpose for which it would be used. Mangin and I arranged the details of the meetings and were responsible for security precautions. Nothing was done to draw attention to the fact that something important was going on. The old servants remained to look after the guests as they would do normally. They were accustomed to house guests, mostly English, so the visitors were treated as usual without any suspicion that they might be very out of the ordinary."

But when the house guests had taken off their coats and mufflers, they were out of the ordinary indeed. There was Dayan, apparently regarding the damp and the cold with distaste; there was Peres, who had probably become accustomed to French weather; and there was Ben-Gurion, presumably as cold as Dayan, but as uncomplaining as Peres.

It was at his request that these secret meetings were being held. He had come to collect "a piece of paper."

CHAPTER EIGHT

The Treaty of Sèvres

The account of the subsequent talks and agreements at Sèvres are based upon the recollections of Pineau, Bourgès-Maunoury, and Abel Thomas, three highly placed witnesses to the events, who agree in detail on what transpired in the next three days.

PINEAU left his office early that afternoon, was driven home as usual by his chauffeur in an official car, changed into a suit more comfortable than the rather sombre, formal one he had been wearing, and then left in his own car. He drove through side streets until reaching the suburbs, where he ignored the main highways. As he had lived in the area some years before, he knew the rarely used alternative routes and short cuts.

"It may sound melodramatic now," he recalls, "but at the time it was vitally necessary. I had to be sure I was not recognized or followed. Apart from the obvious necessity of keeping our own plans secret, it was an inescapable fact of the times that terror was not confined to Algeria. There were plenty of Arabs in Paris who would have welcomed such an opportunity to assassinate Ben-Gurion. I wanted, as well, to avoid being recognized, as that would have led to a lot of speculation about what the Foreign Minister of France was doing driving around by himself in the country when he should be in his office dealing with a world crisis."

When Pineau arrived at the villa, the Israeli house guests, refreshed by their sleep during the morning, were already preparing for the conferences ahead. Pineau formally welcomed Ben-Gurion to France in the name of President René Coty and Premier Mollet, and the rest of the evening was spent in a general exchange of views and plans. Meeting as they were for the first time, Pineau and Ben-Gurion were assessing each other, testing reliability and sincerity of purpose, in the manner of statesmen who, on the verge of making deep commitments, naturally draw a measure of comfort from personal appraisal.

Their talks were adjourned early, each aware that tomorrow would be arduous and critical.

Next morning an inconspicuous car pulled up in the driveway, Mollet stepped out, and Pineau introduced the Prime Minister of France to the Prime Minister of Israel.

The conference, devoid of formality, began with the three Israeli and the two French leaders facing each other across a dining-room table.

Ben-Gurion spoke first, ranging widely over the problems of nation-building, the fears of fewer than two million Jews surrounded by more than forty million hostile Arabs, and the responsibilities of a government faced with an external threat of overwhelming proportions. Egypt had, he claimed, nearly fifty thousand men in the Sinai alone, equipped with the most modern weapons and supported by the most modern air force in the Middle East. There was evidence, too, of Russian destroyers, submarines, and minelayers arriving in Egyptian harbours to become part of the Egyptian navy.

Israel, lacking money and sources for arms, had never possessed a strong air force and navy. Her cities were vulnerable to air attack and bombardment from the sea; there was almost no hope of preventing assault forces landing along her coast.

"Yet somehow," he said in effect, "we have to destroy the springboard for the main threat against Israel: the Egyptian bases in the Sinai and the Gaza Strip. We cannot allow the fedayeen to bleed us to death over the years; nor can we permit ourselves to become the victims of a surprise attack from which we might not recover."

Placing his position in a strategic and historical context, he referred to the growth of pan-Arabism, to the extent of Soviet penetration into Egypt and Syria, to the election only two days before of a National Socialist régime in Jordan modelled on that of Egypt, and to the uncontrolled ambitions of Nasser, which appeared likely to swallow the smaller Arab states, resolve the traditional Arab dynastic feuds, and thereby complete encirclement of Israel by nations subservient to Egypt.

The Israeli government expected that a move would be made soon to set up a joint military command of Arab armies. "If that happens – and it might include Egypt, Jordan, Syria, Iraq, and Saudi Arabia – they will crush us out of existence," he said.

Israel would accomplish its purpose if the Egyptian army and fedayeen bases in the Sinai and the Gaza Strip were destroyed. But this would mean war, the eventual outcome of which would be decided by keeping other Arab states from fighting alongside the Egyptians, and by making arrangements to protect Israeli cities from being destroyed and to guard the coast against invasion.

"Bombardment of Tel Aviv, Haifa, Jaffa, and Jerusalem will result in a death toll we, as a small nation, cannot accept," he said. "An invasion high up on our coast would place an enemy force in our heart. We are condemned to death unless we fight. M. Mollet, you are a member of the Resistance, a Socialist, and a democrat. You cannot allow us to perish. Israel's existence is at stake here today."

Mollet had no intention at the outset of the conference to commit France beyond the supply of additional arms and the loan of more instructors if Israel needed them. At this point he had only the haziest notion of how extensively Bourgès-Maunoury and Abel Thomas had involved the French forces in Israeli defence arrangements.

Uncomfortably aware, as were all his generation of Frenchmen, that a large proportion of Israeli Jews had once lived under the scourge of Nazidom, he was inclined to share their equation of the past with the present threat from the Arabs. Appalled by the prospect of another mass extermination, so vividly portrayed by Ben-Gurion's eloquence, he instinctively answered: "I shall not let these things happen."

By lunchtime they reached formal agreement that the French air force would provide cover for Israel's major cities, that French warships would patrol its coastline, and that France would use these forces to protect Israel from any belligerent Arab state, as well as from Egypt.

Israel would mobilise on October 26, just three days away; French Mystère squadrons would arrive in Israel via Cyprus throughout the 27th and 28th; and French warships would be sailed immediately to reach positions off the Israeli coast by the 29th, the date Ben-Gurion now set for the attack on Egypt. Bourgès-Maunoury would cover these naval movements by announcing that in view of the *Athos* incident, the French navy would maintain patrols in the eastern Mediterranean to intercept further arms shipments from Alexandria to Algeria.

Their agreement ended with a promise by Mollet that any move by the United Nations to brand Israel as an aggressor would be blocked with use of the veto in the Security Council. Mollet was actually giving political endorsement to much of what the French and Israeli defence chiefs were already in the process of doing secretly.

In the afternoon another aircraft, this one wearing the markings of the Royal Air Force, landed at Villa Coublay, where the tireless Mangin was already waiting. When he delivered the new arrivals to the villa at Sèvres for the second session of the conference, Britain, according to Pineau's account, was represented by Selwyn Lloyd and Patrick Dean, an under-secretary of state at the Foreign Office and a political intelligence co-ordinator.

Ben-Gurion repeated much of what he had said in the morning for the benefit of the new arrivals and concluded pointedly: "If Nasser gets away with the Suez Canal, in spite of all your threats, his power and prestige will be so immeasurably increased that his next step will be unification of other Arab states under his leadership for the conquest of Israel."

Pineau, who appreciated the elderly statesman's keenly prophetic wisdom without ever allowing himself to be wholly seduced to the Israeli cause, has since said: "We discussed British intervention very seriously and very frankly. I was struck by the fact that the English sought above all else a method of justifying their action in the eyes of the Arabs and before world opinion. I thought it would be much simpler to say that the Egyptians had taken over the canal illegally, that this was an aggression under international law, and that we were acting purely and simply to recover it. That was not sufficient for the English. So our discussions ended in a rather complex agreement in principle that:

> The Israelis would attack the Sinai in strength with the primary objective of reaching the vicinity of the canal in the shortest possible time.

> The British air force would attack the Egyptian air force while it was grounded on its airfields, and continue the bombing for most of the operation to provide a daily warning to other Arab states that they would suffer a similar bombardment should they attempt to attack Israel.

> The purpose of the Anglo-French landings would be to protect the canal against both sides, against Israel and Egypt. Israel would accept an ultimatum from France and

Britain to cease fire, but might not actually do so until reaching a line ten miles east of the canal.

The ultimatum would be triggered off by an Israeli radio news bulletin saying that its advance units were at the approaches to the canal. They would then have twelve hours to reach the ten-mile line.

"I recall very well this clause that we should appear to be defending the canal against both sides," continued Pineau. "It struck me then, and I do not hide it, that it was a little hypocritical, and I said so. But Ben-Gurion thought the need for British bombing of Egyptian airfields so important that he accepted it; and the British would not participate without this ruse or something like it. So we, Mollet and I, had to agree. Frankly, it would make little difference if we succeeded."

Mollet drove back to Paris that night, Pineau flew to London with Lloyd to discuss their decisions with Eden, and Patrick Dean stayed at the villa with Ben-Gurion, Peres, and Dayan. Mangin, their unobtrusive host, also remained, but Dayan's staff officers were taken to Paris to begin drafting a detailed schedule with the French Chiefs of Staff.

Pineau returned to Sèvres early the next morning, October 24, with Eden's consent to the agreement, and the conference resumed without Mollet and Lloyd for the drafting of a formal three-power treaty. Several hours later the text was unanimously approved and a copy dispatched to London for Eden's final approval.

The military part of it was inflexible and complicated. It began, at Ben-Gurion's insistence, with the Israeli attack on October 29, and ended with the Anglo-French sea-borne assault at dawn on November 6, the date of the United States election. Inside these rigidly pre-set dates the ultimatum, the bombing, and the paratroop drops could be moved about by no more than twenty-four hours either way. Once the sea-borne assault had been carried out, occupation of the Canal Zone from Port Said to Suez would be completed by November 12 at the latest.

The political aspects were even more complex. France would defend Israel's interests at the United Nations, but Britain would not. The British obstinately refused to appear as a collaborator, supporter, or even friend of Israel on the ground that it could not possibly do so if it were to preserve its influence among the Arab states. However, Britain, for whom the non-collaboration fiction was sacrosanct, would exert private influence in Israel's cause, and be friendly to Israel's territorial claims at a peace conference should the United Nations take the opportunity to seek a general settlement in the Middle East.

"When we received Eden's approval of the text," said Pineau, "it was incorporated into a formal document signed that afternoon by Patrick Dean for Britain, Ben-Gurion for Israel, and myself for France. I believe three copies were made, one for each government, and we decided that the agreement should never be published."

As the official signing was taking place, it was learned in Paris that Egypt, Jordan, and Syria had agreed to integrate their armies under the Egyptian Commander-in-Chief. This fatefully timed report completely reassured the Anglo-French leaders that Ben-Gurion had not been over-dramatizing the threat to Israel.

Ben-Gurion landed in Israel on October 25 with a severe cold, a high temperature, and his "piece of paper." He informed the Israeli Cabinet that as the new Arab military alliance placed Israel in "direct and immediate danger," he was preparing an order for general mobilisation. The stage was being set less than twenty-four hours after signing the Treaty of Sèvres.

II

AS the various national leaders dispersed from the villa at Sèvres, Mollet made a biting speech in the French Parliament in which he accused the United States of promoting a narrow concept of NATO and attacked Dulles for provoking Atlantic bitterness instead of solidarity. He concluded: "The game is not yet up. We have a trump card."

In London, Eden summoned a "war" cabinet meeting to discuss British action in the likely event of an imminent Israeli attack on Egypt. Official news from Israel revealed a deteriorating situation, but ministers such as Butler who were not fully informed were astounded. Like the rest of the world, they thought Ben-Gurion was arming against Jordan.

But Eden's supporters in the inner cabinet were serene and confident, the prospect of action injecting buoyancy where for so long there had been desperate frustration. They approved the ultimatum which first called upon both parties to cease fire and withdraw from the Canal Zone, and then warned that failure by one or both parties to comply would result in Anglo-French occupation of the canal towns: Port Said, Ismailia, and Suez.

On October 27, Abel Thomas was instructed by Bourgès-Maunoury to fly to England for yet another attempt to reduce the time gap between the Israeli attack and the Anglo-French landings. Eden still persisted with his refusal to order the invasion fleet to sea until the Israeli attack had begun, but Bourgès-Maunoury considered it should be sailed within the next twenty-four hours, by midnight on the 28th at the latest.

Thomas flew to Croydon and was taken by car to Downing Street, where he met Eden, Head, and the British Chiefs of Staff. They listened quietly while he delivered the French case for a more urgent attitude toward the operation, and eventually Eden agreed that perhaps the slowest ships should be sailed the next evening. It was the only concession Thomas could get, and he next saw Selwyn Lloyd at the Foreign Secretary's residence in Carlton House Terrace for a brief, inconclusive discussion of Israel's right to hold onto the Sinai once the war was over. It was on his return from this visit that on landing at Villa Coublay he was arrested by French security guards who had not been warned that a military plane would be arriving without navigation lights.

By nightfall on October 27, then, Israel was mobilising for a war that even its own people thought would be against Jordan; France and Britain had an ultimatum prepared for belligerents who were not yet fighting; and an Anglo-French invasion plan, which had been ready for nearly six weeks, would be used for what Eden later described as a "new objective," when the world thought a peaceful solution would emerge from the expected meeting of foreign ministers in Geneva or New York on the 29th.

But the evening before this critical day, Ben-Gurion, under the pressure of two "cease and desist" letters from President Eisenhower, who also believed Israel intended to attack Jordan, telephoned Paris to ask Mollet if his "piece of paper" was good, if all three powers were, in fact, in total and determined accord. Mollet reassured him so successfully that the seventy-year-old leader of Israel immediately succumbed to the flu he had been keeping at bay with drugs since returning from Sèvres.

At sunset the next evening, Dayan released his forces. Armoured units burst out of the Negev through the El Auja swing door, ran over Egyptian trench systems, and headed southwards into the darkening Sinai Desert.

At 7:15 P.M. the French and British military attachés in Israel were summoned to Defence Headquarters to be told that Israeli paratroops had been successfully dropped only twenty-five miles from the canal, that light supporting columns were also on their way.

The British attaché asked the briefing officer, "What is the ultimate aim of your operation?"

"I can't tell you that," was the reply. The officer pointed to a wall map and continued, "but there is Cairo."

In spite of all the complicated political plotting and military planning, the Israelis, by reporting themselves close to the Canal Zone so quickly, were already upsetting the timetable. They were not intended to make this report until the 31st, as the ultimatum would then automatically follow; and the Anglo-French bombing was not planned to begin until after the time limit had expired twelve hours later, on November 1.

In Paris, Bourgès-Maunoury reported to Mollet and Pineau that as his Israeli friends were exuberantly certain of completing a clean victory over the Egyptians within three days, the entire Anglo-French timetable should be advanced by at least twenty-four hours to take advantage of the Egyptian rout.

The French leaders flew to London, spent four hours with an apparently calm Eden, and finally persuaded him that the military plan should be revised. He surrendered, even to the extent of advancing the ultimatum and amending the wording of it to a dangerously revealing degree. Had he at that instant summoned his military advisers, they would have then, as they did later, stubbornly declined to alter the timetable on the ground that any attempt now to tamper with the interlocking phases of the plan would serve to brake the operation rather than accelerate it.

He made the mistake of issuing the revised ultimatum that afternoon while Mollet and Pineau were still in London, and the key condition for intervention – failure of one or both belligerents to comply – was missing.

It didn't matter any more who accepted it or who rejected it; France and Britain would occupy the Canal Zone anyway. And it was not until the next morning that Eden was confronted by the dismaying refusal of the military machine to change its pre-set pace and schedule.

The ultimatum expired at dawn on October 31, and Cairo blacked out, waiting for the first wave of bombers to appear. Nothing happened in the morning, in the afternoon, or in the evening. The drubbing began that night when a form of psycho-aerial warfare was launched – high-level precision bombing of Egyptian airfields, accompanied by fiercely worded broadcasts in Arabic from Cyprus Radio warning Egyptians to stay away from military targets, remain in their homes, or seek shelter in built-up city or village areas which wouldn't be attacked.

After some time, leaflets depicting caricatures of a frightened Nasser were dropped by the thousands, inciting Egyptians to revolt, saying: ". . . We are now obliged to bomb you wherever you are. Imagine your villages being bombed. Imagine your wives, children, mothers, fathers, and grandfathers escaping from their homes and leaving their property behind. This will happen to you if you hide behind your women in the villages. . . . You have committed a sin . . . that is, you have placed your confidence in Abdel Nasser."

These leaflets had been printed weeks in advance, and a deep sense of outraged shock rippled from one capital to another, as suspicion hardened into conviction that efficient operation of the canal had been a public pretext for an actual war aimed at the overthrow of Nasser.

While Paris pressed for faster action, while Washington watched incensed and alarmed, and while condemnation resounded across the world, the British government headed unswervingly toward moral disaster.

III

IT was a strange, unprecedented war fought under a political directive from Downing Street which said, "Thou shalt not kill." Egyptian ground crews on the airfields were warned to take cover before the air bombardment began; the assault forces were under orders to attack centres of resistance, but to refrain from street fighting if civilian lives were endangered; and Dayan had told his unit commanders: "There are so many Arabs that killing Egyptians will not make too much sense. Your job is to clear them out of the Sinai, destroy their bases and war material, and teach the Egyptian army a punitive lesson."

Politically, it had been impossible to inform the United States of Anglo-French intentions, but the French leaders at least were convinced that Washington was far better informed than has been admitted, that the readiness with which the United States responded to requests made through diplomatic channels for military supplies indicated unofficial approval for a course of action that could not be officially endorsed.

"There was no foundation for this belief," Robert Murphy says. "Washington simply was not informed of what the British and French were doing. We didn't know they intended going so far."

There was some concern at Cyprus military headquarters about the presence of the United States Sixth Fleet, which was evacuating American citizens from the Levant and Egypt, but the commanders of the invasion fleet were given to understand, by implication and rumour, that as "the United States is with us, you will have no trouble from the Sixth Fleet."

Before dawn on October 31 the French cruiser *Kersaint*, patrolling in Israeli waters to give coastal protection, sighted the silhouette of a warship closing in on Haifa, and indentified it as an ex-Russian "Skory" class destroyer known to have been supplied to the Egyptian navy. When the *Kersaint* opened fire it attempted to break away in the darkness. The French commander, in a quandary because the ultimatum had not yet expired and France was not officially at war with Egypt, summoned Israeli motor torpedo boats from Haifa. And while the destroyer lay under his guns, he signalled a report of the action to Admiral Barjot, French deputy supreme commander at Cyprus. The admiral was immediately concerned at the similarity between the silhouettes of some American warships and those of the "Skory" class destroyers. A case of mistaken identity was highly unlikely; nevertheless he signalled Paris: "Have crippled Egyptian destroyer. But not entirely sure it Egyptian. If this should prove a mistake, this is not a deliberate attack on our part on stray ships of the Sixth Fleet."

This first operational report of the war was made six hours before it actually began.

Washington, from the President down to the most junior official at the State Department, heard about the ultimatum on the ticker tapes. Not long afterwards the French Ambassador, Hervé Alphand, and the British Chargé d'Affaires, John Coulson, presented Dulles with letters from their governments giving formal explanations as to why there had been no prior consultation or warning. The British letter was rambling and unconvincing, the French perfunctory, saying in effect that whereas there was no wish to embarrass the President on the eve of an election, "we did not wish to incur further delays and interminable talks designed to prevent us from acting or have to wait for you as we did from 1914 to 1917 and from 1939 to 1942."

Eisenhower greeted this with a typical outburst. According to Allen Dulles, who was with him, he said: "If people think I am going to be put off from a course I think is right just because we're on the eve of an election, they are greatly mistaken. We're going to push this thing right through the United Nations until they stop. They're not *our* allies in this."

That afternoon the New Zealand Ambassador, Sir Leslie Munro, spoke with Walter Robertson, Assistant Secretary of State, and William Rountree, who had replaced George Allen as head of the Near Eastern Affairs division. When Munro asked what prior notice the United States had received from London or Paris, Rountree replied: "None. In fact, there's been a great number of things happening over there during the last two weeks that we don't know about.

"The Israeli Ambassador, Mr. Eban, was in here with me on the day it started, explaining that his country was only interested in cleaning out fedayeen nests, when we got the news by ticker tape that the Israeli army was on its way to the canal. I told him he'd better understand that we wouldn't like this sort of treatment at all."

While it was true, said Rountree, that the Egyptians had provoked the Israelis from time to time, the situation had been quiet for some weeks, and the problems of dissension in Jordan militated against any unified action. It was a question of whether full-scale aggression was justified.

"If someone throws stones across the border it can be called an aggressive act," said Rountree, "so it is really a case of degrees of aggression. We think here that Israel is guilty of flagrant aggression. Furthermore, we don't like the Anglo-French deal because it puts us on the same side as the Soviet Union."

Walter Robertson broke in to say: "This is one of the gravest situations in my experience. A breach of the greatest magnitude has occurred in United States relations with its allies, and for many friends of Britain and France here in Washington, there can be little else but depression and despair. That ultimatum is so worded that no one in his right mind can imagine Nasser accepting it – if he was ever intended to."

Rountree added that it was not a question of pushing Nasser toward reason, or of a simple action to ensure that the canal was effectively operated. "There are far more serious factors in this Anglo-French action than appear on the surface. The implications are legion, and let's be honest – worse is yet to come."

When news of the first bombings reached the White House, the astounded Eisenhower roared: "Bombs, by God. What does Anthony think he's doing? Why is he doing this to me?" Then he told Dulles: "We have to stop them – fast."

The United Nations, all hopes of peace now in total collapse, and confronted with a fresh crisis of alarming proportions caused by an ultimatum already being called the most "brutal in modern history," was still reeling from the shock when the Security Council met late on October 30. M. Cornut-Gentille, the French Ambassador, who was also President of the Council, and Sir Pierson Dixon of Britain were subjected to withering hostility by the other members. Dixon, attempting to speak in the corridors with Cabot Lodge, had been brushed rudely aside; Cornut-Gentille had been pointedly ignored throughout the day by friends as well as opponents.

Yet he was able, when Cabot Lodge insisted that the Council rush through a vote on a United States resolution calling on Israel to withdraw its forces from Egyptian territory and upon all members of the United Nations to refrain from force or the threat of it, to argue forcibly against it. The Soviet delegate was the first to vote with the United States, and six other members of the Council followed suit. Then Britain and France opposed the vote, and their veto killed Lodge's first move.

Under pressure from the White House, Lodge made it known that he might even consider voting for a Soviet resolution if the wording was acceptable, and when a second resolution was put up for the vote, the British and French applied their vetoes for a second time. In the Middle East the ultimatum was rapidly expiring.

Israel announced it would accept the conditions providing

they were also accepted by Egypt. Nasser sent for Sir Humphrey Trevelyan and told him: "We're going to fight. The last time we let you British in on a temporary basis, you stayed for more than seventy years. I won't have that happen again."

At 5:30 A.M. next day the ultimatum ran out, and the British Parliament, quite naturally, wanted to know if the country was at war. When Eden appeared in the House of Commons later in the morning, he evaded the question until in final exasperation a Labour member acidly remarked: "How can we debate a war when the government won't even tell us whether it has started?" Eden retorted that he was not prepared to give any details of what was happening in the Middle East. Hugh Gaitskell, the Labour leader, said: "This is really a fantastic situation. . . . The whole House and the whole country are waiting for an answer to this question. Are we at war?" Eden reluctantly admitted that a state of "armed conflict" existed.

The second session of the Security Council opened that afternoon in New York with all delegates aware that they were deadlocked. Hammarskjold attempted to force the issue with a speech that clearly indicated he would resign his office if positive action was not forthcoming without delay.

Then the Yugoslav delegate invoked the previously unused "Uniting for Peace" procedure, which enabled the Council to hand over the crisis to a special session of the General Assembly, and which, being procedural, was not affected by the veto. The Council overruled French and British objections to the Yugoslav proposal, and the crisis was passed to a forum where all nations could become seized of it.

Before the Council adjourned the Soviet delegate, Sobolev, gazed bleakly at Cornut-Gentille and said with cold, deliberate menace: "France and Britain must be made to carefully examine their deeds in view of the grave consequences to which armed aggression in the Suez Canal area may lead us . . . extremely grave consequences for all mankind. . . ."

The Frenchman looked back, eyes unnaturally brilliant in his ashen face. Then he collapsed from nervous exhaustion and heart trouble. So critical was the threat of a general war, however, that the coincidence of the attack, coming as it did straight after Sobolev's portentous warning, was too dangerous a combination to permit public speculation. The news filtered through the corridors that the Ambassador was suffering from jaundice.

Once it was known in Ottawa that the crisis had been handed over to the General Assembly, Pearson prepared to fly to New York. He had kept Canada uncommitted for three months, while most other countries had sacrificed their freedom to manœuvre in debate by taking sides. By refusing to pursue a partisan policy, he had given Canada a position of independence and non-commitment from which its representatives could work toward a United Nations solution and a general peace settlement. His first consideration, however, was to forestall any move to have Britain and France arraigned before the United Nations on charges of conspiring to commit an act of war against a weak and sovereign state. The arresting officers were the Afro-Asians; and leading the prosecution was an impropable alliance of the United States, the Soviet Union, and India.

Pearson gave himself a difficult task. Of the seventy-six members of the United Nations, only two were supporting the Anglo-French action: Australia and New Zealand. He could not hope to stand by himself between the United States and Russia, then moving in massive condemnatory unison, and those whom they sought to punish. He had no precise plan in mind, and no idea at all that an immense invasion armada had just put out to sea.

A hundred thousand men, a hundred and thirty warships, including six aircraft carriers, more than a hundred freighters carrying nearly twenty thousand vehicles, and a multitude of landing craft would attack Egypt on November 6. Pearson, aware that few nations would be able to stay aloof from the crisis, and having determined that Canada's two mother countries would need sympathetic help and understanding in so dark an hour, had six days in which to rescue them from the brand of aggression, from the threat of moral ruin, and from the shadow of nuclear war.

PART TWO

The Soft
Impeachment

CHAPTER NINE

The Concept

DIPLOMATIC activity in and between the crisis capitals was confused, often frantic. Selwyn Lloyd confessed to Commonwealth diplomats in London that in his view the British policy of retreat from the Middle East was a disastrous failure. "It was a mistake to give up the Palestine Mandate for the sake of creating Israel," he said. "It was a mistake too to withdraw from the Suez Canal Zone. On both occasions we submitted to strong American pressure, and ever since we have striven hard to arrive at a common Anglo-American policy without success. We have to look after ourselves now."

Eisenhower sent fretful messages to Eden and Mollet, urging them to refrain from carrying out the terms of the ultimatum, and Dulles, thinking they might be ignored, told Arnold Heeney in Washington: "The French and the British feel they've got to destroy Nasser's power and prestige fast. He may be replaced by a more amenable pro-Western government, so we've got to be ready to deal with a new Suez situation at any moment. The Arab-Israeli situation is separate and different. In this one we're faced with the expert opinion of General Burns that the Israelis deliberately put obstacles in the way of peace-keeping. And we've got to find out if the Arabs can be made to admit that Israel exists."

In Paris, NATO discovered that in addition to the three Mystère squadrons it had "lost," another three French-manned F-84 squadrons were "out of service." Inquiries at the Rue Saint-Dominique headquarters of the Defence Ministry were deflected by friendly suggestions that "it is impossible for such a thing to happen. They must be moving to another station." When the United States Ambassador called upon the Director General of Political Affairs at the Quai d'Orsay to ask why there had been no prior consultation, he was told: "*Mon vieux lapin, je n'en savais rien. Les fonctionnaires n'étaient pas dans le jeu.*" The minister's office had made all decisions; the Quai had not been informed. Ambassador Dillon persisted with the comment: "We believe Israel has suddenly acquired two or three hundred Mystères." The Director General shrugged. "That's nice. I know nothing of it. None of us do."

Prime Minister Gerhardsen of Norway was on an official visit to London. The Labour Party's shadow Foreign Minister, Alfred Robens, told him during a lunch on the 31st: "There is good evidence that the government had information about the intended Israeli attack on Egypt. It set the stage for, and determined the timing of, the British and French action."

That evening, during a dinner at Downing Street, Eden said that while he didn't expect Norway to approve of the action Britain and France had taken against Egypt, he wanted to assure Gerhardsen that he knew of nothing which might give credence to the charges of collusion being levelled at the British government.

Eden, in fact, was telling the truth. He had himself not met any Israeli leader, and the two governments had not conspired. Eden and Lloyd had not acted with the authority or knowledge of the full British government; Mollet, Pineau, and Bourgès-Maunoury had not acted with the authority or knowledge of the full French government; and Ben-Gurion had acted entirely on his own.

But Gerhardsen thought that not "all British authorities could claim equal innocence." After dinner, his chief political adviser and interpreter for the visit, Andreas Andersen, was taken by Butler into an unoccupied room for a private talk. The British deputy leader created a conspiratorial atmosphere by recalling the great decisions of historic importance that had been made in this setting, and then stated dramatically that he was not at all happy about Eden's decision to participate with the French in a sudden action against Egypt. He did not intend to resign in protest yet, but would reserve his decision pending the outcome of the action. In the meantime he hoped for the best, and under the circumstances felt that, while he had grave reservations, the best immediate policy was to keep the government intact for the crisis.

Gerhardsen's report to Oslo of what he had heard in England inspired Foreign Minister Halvarde Lange to react violently at the ultimatum, using what one ambassador described as "the strongest language I have ever heard from him." Lange believed there was collusion between France, Britain, and Israel which, he said, "makes a mockery out of NATO and the principle of full and frank consultation between allies."

In New Delhi, the Indian government exerted pressure on Canada, Australia, and New Zealand by telling their High Commissioners that India would be forced to quit the Commonwealth if their governments presented a united "white" front with Britain at the United Nations.

It seemed, however, that an influential group of Tory members of Parliament in London might lead Britain out of the Commonwealth first. More than fifty of them discussed Churchill's 1940 offer of common citizenship with France, and proposed a political, economic, and military union between the two countries.

And from this frantic mêlée, a Canadian policy solidified.

Recalling it, Pearson said: "There was only one course – to do our best to ensure that the British and French action was not examined by itself under a spotlight narrowly focused on recent events alone. I felt it should be examined in the fullest possible perspective against the situation that had led to the intervention, and against the past records of both countries. It was clear even then that if they had suffered considerable provocation at the hands of Egypt, they had endured too the frustrating sequels to what undoubtedly comprised the worst chapter in Dulles's diplomatic career. I regretted they thought it necessary to take the keeping of peace into their own hands, but it was equally obvious that the peace needed keeping in the Middle East.

"That was principally because members of the United Nations had failed to discharge their collective responsibility. They had failed to protect life on both sides of the Arab-Israeli borders, failed for five years to enforce their own resolution that the canal should be kept open to traffic of all nations. All members, ourselves included, were to blame for these failures, and none of us had the right to act the accuser or to throw the first stone.

"In the past, there were members who were always too concerned with apportioning the blame for the last incident and too little concerned with preventing the next. I wanted to persuade my friends in New York to turn their minds toward something more than an immediate way out, toward a lasting settlement, no matter what the sacrifices involved.

"It was essential to prevent a recurrence of a situation such as this, where two nations, rightly or wrongly, had felt themselves obliged to intervene to keep the peace. We should not seek to make life more difficult for the British, the French, the Arabs, or the Israelis, but contribute to a just solution.

"We were very nearly in a world war. If the United Nations failed again this time, there was no knowing where it would all end. . . ."

Pearson was worried, as were most people, by the glaring discriminatory intent of the ultimatum. The demand for both sides to withdraw from the Canal Zone meant that Egypt would have to retreat from her own territory while Israel was invited to advance and occupy.

Then, without warning, relations between Canada and Britain were suddenly strained.

Eden, alarmed at the unexpected prospect of the Commonwealth collapsing about him, tried to rally the "old" members to Britain's side. On October 30 he sent a letter to Prime Minister St. Laurent in which he said that he had warned a restive Israel against attacking Jordan and had obtained assurances from Israel that it would not attack Jordan. On the other hand, he had assured Israel that Britain was under no obligation to defend Egypt, although a war between Israel and Egypt would not be permitted to block the Suez Canal. In such an event, Britain and France would feel bound to require both countries to cease hostilities and to withdraw from the canal.

The curious aspect of this comment is that Israel and Egypt actually faced each other in the Sinai, more than a hundred miles from the canal. Eden's mention of the canal – and clear assumption long before the war ever reached the canal that the war would be fought around it – indicated that he anticipated the event either through excellent intelligence or by foreknowledge.

Referring to "our grave concern," he continued that in order to ensure the safety of the canal he expected to intervene, stop the fighting, and then raise "all this at UNO in the most appropriate way." To achieve these objectives Eden proposed to send "a requirement to Israel and Egypt demanding that hostilities must cease" and "that troops should be withdrawn from both banks of the canal." At the time of writing, only Egyptian troops were in the vicinity of the canal, yet he informed St. Laurent that Britain and France reserved the right to take military action "to compel the offender to conform."

A rather curious attempt to place responsibility on Egypt was made by referring to Israeli counterattacks against Egyptian aggression, and the letter then continued with a self-righteous plea for sympathy on the ground that the war "must be stopped before it has time to develop into a wider conflict involving others."

Eden ended the letter with another of his unfortunate presumptions, saying in effect, "I know I can count on your understanding and support."

It arrived just as St. Laurent, normally equable, not easily aroused in spite of his part-Irish ancestry, was reading ticker-tape news of the ultimatum and quietly simmering. He read it quickly, threw it down on his desk, and, according to the official who delivered it, "then exploded, he was so mad."

His earlier objection to Eden's attempt to extract Canadian endorsement for a possible use of force was mild compared to his rage at Britain's treatment of the Commonwealth. When Pearson saw the telegram, he said, "I agree he presumes a bit much, but let's look at it from the British side. They couldn't very well tell us, the Americans, or anyone else in advance, because if they had we would have stopped them. And they're in no mood to be stopped."

When finally drafted and approved, St. Laurent's reply was essentially reasonable, expressing sympathy for the Anglo-French predicament rather than hostility. He regretted that Britain should have acted without prior consultation, but understood the difficulties which precluded it.

Having said that, however, Prime Minister St. Laurent indicated that Canada could not conclude that Israel was justified in attacking Egypt or that Egypt's natural resistance justified British and French intervention. He informed Eden that shipments of Canadian arms to Israel had been suspended and, after pointing out that the Canadian government would shape its course in conformity with the United Nations Charter, he continued: "We are never unmindful . . . of the very special relationship of close friendship and intimate association which we have with the United Kingdom and with your government. Nor do we forget the vital importance of the Suez Canal to the economic life of the United Kingdom."

There were three aspects of the situation, said St. Laurent, which caused particular anxiety to the Canadian government. The first was the effect of Eden's decisions upon the United Nations, of which the United Kingdom had been such a staunch and steady supporter. The fact that Britain had acted while the Security Council was formally seized of the matter was, in St. Laurent's view, most regrettable.

Then there was the danger of a serious division within the Commonwealth which might "prejudice the unity of our association." And finally there was the "deplorable divergence of viewpoint and policy between the U.K. and the U.S.A.," which · was a matter of deep and abiding interest to Canada.

After stressing that Anglo-American co-operation and friendship was the foundation upon which the free world based its hopes for a peaceful and secure future, the Canadian Prime Minister emphasised that it would be a tragedy beyond repair if this co-operation and friendship were to disappear, or be weakened. It would be difficult, he said, for a Canadian to think of any consideration, other than Canada's national survival, as of more importance.

He concluded by hoping that he had in no way added to Eden's burdens and that he had been of some help by explaining as a friend the worries of the Canadian government.

But what Eden wanted most – Canada's commitment to support of his actions – was missing. The Prime Minister simply avoided any mention of it, as he had ignored sharing Eden's "indignation" at the seizure of the canal.

The reply reached London the next day, before the bombing of Egyptian airfields began, and created instant consternation. Reports rippled back through diplomatic channels that Eden was "aghast" at its tone, the Foreign Office "shocked." Rumours of a rift inspired the Conservative opposition in Ottawa to renew its attack on the government by subjecting St. Laurent to a biting cross-examination on his "betrayal of Britain."

The British High Commissioner in Ottawa curtly informed the Department of External Affairs that "this is the first occasion on which Canada has parted company with the United Kingdom on such a crucial issue," and warned that "we should begin at once to pick up the pieces." He was politely assured that "any action Mr. St. Laurent or Mr. Pearson initiates is bound to be positive and constructive."

Pearson was, in fact, vaguely aware that in some as yet indefinable way the present situation resembled another he had experienced twenty years before, while attending the old League of Nations. He had felt then that Mussolini could have been stopped in Ethiopia had the democracies been willing to take collective action against Italy. Their failure even to agree among themselves, and their weak indecision, had so encouraged the dictators that, in his view, world war had been made inevitable.

He was convinced now that if the United Nations could impose its collective will on the belligerents in the Middle East, a critical deterioration in the international climate might be immediately halted. It was time, he thought, that an effective instrument existed to enforce United Nations decisions: an international police force, perhaps, which need be merely temporary for this specific emergency.

At about 7:00 P.M., Wednesday, the 31st, Pearson telephoned Norman Robertson in London to discuss the idea and instruct him to find out whether the British government might welcome it as a substitute for their own action. A second call was made to Washington, where Arnold Heeney was asked to inquire whether the State Department would incorporate a clause providing for an international force into the United States resolution being prepared for the Assembly.

When the ambassadors replied the next morning it seemed

that, whereas both governments welcomed the concept as an eventual or ultimate solution, they considered it too complicated to serve their respective interests in the immediate future.

That Thursday, the British House of Commons was the scene of an ugly exhibition of impassioned and irresponsible political behaviour. The Labour Party were angry and bewildered; Eden, Lloyd, and Head were obstinately uninformative. The government's ambivalence infuriated the Opposition until, amid a shrill cacophony of political and personal abuse, the House was suspended, the Speaker ruling that further debate was impossible.

Eden, at one point, however, seeking to make the government's actions at least sound respectable, managed to say: "The first and urgent task is to separate these combatants [Israel and Egypt] and to stabilize the position. That is our purpose. If the United Nations were then willing to take over the physical task of maintaining peace in the area, no one would be better pleased than we. But police action there must be. . . ."

This was not quite the formula Norman Robertson had transmitted to the Foreign Office, but at least it was a public declaration of willingness to accept the principle of a United Nations force.

When Pearson flew to New York in the afternoon, accompanied by John Holmes, Assistant Under Secretary of State, it was already night in Cairo, where the thud and flash of bombs on airfields five to ten miles from the city centre was not nearly so terrifying as the Egyptians had expected. At the last minute, the size of the bombs to be used was reduced from one thousand pounds to five hundred, and then to two hundred and fifty pounds. And Nasser, believing that imminent invasion would be accompanied by a convoy escorted by warships, ordered his chief engineer, Younes, to sink blockships in the canal.

II

MORE than three thousand people thronged the Assembly: delegates, advisers, Secretariat staff, press, television crews, and spectators. The "Uniting for Peace" procedure was specifically designed to enable the General Assembly to act when the Security Council was blocked and if international intervention of some sort was imperative to prevent war. There could be no doubt that the crisis had reached a decisive peak, that the danger of war was real.

The United States forced the pace of proceedings. The presidential election, the certainty that unless a moderately toned sensible resolution was moved quickly, less responsible nations would introduce something that might exacerbate the situation, and genuine concern that the United Nations should prove itself capable of acting for peace, inspired the State Department with a dangerous sense of urgency.

Many governments would have preferred less haste and greater attention paid to the overriding need for a firm basis upon which the issues could be settled once and for all.

Expecting Britain and France to challenge the legality of the special session on the ground that the "Uniting for Peace" procedure had been improperly invoked in the Security Council, Cabot Lodge drafted a letter which expressed endorsement of the legality of the session. Copies were distributed to fifty heads of missions with a covering note asking that they sign it and have it delivered to the Secretary General. Lodge thought that if the debate threatened to become bogged down in complicated legal argument, he could keep it under control by calling upon Hammarskjold to reveal how many members approved the proceedings. The precaution was unnecessary, as the British and French avoided a procedural debate.

When Pearson and Holmes arrived at 5:30 P.M. to take their seats with the Canadian delegation, the Egyptian delegate was already at the rostrum delivering a lurid, imaginative catalogue of alleged French and British crimes against humanity. Geoffrey Murray, the Canadian delegation's senior adviser, who had been circulating through the corridors for most of the afternoon, reported that this heralded a combined Afro-Asian intention to employ fulsome propaganda in an attempt to have the Allies branded as aggressors. The mood of the Assembly, he said, was sultry and unpredictable.

The British delegate was the next speaker, and almost immediately Pearson heard the echoes of Robertson's efforts in London during the morning. "The first urgent task is to separate Israel from Egypt and to stabilize the position," said Sir Pierson Dixon. "If the United Nations is willing to take over the physical task of maintaining peace in the area, no one will be better pleased than we. But police action there must be. . . ."

The wording was identical to that used by Eden in the House of Commons a few hours earlier.

At 7:40 P.M., the Assembly recessed for dinner and to give delegates an opportunity to consult with each other or with their governments. Pearson, accompanied by Holmes, Mackay, and Murray, walked across the hall to the United States desk, where he held an impromptu conference with Dulles. After Pearson had explained that he was apprehensive at the haste with which the United States was pressing for a vote, Dulles said: "We've got to have a resolution passed quickly. Events are moving so damn fast out there that there's no telling what might happen if we don't get something done to stop them. We think there's a strong possibility that military operations will be stepped up by the British and the French. If they are, then we may as well face the fact that the danger to world peace is going to become intolerable.

"We're worried about the Afro-Asians. They don't like our resolution because they think it's too soft. They're going along with it right now because they haven't got an alternative of their own that has a hope in hell of being approved. But if we're too slow, they might come up with something that will only aggravate the situation."

"You may be right," replied Pearson, "but surely it's essential to have a resolution providing for some sort of negotiating machinery, perhaps an *ad hoc* committee which can investigate and recommend terms for a settlement."

Dulles agreed, but remained unconvinced that there was time to draft such a resolution in a manner that would have any hope of being accepted.

"We don't need a new resolution," Pearson said. "We can put a brief clause into yours. There's not a chance of it being brought to a vote before midnight, so we have three or four hours to work on it."

"Not time enough," Dulles insisted.

"I can't see much point in merely working for a return to the status quo in the Middle East," said Pearson. "We've got to get a settlement across the board out there and we've got to ensure the security of the demarcation lines while negotiations are in progress."

"That's fine. If you people care to propose something like that, go ahead. We'll support you."

"You mean we should put forward a brand new resolution. We're agreed there's no time for that. The Assembly is about to vote on your motion, and anything new will require thinking through. If you don't think there's time for incorporating something constructive into your resolution, then I don't think there's time for us to produce a detailed proposal tonight. I shall probably confine myself to speaking in general terms later on."

When Dulles asked if Canada would support the United States resolution, Pearson replied that he had not yet received instructions from Ottawa. He had personally hoped for something more constructive, and added: "We're interested in helping Britain and France. I would like to make it possible for them to withdraw with as little loss of face as possible, and bring them back into realignment with the United States."

"That's not possible at this time," said Dulles. "They've damaged the whole cause of freedom by placing us in an inferior position morally to the Communists. We could be having a showdown with Russia right now over this Hungary situation but for their actions."

"I don't see it that way," replied Pearson. "They're in a difficult situation, and we feel it necessary to help them out of it. Anything else is purely negative."

They parted on this inconclusive note, and Pearson telephoned Ottawa to speak with Prime Minister St. Laurent. After explaining the United States position, reporting on the urgent need to head off the introduction of irresponsible moves by the more vehement enemies of Britain and France, and summarizing his own feelings, he proposed that Canada should abstain from the vote on the American resolution. "By abstaining we keep our freedom to put forward our own proposal for a United Nations force," he said. "The British and French will vote against it, as they did in the Security Council, so it really gets us nowhere. They'll simply pursue their present course, get inextricably involved, and have the Assembly really after them. If we can persuade them to accept our idea of an international force and word a resolution so that they can support it, or at least avoid voting against it, then they can be seen to be complying with United Nations wishes and thereby upholding the Charter. That way they're off the hook."

"Can you persuade the Assembly to go along?" asked the Prime Minister.

"We'll try."

St. Laurent promised to telephone instructions to New York after he had consulted the Cabinet, and at 10:00 P.M. the Assembly session was resumed.

During the next five hours, tension deepened as rumours flew from one delegation to the next: the Russians were leaving Hungary, the Russians were turning back in strength, Nasser was seeking a means to surrender, Nasser had vanished, the

Israelis were on their way to Cairo, the French were dropping paratroops in the Canal Zone, the British were holding back. But a few reports were true.

Throughout the evening Cairo Radio had appealed to all Arab states to join the war against the aggressors. The Egyptian Commander-in-Chief, General Amer, had ordered the Syrian and Jordanian armies to attack Israel. Jordan had replied that as its own security was threatened, its army was required for home defence; and the Syrian government had regretted that its armed forces could not be committed into action without authority from the President, who, quite inexplicably, in view of the dangers facing Nasser, had left on Tuesday for an official visit to Moscow. The Arab states, it seemed, were willing to join the battle of words in the General Assembly, providing they could keep out of the shooting war.

Most of the Egyptian army's four hundred modern tanks were in Cairo, one on each street corner, ostensibly to protect the seat of government. Only later did Western correspondents report that the army, knowing the Anglo-French air forces would not bomb built-up areas, preferred the safety of the city to the open ground in the Canal Zone.

Shortly before midnight St. Laurent approved Pearson's proposal to abstain and to speak in general terms of the necessity for an international police force. Three hours later, at approximately 3:00 A.M. on Friday, the Assembly adopted the United States resolution by sixty-four votes to five, with six abstentions. Only Australia and New Zealand voted against it with Britain, France, and Israel, and the most surprising vote of all was Canada's abstention. The reason, however, became dramatically apparent when Pearson rose to explain it, and for the first time since the session opened, the clamour was stilled.

"As my delegation sees it," he said, "this resolution which the General Assembly has thus adopted in its present form – and there was very little chance to alter that form – is inadequate to achieve the purposes which we have in mind at this session. . . .

". . . I confess to sadness, indeed even distress, at not being able to support the position taken by two countries whose ties with my country are and will remain close and intimate; two countries which have contributed so much to man's progress and freedom under law. . . . I regret the use of military force . . . but I regret also that there was not more time . . . for consideration of the best way to bring about that kind of cease-fire which would have enduring and beneficial results. . . .

"This resolution does provide for a cease-fire . . . it does not provide for any steps to be taken by the United Nations for a peace settlement. . . .

"Today we are facing a feeling of almost despairing crisis for the United Nations and for peace. Surely this feeling might have been harnessed to action. . . . We need action, then, not only to end the fighting, but to make a peace.

"The armed forces of Israel and Egypt are to withdraw or, if you like, return to the armistice lines, where presumably . . . they will face each other in fear and hatred. What then? What then six months from now? Are we to go through all this again? Are we to return to the status quo? Such a position would be . . . a return to terror, bloodshed, strife, incidents, charges, countercharges. . . .

"I would like to see a provision in this resolution . . . authorizing the Secretary General to begin making arrangements with Member States for a United Nations force large enough to keep these borders at peace while a political settlement is being worked out. . . . My own government would be glad to recommend Canadian participation in such a United Nations force, a truly international peace and police force. . . ."

In view of their earlier discussion, even Pearson was surprised when Dulles immediately returned to the rostrum to say he was aware of the need for a constructive and positive approach to the situation, that it was not the intention of the United States to merely "turn the clock back." He was in complete agreement with Mr. Pearson's comments. It was "not only my personal agreement, but . . . also the feeling of President Eisenhower, with whom I have spoken about this aspect of the matter." The United States, he said, would be "very happy indeed if the Canadian delegation would formulate and introduce . . . a concrete suggestion along the lines Mr. Pearson has outlined."

The particular tactic of abstaining from a crucial vote in order to preserve independence of action was at the time the least understood and most bitterly criticised of all Canadian actions during the crisis. Subsequently it became accepted at the United Nations as a classic example of skilful application of international diplomatic techniques.

The concept of a world force to police a world peace has its origins buried deep in antiquity. In more recent times France tried unsuccessfully to persuade the allied powers to create such a force in 1919, and the League of Nations made several futile attempts in the 'thirties. The United Nations Charter provides for a police force, but no one seriously considered the idea practicable in a climate of East-West hostility. The Military Staff Committee, consisting of the Chiefs of Staff of the permanent members of the Security Council, had been deadlocked on this issue since 1948.

Pearson's originality lay in his early recognition, after the Anglo-French ultimatum, that perhaps the political climate had changed sufficiently to make an international force feasible. And once he had implanted the idea in London and Washington, the reactions were so swift that he was virtually forced to accept as irrevocable that if there were to be effective United Nations action, if there were to be a negotiated settlement in the Middle East, and if Britain and France were to be rescued from the cruel consequences that would surely follow if they continued to ignore world opinion, Canada had to take the initiative.

The tactics were possible only because of Pearson's special

knowledge of the curiously obscure manner in which United Nations diplomacy operates. Power shifts and unfamiliar re-alignments of doubtful loyalties were taking place constantly, confusing the normal pattern of international behaviour. The Ottawa-London-Washington triangle of Anglo-Saxon diplomacy had broken apart; the Paris-Washington link, never strong, had been severed; India, Pakistan, and Ceylon were voting against the Commonwealth and threatening to leave it; Britain was allied with Israel against the entire Arab world, much of which she had created; France had permitted her war against the Arabs in North Africa to become extended to the Middle East; and most formidable of all, Washington and Moscow were being drawn together by identical interests in circumstances that were cause for disquiet rather than comfort. Precisely where did an international police force fit into such a convulsed picture, heavy with forbidding implications that were not yet clear?

The first decision by the Canadian delegation was whether Pearson should speak before the vote on the United States resolution or after it. They had decided that if they were seriously going to develop the concept of an international force, Canada would have to abstain. To have voted against the resolution would have amounted to commitment with Britain and France; to vote for it might have so angered the British that it would be impossible for Canada to keep lines of communication open between Washington and London. There was by then no direct dialogue between the United States government and the governments of Britain and France. Once the decision to abstain had been taken, it led naturally to unanimous agreement that Pearson should speak in explanation and at the same time introduce the police force concept in general terms to test Assembly reaction. If it proved favourable, then automatically Britain and France were presented with a face-saving formula for avoiding further involvement. They were allegedly acting to separate belligerents, to prevent the spread of war; a United

Nations force would perform the same function. If pride could be satisfied, passions might cool.

There was considerable risk in pursuing this line of policy. Pearson would be staking the reputation of the government of Canada and his personal prestige at a time when Assembly approval could not be guaranteed. Rejection would prove so damaging that volatile critics of the government in Canada might force him to resign and result in a demoralizing re-appraisal of Canadian foreign policy.

Mackay and Murray, as members of the permanent mission, were responsible for advising Pearson on the reception his proposal could expect from the Assembly, and in so fluid a situation they had to rely upon professional intuition rather than practical assessment. The Soviet Union was matching American haste with unfamiliar restraint and moderation; Pakistan, Iran, and Turkey were acting as brakes on the more impetuous Afro-Asians; the Latin Americans, accustomed to taking their leads from the United States and Britain, were un-decided in the face of an Anglo-American division; and only Canada, the Scandinavian countries, and the European mem-bers of NATO could be relied upon to react responsibly. In this context, the Canadian delegation estimated that if Britain, France, and the United States supported a Canadian resolu-tion, at least thirty other nations would follow suit.

On this friable basis Pearson decided to produce a detailed proposal. And at 5:00 A.M. the Assembly adjourned, most dele-gates having been busy, because of time differences between New York and their capitals, for more than twenty hours and without food for the last ten. Before Pearson left the United Nations building, there was a telephone call from London. It was Robertson, saying he had received a message from Selwyn Lloyd to the effect that Pineau was arriving to see Eden and himself in the afternoon. They were all worried about the criti-cal proportions of the crisis – about the vehemence of the speeches in the Assembly, about the split that had developed domestically in Britain – and thought that the best hope for finding a way out of their predicament lay in the Canadian proposal. They would like to be kept closely informed on the details.

"We don't have any yet," said Pearson, "but tell them we'll have it all set up by tomorrow."

Then he joined Hans Engen, the Norwegian permanent representative, for breakfast with Hammarskjold on the thirty-eighth floor. The Norwegian was enthusiastic, offering to work with Pearson and to advise his government to act as co-sponsor of a resolution; Hammarskjold, still feeling that Britain and France by using the veto in the Security Council had damaged United Nations prestige and moral leadership, was morose and pessimistic. The Assembly was in a mood to punish, and could not be expected to react favourably to any proposals that might divert attention from flagrant aggression. Besides, he said, there was no time.

On his desk was a message from the United States delegation, drawing his attention to State Department information that French convoys from Algiers and Marseilles had joined British convoys from Malta to form an invasion fleet bound for Egypt.

Peace was chasing war.

III

NO ONE knew if or when the emergency session would resume. The United Nations had made its bid for peace; now it was simply a matter of waiting to see whether the cease-fire would be obeyed.

Red China was reported to be registering "volunteers" for

service in the Middle East if Egypt was invaded; the Soviet Union was opening offices where "volunteers" could enlist in the Egyptian armed forces; and Western diplomats warned their governments that "it would be dangerous to construe this move as bluff because volunteer units are in fact standing by at airports." Allied Headquarters suspected that Communist bloc personnel were already operating in the area. A British Canberra bomber returning from a photographic reconnaissance mission was brilliantly intercepted by MIGs at a height of 45,000 feet above Syria and badly crippled. Highly skilled pilots guided by an efficient radar system? The implications were ominous.

At 10:00 A.M. in New York, Hans Engen of Norway joined Pearson at the Drake Hotel, where the Canadian Minister was already speaking by telephone with Norman Robertson. The High Commissioner reported that Selwyn Lloyd had again assured him Britain would hand over its police action to a United Nations force. Pineau was in conference with Eden at Downing Street, and Robertson hoped that France would also be persuaded to agree. Eden was said to be in a "high state of agitation" at the unexpected strength of opposition to Anglo-French operations; Lloyd confessed to being worried himself at the way events were developing; and the French were insistent that the entire timetable of military action should be advanced.

The NATO Council met in Paris that same morning, Friday, November 2, to hear the United States Ambassador report that Dulles was in complete agreement with the Canadian concept of a United Nations force. He was followed by other representatives, all of whom expressed the opinion that Britain and France had gravely prejudiced their case against Egypt by the methods of their intervention rather than the motives that had inspired it. Several described the prolonged bombing as "sickening."

When the question of Soviet participation in a United

Nations police force was raised, the British Ambassador cautioned that such a possibility should not be rejected.

In London and in Paris there was general misconception about Pearson's proposal. Pearson envisaged some sort of United Nations force being inserted into the situation within a week, rendering further Anglo-French action unnecessary; the British and French interpretation was that a United Nations force could not be formed in less than a month and would have to take over after occupation of the Canal Zone.

In New York, the Pakistani Ambassador called at the Drake to inform Pearson that he was instructed to support the Canadian plan, and to offer background information. His government had been informed that the British expected that four weeks of occupation would be sufficient to bring down Nasser and establish a new régime in Egypt.

Replying to a question from Engen, the Ambassador said, "The French can justify what they are doing on the ground that they are so committed already, they have nothing to lose by further involvement. But the British are making a major error. If they go any further there's a good chance that India and Ceylon will break away from the Commonwealth. In that event, the pressure on us to do the same will be irresistible. The last vestige of European influence in the Middle East and South East Asia is likely to disappear and, despite the loss of prestige the Soviet Union is suffering because of events in Hungary, the Communists will become the protectors of Asia."

As Pearson and Holmes left New York at about noon for Ottawa, Ambassador Heeney was summoned to the State Department for a private conference with Dulles, who showed him two draft resolutions in the form of "working papers": one related to the canal issue, the other to Palestine and security of Israel's borders. His dispatch to Pearson said:

Mr. Dulles is thinking of having to introduce resolutions along these lines as early as tomorrow [Saturday, November 3] or perhaps Sunday. Otherwise he fears that the initiative will be lost to those who are already rumoured to be preparing resolutions of a condemnatory character involving sanctions, etc., against the United Kingdom and France.

Dulles and his advisers . . . believe it is the part of wisdom to divide the two subjects. . . . With regard to the Suez Canal, the Secretary was optimistic that a proposal along the lines of his Working Paper 1 would receive wide support. He was prepared to gamble that the United Kingdom itself would welcome it, and Egypt, after the events of the past few days, might be similarly disposed. He is thinking of a three-man commission for the Suez Canal to consist of Pearson (Canada), Lange (Norway), and an Asian, or perhaps Popovic (Yugoslavia). The manning of the second commission for Palestine to consist of five members would be on a geographic basis, as outlined in his Working Paper 2.

Dulles sees these resolutions as the second element in the strategy initiated in the Special Assembly yesterday by the United States call for a cease-fire. In this connection he continues to recognize the force of your own argument. He feels that action taken so far has avoided something much worse. But we must press on to the next stage . . . and we have not much time.

I put to the Secretary the points you had made to me earlier . . . on the phone from New York. A primary objective was to realign the United Kingdom and the United States; this means that there must be United Kingdom acquiescence, if not actual support. We were in urgent touch with London. It was important to avoid taking a fixed position too soon until sufficiently wide support was reasonably assured. . . . I also described your preliminary thinking with regard to a United Nations "police force."

Dulles was most sympathetic . . . but again he emphasized the severe time limitations under which we were working. . . . He thought this idea would take a long time to work out, though he did not exclude it as part of an ultimate solution. . . . He would welcome your reaction to his proposals, as well as any reaction we could get from London. . . . We were not asked to take any initiative in Paris.

When the Canadian Cabinet met at 4:00 P.M. Pearson reported on what had transpired in New York, avoiding general mention of Canada proposing the creation of the United Nations police force, in case his final instructions were delayed by protracted argument. When he had finished, Prime Minister St. Laurent formally thanked him and concluded, "We can all see how grave this situation is. Let us hope that the efforts being made at the United Nations will spare us the worst effects of so dangerous a crisis. I take it you will be leaving again for New York. . . ."

The meeting ended and, while ministers were breaking up into groups, Pearson steered the Prime Minister into a corner to explain that he intended to introduce a resolution, at the earliest possible moment, concerning the establishment of an international force. St. Laurent replied, "Do as you think best. I will support you here."

Pearson has since said, "I had to get my instructions informally that way because one or two of our Cabinet colleagues opposed us taking the initiative. They thought it might prove embarrassing politically."

Pearson had decided by then that Canada could not countenance Britain and France being branded as aggressors. He informed the Cabinet that the delegation in New York would be instructed to urge this view upon other delegations in the strongest possible terms. Canada would also work for a general peace settlement in the Middle East, not just a cease-fire, and in this sense he contemplated a resolution, clearly aimed at opening up a way for negotiation, that would give the United Kingdom and France an opportunity to withdraw from their predicament. "We cannot expect them to agree to cease firing and return to the status quo," he said.

These principles became the guide lines for the consultations of the Canadians with other delegations in the corridors and lobbies, in which they stressed the importance of avoiding any sudden action that might parade Britain and France before the world as criminal nations. While pursuing this course, the team also had to avoid giving the impression that their main motivation was to protect British and French interests.

Hammarskjold, too, although the target of unfriendly comments in British and French newspapers, allied himself with Pearson by using his influence to deter drastic proposals that might cause irreparable damage to the United Nations by so arousing public opinion in Britain and France that these two founder-nations might be forced to resign their membership.

In the sullen, angry atmosphere such as then existed in the Assembly, this task would have been a difficult one but for the conduct of two men: Sir Pierson Dixon of Britain and M. Louis de Guiringaud of France. Though it was quite apparent that these men were appalled by the actions of their governments, they defended the Anglo-French cause with such courage and clarity that they earned considerable sympathy for themselves, if not for their countries. In those hectic days they were admired and respected as the representatives of two governments most of the delegations wanted to publicly condemn.

Before the Canadian Cabinet resumed its meeting on Saturday morning, Pearson received a message from St. Laurent. Eden had made a thirty-minute transatlantic telephone call to the Canadian Prime Minister to ask if Canada intended to propose the creation of a United Nations force. If so, there was no reason why Britain and France should not "continue our operations against Egypt under the United Nations flag." Eden had said that as "we have the forces already in position, we are better placed than anyone else to implement a United Nations resolution in this regard."

"Good Heavens!" exclaimed Pearson in honest astonishment. "Some people will say that the burglars want police protection while they rob the safe."

St. Laurent said that Eden could see no other way out; that he would have to make acceptance of the cease-fire conditional upon the United Nations being in a position to take over the physical tasks already embarked upon by the Anglo-French forces.

The precise location of British and French forces in the Mediterranean was not known, but it was anticipated that British and French ground troops would occupy the Canal Zone within the next two or three days. Although other Arab states, including Jordan and Syria, were considered likely to be vocal in support of Egypt, no one really thought they would initiate large-scale military operations. If, however, the British and French struggle for control of the immediate area of the canal was protracted, the eventual involvement of other Arab military forces was possible.

There were no indications that the Soviet Union intended to provide large-scale material or military aid. Egyptian forces would presumably be defeated quickly but if the Nasser government, or anything less than an efficient pro-Western government, remained in Cairo, Egypt would retain a long-term harassing capability of considerable magnitude. This would be particularly true if part of the Egyptian forces were withdrawn into the Delta area and if the Soviet Union elected to continue shipments of military equipment.

A report from Washington indicated that the cease-fire was regarded as extremely urgent on military as well as political grounds. The United States felt that British and French forces should not be committed in the Middle East at a time when Soviet aggression in Eastern Europe could prove to be a dangerous threat to peace. London and Paris, however, con-sidered that the Red Army was so committed in Hungary and in other restless satellites that the situation was tailor-made for action in the Middle East.

If the United States was concerned over the weakening of NATO defences in Western Europe during a stage of critical internecine relations on both sides of the Iron Curtain, the only obvious method of stopping Britain and France would be to offer an overwhelmingly good reason which they could accept politically. There was, instead, a complete breakdown of diplomatic contact.

The Ottawa bridge was virtually the only means of com-munication between Washington and its belligerent allies. Pearson had persuaded the Americans that a United Nations police force was feasible and desirable, and had persuaded the British that United States support for his concept provided them with an opportunity to accept the cease-fire on condition that there would be no return to the status quo. Had the cease-fire been rejected outright, strongly condemnatory resolutions would have followed merely to inflame a worsening situation. Overnight, he had achieved the tenuous triumph of an Anglo-French acceptance of the cease-fire on condition that a United Nations force was created, and of United States support, provid-ing Britain and France accepted in principle the provisions of the two "working papers" Dulles had asked Heeney to transmit to London.

Early on Saturday he telephoned Norman Robertson and said, "We're going to go ahead with a resolution calling for the creation of a United Nations force. You should tell the government there that there's absolutely no hope of Assembly approval if landings take place before the vote. If they are sincere about handing over to a United Nations force, they've got to play their part in helping to establish it. Once we have a resolution adopted we can link the cease-fire with the United Nations force and the American working papers proposing committees to negotiate settlements. It's vitally important that they slow down now to give us a chance."

Pearson, conscious that no one really thought that a United Nations force could be put together quickly enough to halt the agonising slide toward tragedy, declined to be discouraged or deflected from his purpose while the lines between Ottawa and London, and Ottawa and Washington, remained intact. He felt instinctively that his straw could be conjured into a torch of peace if there was the time. The invasion fleet in the Mediterranean was steaming toward Port Said with less than seven hundred miles to go. Somehow it had to be slowed down.

But a new day had already dawned in London and Paris; and Bourgès-Maunoury, assisted ably as always by Abel Thomas, and with the political support of Pineau, was exerting all the pressure he could muster to speed up the assault on Egypt.

The Resolution

PINEAU returned to Paris on Friday evening worried by what he had seen and heard at Downing Street: of Lloyd he said, "*Il est calme, un peu lent*"; but Eden revealed hesitancy where there had been resolve. Condemned overwhelmingly by the bulk of world opinion, subjected to an astoundingly violent assault by British socialists, criticized by his own party, deserted by Eisenhower and Dulles, who were ranged alongside the Afro-Asians and Communists against him, and frigidly treated by dissident members of his own Cabinet, the tide of the British leader's will and strength was changing, determination ebbing before the flow of indecision.

Eden's insistence that they should accept the cease-fire, on condition that the United Nations would take over military operations, was not so disquieting to Pineau as his obsessive reiteration that Britain and France were in reality acting as the United States had done at the time of Korea, as the van of a more slowly organised United Nations army. In the final analysis they were holding Communism in check as Truman had done. The apprehensive Pineau wondered what had happened to the original objectives: repossession of the canal, protection of Israel, and overthrow of Nasser.

Bourgès-Maunoury reacted swiftly after Pineau had reported his fears. Personal messages were sent to the commanders of French ground forces, instructing them that once landed they were to go forward and achieve their objectives regardless of orders to the contrary they might receive from Allied Headquarters in Cyprus. Admiral Barjot, Deputy Supreme Commander, was told to demand of General Keightley that the paratroop attack be advanced from the 5th to the 4th, even the 3rd, if possible, and at the same time the Israeli army was informed that there was no rigid obligation to stop at the ten-mile line, that the Egyptian army could be chased right across the canal.

In fact, Israelis were in the process of completing their astonishing victory in the Sinai. Six thousand Egyptians were prisoners-of-war as against four Israeli pilots shot down behind Egyptian lines. Though it was true that Israel's cities had been protected by the French air force, its coast by the French navy, and that the psychological effect of the bombing offensive had been to discourage Syria and Jordan from entering the conflict, Dayan had nonetheless inflicted a humiliating and decisively punitive defeat upon the Egyptians.

The Canal Zone, from Suez to Port Said, was jammed with columns of armour and infantry fleeing westwards from the desert. Instead of diverting a third of the Egyptian forces as Britain and France had hoped, Israel had driven forty thousand bedraggled, bootless soldiers into the line of allied attack. As a result, Bourgès-Maunoury discovered that his attempts to hurry up the operations were blocked by a normally cautious Keightley, made doubly cautious by evidence that the strongly manned defences at Port Said were now reinforced by the military pile-up along the canal.

When the Egyptian air force was estimated to have been destroyed on the ground, Keightley simply switched the bombing attacks from airfields to troop concentrations. During the planning the British had insisted that the Egyptian air force

posed such a threat that it must be destroyed before the landings; now they argued that the amount of armour in Egypt
posed a similar threat and must also be destroyed before the
landings. No wonder Barjot and other French commanders
were exasperated.

Far more was at stake, however, than military impatience.
The Anglo-French ultimatum demanding a cease-fire had been
accepted by Israel, as arranged, and rejected by Egypt, as
expected. The Assembly cease-fire resolution had not been accepted by anyone, and Ben-Gurion was running out of excuses
for failing to comply. The swiftness of Dayan's victory was too
valuable in propaganda terms to be suppressed, and it would
be difficult to sit on the edge of the Canal Zone with no one to
shoot at while ignoring world opinion.

On the other hand, a war had to be in progress in or near
the Canal Zone to justify the Anglo-French landings in two or
three days' time. Somehow the pretence of opposing armies
needing to be separated had to be maintained. The original
excuse of acting to safeguard shipping had already become
invalid because Nasser had blocked the canal at both ends.
Moreover, there was no longer any question of protecting oil
supplies, as the pipelines from Iraq through Syria had been cut
and the pumping stations blown up.

The Israelis had accomplished their basic objectives of
clearing the Sinai, capturing vast stores of Soviet arms, occupying the Gaza Strip and destroying fedayeen bases, and
freeing the Gulf of Aqaba to Israeli shipping. As the Anglo-
French bombing had destroyed the Egyptian air force, there
was no longer a major Arab threat to Israel. If Ben-Gurion
were now to accept the Assembly cease-fire call, he could earn
a measure of goodwill for Israel from United Nations representatives at any subsequent peace talks.

Mollet, Pineau, and Bourgès-Maunoury were primarily concerned that Ben-Gurion would be tempted to seek this advantage rather than further outrage the Assembly by continued

procrastination. In this event their own basic objective of removing a malevolent symbol of insurrection in Algeria by overthrowing Nasser would evaporate along with the pretext for French intervention. The only insurance against Israel contracting out of the Sèvres agreements was to advance the military timetable so that landings could take place while Israel prolonged the fiction of mopping-up operations for as long as might be decently possible. The seaborne assault was too far off, so the French pressure on the British was for something now: a massed paratroop assault – occupation by air, in fact.

They had not bargained for the turmoil Pineau had seen in London, where it seemed probable that Eden actually wanted to contract out. The United Nations, experiencing United States–Soviet Union togetherness for the first time, had reacted with unprecedented speed, and might yet brand Britain and France as aggressors. The French leaders, convinced that their national interest came first, were undismayed at the prospect. Eden, who had undergone metamorphosis during the night of November 1 – for the second time in six months – could see clearly that he was gambling away Britain's moral leadership of the world. Nasser was not going to be overthrown by revolt from within, and the United Nations was acting too quickly to be presented with occupation of the Canal Zone as a *fait accompli*. Eden, seeking a way out, seized upon the slender hope presented by Pearson's concept of a United Nations police force, and despite all that had been said and done since the evening of July 26, busily proclaimed that his actions had been necessary in order to stimulate United Nations awareness of the dangers of Communist aggressive intentions in the Middle East.

Trapped by his own propaganda that Nasser was another Hitler who had to be stopped, and by the agreements with his allies, he could not simply halt the operations, which were themselves compressed into a straitjacket. Eden had withdrawn British troops from the Suez base on the grounds that there was no place for such an ancient monument to past imperialism in an age of nuclear deterrence, that Cyprus was more suited to the doctrine of NATO task forces and strategic bomber bases. Little or nothing, however, had been done to build air and naval facilities on the island, and the invasion fleet now at sea had been forced by this omission to sail from as far afield as Marseilles, Algiers, and Malta. Once launched, so vast an enterprise gathers its own momentum.

The French plan of flying out additional paratroops to Cyprus for occupation of the Canal Zone from the air was bold and imaginative. It offered the British their best chance of achieving the objectives they had originally intended. It seemed that either no British commander or political leader was bold or imaginative enough, or Eden had altered course away from France and toward the United Nations, which, in fact, he had.

Confronted by British military immovability, Bourgès-Maunoury conceived an ingenious plan to serve two purposes. The Middle East war could be kept alive as an excuse for Ben-Gurion to hesitate further on the cease-fire if the bogey of a Jordanian attack on Israel was reactivated. It might also throw a scare into the British that a general conflagration threatened unless it could be extinguished by quick action.

He discussed the plan with Louis Mangin and Abel Thomas, who then telephoned Peres in Tel Aviv. Within hours rumours flashed from the Middle East of Jordanian troops massing on the Israeli border, and of Iraqi troops standing by to assist if required. Later in the day a Central Intelligence Agency report in Washington said: "It is highly possible, if not probable, that Israel will attack Jordan tonight [Saturday, November 3] in order to get maximum benefits from campaign before U.N. action can become effective."

Israel's excuse for delaying acceptance of the cease-fire was now established, but the British refused to be scared. "We have obligations to Jordan," said a Foreign Office spokesman curtly.

CHAPTER TEN *The Resolution*

Pineau returned to London on Saturday morning accompanied by two members of the French General Staff to argue the case for advancing the timetable with Eden, Lloyd, Head, and General Templer, the C.I.G.S. whose visit to Jordan six months previously had nearly cost King Hussein his throne. In Cyprus, the French paratroop commanders alerted their units for immediate action.

By then, however, Norman Robertson had called at the Foreign Office to deliver Pearson's message that the only hope for a realignment of British and American policies, of the Anglo-French operations receiving even a threadbare cloak of United Nations respectability, was to delay any form of landings in Egypt until after the United Nations had voted on the creation of a police force.

Eden, anxious to restore contact with Washington, and seemingly uncertain about the righteousness of his war, was willing to place the future of his government in Ottawa's hands.

While Pineau and the French staff officers were told that nothing could be done in terms of a mass paratroop occupation of the Canal Zone until sufficient numbers of transport aircraft had arrived in Cyprus, Sir Ivone Kirkpatrick informed the Canadian High Commissioner: "We can undertake that no landings will take place before your resolution reaches the Assembly, providing it is voted on not later than tomorrow evening London time."

The braking pressure exerted by Ottawa was proving greater than the power of French acceleration. Now it had to be exerted on Washington.

II

EDEN was sick, Ben-Gurion had been sick, Eisenhower was sick, and now it was the turn of the Secretary of State. During the night Dulles had been rushed to hospital, and by Saturday morning the United States role in the crisis was being handled by his deputy at the State Department, Herbert Hoover, Jr., and in New York by Cabot Lodge, who enjoyed such close relations with Eisenhower that he could talk directly to the White House. At his instigation it was decided that as Britain, France, and Israel had not yet complied with the cease-fire, the two "working papers" drafted by Dulles should be introduced at another special session of the Assembly that night.

But Mackay and Murray had been as busy overnight as Lodge, and Pearson was already in possession of a detailed formula for the presentation of the Canadian resolution. It said, in part:

> Clearly the negotiating groups [the committees proposed in the Dulles "working papers"] cannot achieve a solution of these complex problems in a short time. It may take months. During this period it will be essential to maintain a cease-fire and withdrawal of troops upon which all this process of negotiation is predicated. It would be absolutely necessary to restrain elements on both sides of the demarcation lines in Palestine, and while this may be the most important policing operation, it may also be necessary to maintain law and order in the Canal Zone. Accordingly, parallel with measures which are being developed for negotiating a settlement, it would seem desirable to take steps at once to establish an international police force under U.N. auspices which could be employed in the area . . . during the process of negotiation.
>
> One of the most difficult questions is what body or

person will be responsible for giving orders to this police force. The Security Council as the executive body of the U.N. is the obvious choice. But the problem of the veto is equally obvious, and in this case it is not only the veto of the USSR which might cause difficulty. . . .

The link between all the proposed measures will be the Secretary General. It may well be, therefore, that the primary responsibility for alerting and using the police force should rest with the Secretary General. . . . He would, of course, act in close consultation with the negotiating groups and with the Security Council, and, if necessary, the General Assembly. . . . He would be in a sense an international police commissioner.

And here we should emphasize that the international police force must be able to act *with or without the consent of the parties concerned.* There can be no question of a return to the hampering conditions imposed upon the United Nations Truce Supervisory Organization by the armistice agreements. . . .

We have included India in our calculations because we consider that Nehru's oft-expressed desire to be a peacemaker should be translated into effective action, and because India is the one Afro-Asian country with military forces qualified to carry out the tasks we have in mind.

The problem of sponsorship exists. Canada could introduce this resolution on its own, but because of our links with the United Kingdom and France, and of the position Canada adopted on the United States resolution of November 2, there is some possibility that the Afro-Asians . . . might think that the Canadian proposal is designed merely to assist them out of their difficulties. Since the proposal for an international police force is also open to the charge of "collective colonialism" it would be desirable to have the resolution introduced by a number of countries whose reputation in the field of colonialism is unassailable.

Canada is certainly one of these. Norway, Sweden, Iran, Burma, India, and Pakistan are others. The Norwegians are ready to help us. . . .

Taking the time difference into account, Kirkpatrick's undertaking that no landing would take place before "tomorrow night" gave Pearson approximately thirty hours in which to draft a resolution so worded that it would be acceptable to the British, French, and United States governments, be likely to muster support in the corridors of the United Nations, and finally earn a majority vote in the Assembly. He knew nothing of Bourgès-Maunoury's efforts to advance the timetable, which might succeed at any time, or of Keightley's disinclination to be harried into hasty action, which could also be swayed by events.

At the Canadian Cabinet meeting early on Saturday morning (late afternoon in London), St. Laurent insisted that as a cease-fire and a halt to further British and French military operations were imperative, at least some of their units should be brought into a United Nations force if it was at all possible, as they were immediately available in the area. It was then agreed that Canada should propose the formation of a police force in two stages. The first would be a short-term, temporary force consisting of British and French units added to the existing United Nations Truce Supervisory Organization and placed under the command of General Burns. The second stage would be the creation of a long-term emergency force which would take over police duties between Israel and her Arab neighbours while negotiating groups were working out a political settlement.

Pearson informed Robertson in London of this decision, instructing him to pass it on to the British government with another warning that no landings should take place until after a resolution had been introduced into the Assembly. He also called Heeney in Washington and asked him to inform the

State Department. Before Heeney could see Hoover, however, Eisenhower and Cabot Lodge had already decided to push forward the Dulles "working papers" and set up the committees for Palestine and the Suez. No attempt was made in either of these proposals to explain how peace would be maintained in the Middle East while the protracted diplomatic negotiations were continuing.

The State Department reaction to the Canadian proposal was interested but skeptical. Although the United States was as anxious as Canada to extricate the United Kingdom from its position, it was important to the Americans that no ground should be given for the charge of collusion to that end. This might deprive the United States of such sanction as it had in its present position. United States officials were skeptical that the landings could be stopped, and the addition of token forces to the Franco-British occupation might be taken as legitimising the present operation. It would be taken, in their view, as an attempt to give United Nations auspices to an action to which the majority of the United Nations took exception.

These views forced the Cabinet in Ottawa to remain in session, searching for an alternative. By 11:30 A.M. that Saturday, November 3, Pearson was able to telephone Washington again to tell Heeney that a new Canadian proposal would ask the Assembly to set up a "Committee of Five" to establish an "intervention force." As worded then, this second draft resolution read:

> The United Nations General Assembly . . . recommends that a Committee of Five Members of the Assembly be appointed to submit within forty-eight hours a plan for the setting up in the Middle East of an emergency international United Nations police force recruited from national military forces immediately available and adequate in number to carry out the purposes. . . .

On Saturday afternoon Pearson and Holmes returned to New York, where they were at once consulted by Engen, who promised to act as co-sponsor and proposed asking a Latin-American country to act as a third. Then Robertson telephoned from London to say that preliminary British reaction to the new proposal was favourable. At about the same time, Heeney learned in Washington that the United States had decided to "encourage it" but could make no commitment yet on actual support for it. The Americans had suggested two changes: that it should provide for the agreement of all parties concerned to any intervention by a United Nations force, and that reference to recruiting "from national military forces immediately available" should be deleted.

"If the intention is to get the British and French into this force, we can't support it," Robert Murphy said. "We don't think the Assembly will go along, either. And you can't put a police force into the Canal Zone, which is Egyptian territory, without the consent of Egypt. If you shoot your way in, then the U.N. will be as guilty of aggression as it says the British and French are now."

"I'll pass that on to Mr. Pearson," said Heeney. "Meanwhile you should know that we're urging the British in the strongest possible terms to refrain from any further military operations until the Assembly gets a chance to act on this."

Murphy smiled. "We guessed something like that had happened," he said. "Only a couple of hours ago we got a report that the British were revealing an unaccountable disposition to suspend operations."

The Canadian delegation discussed the changes Murphy had mentioned with Cabot Lodge, and Pearson subsequently agreed that they were desirable.

He recalled: "They were minor changes, and by letting Cabot have them I hoped to keep his mind off the major purpose of creating a force quickly enough to get the British and the French out of their predicament. The Americans kept hinting that they suspected this was our intention, and to some extent they were right."

Before entering the Assembly Hall he received another telephone call from Norman Robertson, who had just spoken with Selwyn Lloyd, at about midnight in London. The High Commissioner had been told that Eden would accept the Canadian resolution, and Lloyd had assured him that no landings would take place before Sunday night. Furthermore, if the Assembly acted quickly to set up the force, no landings would take place during the forty-eight-hour period in which a blueprint would be produced – that is, until Monday night.

A world police force was closer to realisation than at any time in history – except for one important omission in Pearson's endless manœuvring. There was no time left to inform the British and the French of the changes suggested by the Americans, and if the deletion of the intent to recruit from "military forces immediately available" resulted in their being excluded, they might not accept United Nations intervention.

Pearson banished this bleak prospect. It seemed there were so many obstacles, peace could never catch up with war.

III

THE special session of the Assembly had resumed; the crescendo of debate was rising as one delegate after another vehemently condemned Britain and France; the hall was, if anything, even more crowded than on Thursday night. Public spectators as well as delegates were now aware that an invasion fleet was somewhere at sea, that the British and French were making acceptance of the cease-fire conditional upon creation of an international force, that there was precious little time in which to do it. They wondered if Red China would really send the three hundred thousand volunteers it claimed had registered for service in Egypt, whether the Soviet Union would intervene in the Middle East, and whether the United States, the United Nations, or NATO would intervene in Hungary.

The mood was sombre, heavily laden with anxiety and expectancy. Anglo-French attempts to dictate the terms of the cease-fire were bitterly resented; the bombing of Egypt, seemingly endless, aroused severe condemnation. The brutally worded leaflets dropped on Egyptian cities shocked and appalled everyone no less than the frightening broadcasts beamed at Egypt from Cyprus Radio, now calling itself "The Voice of Britain." The accused governments needed friendly witnesses in New York that night, but their actions made friendship difficult to sustain or justify.

The Australian delegate, desperately trying to divert the flow and force of the prosecution, interrupted proceedings to read a bulletin from Vienna, which said, "Premier Imre Nagy, speaking in English over Budapest Radio, today announced: 'In the early hours of this morning [Saturday, March 3] Soviet troops started to attack the Hungarian capital with the apparent purpose of overthrowing the democratic government of the Hungarian People's Republic. Our troops are in battle with Soviet forces. The Hungarian army is in position. This is my message to the Hungarian people and to the world.' "

Stung into angry retort, the Russian delegate condemned Anglo-French "hypocrisy" and "barbaric bombing"; and Cabot Lodge, in a moment of anguished fury, cried out, "God knows I want to see the bloodshed in Egypt stopped. But there is cynicism in the Soviet representative's words while his army is spilling blood in Budapest."

Like two wounded beasts, the United States and the Soviet Union snarled their rage at each other as events beyond their control continued to pull them closer together.

These flashes of sudden lightning in so thunderous an atmosphere served to aggravate the deepening sense of gravity in man's affairs. For Pearson, shrewd and calculating behind a disconcertingly habitual expression of open, boyish naïveté, it would be a long, decisive night, with his political future suspended in the interim hours until the vote on the Canadian resolution was taken.

The essential first step was to enlist co-sponsors. Engen had already agreed to approach Colombia, and while Pearson would have liked to include India, that country was in the forefront of a new move to bring about immediate withdrawal and therefore its support did not seem feasible then.

The next stage was to mobilise votes, the three co-sponsors – Canada, Norway, and Colombia – had to make the best possible use of their respective contacts among the delegations, and from the moment Pearson took his seat in the Assembly hall at roughly 6:00 P.M. the Canadian desk became the focal point for intensive consultations, with one delegate after another arriving to inquire as to the nature of the anticipated Canadian move.

Pearson and his advisers had to refer constantly to the draft resolution, answering each inquiry with an explanation of its purpose and meaning. When opportunities arose Pearson instructed his advisers to seek out the views of other delegations in the hall. This entailed a constant movement to and from the Canadian desk, all under the surveillance of batteries of television cameras, and if they looked, as one announcer commented, "gravely concerned," it was because, of all the language in the resolution, the phrase "consent of the parties concerned" was proving the most difficult to explain as its ambiguity aroused persistent suspicion.

Murray has recalled: "This phrase meant different things to different people. To the United Kingdom, France, and Israel it referred to themselves. But the Egyptians thought it should refer to Egypt. Others interpreted it as referring to those countries which might eventually make up the international force. We allowed these varying interpretations to stand, mainly because we were not terribly sure ourselves of who it should refer to.

"This is how United Nations resolutions are made. Ambiguity and vague terminology are often deliberate, because lack of precision permits governments which have to deal with public opinion to place their own positions in the best possible light."

During the preceding year, events at the United Nations had given the Canadians a solid opportunity to exert wide influence in the Assembly. The delegation had sparked a move that eventually led to the addition of some sixteen new members, and in pursuing this earlier initiative Canada had worked closely with at least a third of the existing membership, and had earned the acclaim of the Assembly and the gratitude of the incoming nations. Close and useful contacts had been cemented.

But, despite this influence and concentrated effort, the advisers had to concede before the police force resolution was submitted that the outcome would depend largely upon broad support from the Arab-Asians, as without it the necessary two-thirds majority would not be forthcoming.

The Indian Ambassador, Arthur Lall, was organising a resolution giving the British, French, and Israelis twelve hours in which to comply with the cease-fire call. Nineteen Arab-Asian countries – including Egypt – were sponsoring it, countries which Pearson now needed desperately to support his own draft resolution. As he had agreed to insert the proviso that intervention would depend upon the "consent of the parties concerned," he wanted Egypt to vote for it on the ground that Nasser could not then refuse to accept a police force. Lall might hold the key to the two-thirds majority which the resolution required.

When he discussed the problem with the Indian Ambassador, he discovered that Lall was also concerned that the Arab-Asian resolution would not command a two-thirds majority, that he was anxious to avoid obtaining so slender a margin of victory that his resolution would lack weight and substance. To give it moral force he needed the thirty or so votes committed to the Canadian resolution.

They made their deal. Pearson would deliver the votes of his supporters to the Arab-Asian resolution, while Lall would deliver the nineteen Arab-Asian countries to the support of the Canadian resolution.

Pearson's next concern was uncertainty about the British and French positions. He was by no means sure that the British and French governments would accept the amended resolution.

Dixon crossed the floor to speak with him, saying: "The text doesn't agree with the one I understand you sent to London. I'm not sure they'll like it."

"The substance is the same," said Pearson. "In any case the main thing is that you and the French should not oppose it. Your abstention would be good enough."

"I may get instructions to oppose it," said Dixon. "If the vote is taken soon enough, I can abstain through lack of instructions. I'll try working toward a snap vote if you will help me prevent this Indian resolution being passed unanimously or by a huge majority."

Another deal was made. In return for Dixon's promise that France and Britain would abstain rather than oppose the Canadian resolution, Pearson would try to persuade the Scandinavian countries to abstain on the Indian resolution, for which the Danes and Norwegians at least had little sympathy. His next step was to insure against the mercurial Afro-Asians changing their minds about supporting Canada. Murray met Lall in the corridor outside the hall, and after twenty minutes of persuasive talking returned with the Indian's agreement that the Canadian resolution should be voted on before the Afro-Asian draft. Pearson and most of the delegates supporting him had no real liking for the Indian resolution with its twelve-hour time limit on a cease-fire expressed in strong and condemnatory language. They considered support for it, however, a small price to pay for the votes needed to ensure approval for a United Nations force. If Lall failed to deliver all nineteen of them, Pearson's supporters would thwart the Indian resolution by abstaining.

Abba Eban, leading the Israeli delegation, confronted
Pearson on the floor to suggest bluntly that the Canadian
resolution invited the United Nations to intrude upon Israel's
sovereignty. Eban made it clear that unless Israel was included
among the "parties concerned" there would be no United
Nations force on Israeli soil. Pearson ruefully noted later: "The
Israelis are obviously in a confident mood and unlikely to
co-operate with us unless they are forced to do so. With the
United States, Britain, and France so bitterly divided, it is going
to be difficult to apply the necessary pressure."

Throughout these manœuvrings the speeches from the rostrum droned on above the sibilant whispering of delegates, one
speaker after another pressing home charges against the three
governments no one had yet managed to brand as aggressors.

The time was rapidly approaching when the draft resolution
would have to be presented to the Assembly. Pearson, feeling
that Hammarskjold should be aware of its contents in advance,
as it laid a unique, heavy, and urgent responsibility upon his
shoulders, sent Murray behind the dais to deliver a copy of it
to the Secretary General. Attached was a note which said: "In
a few minutes I shall be proposing this resolution. But before I
do, could we discuss it?"

Hammarskjold, frowning as he read the text, left the rostrum. Pearson met him in the small office behind it.

Revealing resignation and depression, Hammarskjold said,
"It won't work. We'll never get a force going in time to stop the
British and the French. They'll attack Egypt, people will get
killed, and what can we really do about it? People will say what
use is the United Nations? We can't keep the peace in Egypt,
we can't keep the peace in Hungary, and all our diplomats do is
condemn each other."

It was so unlike Hammarskjold that Pearson spoke quickly,
urgently.

"We may not be able to do much about the Soviet moves in

Hungary," he said, "but we can do a lot about Egypt in the next forty-eight hours. Canada will give you troops, so will Norway and Colombia. There are British and French detachments in the area already, and there's the Sixth Fleet. We can impress the lot into United Nations service if necessary."

"How are we going to get them into Egypt if Nasser won't have them?"

"He will. Arthur Lall just told me he's willing to accept American and Canadian troops as well as Scandinavian."

Hammarskjold was suddenly alert. "I wonder if Eisenhower will let us use some people from the Sixth Fleet?"

"I don't know yet," said Pearson. "But if it is really necessary, we'll do our best to persuade him."

The final step in these preparations was taken when Pearson left the hall to telephone Ottawa and speak with Prime Minister St. Laurent. After reporting on the situation in the Assembly, Pearson mentioned that the British would hold off their landings at least until Monday night. St. Laurent agreed that this information was sufficiently important for Heeney to deliver direct to the White House.

Shortly before midnight, Pearson walked to the rostrum, betraying none of the anxiety he felt, and began his address.

". . . My delegation would like to submit to the Assembly a very short draft resolution, which I venture to read at this time. It is as follows:

The General Assembly,

Bearing in mind the urgent necessity of facilitating compliance with the resolution of 2 November 1956,

Requests, as a matter of priority, the Secretary General to submit to it within forty-eight hours a plan for the setting up, with the consent of the nations concerned, of an emergency international United Nations force to secure and supervise the cessation of hostilities in accordance with the terms of the aforementioned resolution.

"I would assume that during this short period the Secretary General would get in touch with the parties concerned and endeavour to secure their co-operation. . . ."

Cabot Lodge claimed the floor to say, "The United States likes this Canadian draft resolution very much. We have presented two draft resolutions dealing with the long-range questions . . . and we are not pressing them for a vote tonight. We do think the draft resolution submitted by the Canadian Secretary of State for External Affairs is one that should be acted on promptly . . . because it contains a real hope of meeting the very grave emergency that confronts the world."

At 2:00 A.M., Sunday, November 4, before the British and French governments could send instructions to their delegates, the Assembly voted unexpectedly. Nineteen nations abstained for lack of instructions, and the remaining fifty-seven nations voted in favour. Not one vote was cast against it, not even that of the Soviet Union, which has since sought to evade its financial responsibilities by claiming that it had opposed UNEF. Arthur Lall delivered all nineteen of his promised votes; but more significantly, the Communist bloc abstained, and for the first time in the crisis the Soviet Union was split from the Afro-Asians. Delegate after delegate walked across the hall to congratulate Pearson, and in the corridors the vote was referred to as one of the most skillfully organized coups in United Nations history.

Weariness and despair lifted slightly, giving way to general relief that something positive had been achieved at last. No one could quite forget, however, that bombs still fell, that a fleet was still at sea. Nor did the peacekeepers in New York know that the warmakers were meeting over a strange breakfast in Cyprus.

IV

_____

WHEN Pineau and the French generals arrived at Downing Street on Saturday, what amounted to a small, informal Cabinet meeting was in session. In addition to Eden, Lloyd, and Head, there were Butler, Macmillan, and his deputy at the Treasury, Sir Edward Boyle, and the Chief of the Imperial General Staff, Sir Gerald Templer. Though Pineau had not been told that the Canadian High Commissioner had urged that no landings take place while the United Nations was working out the details of the emergency force, he brushed aside a suggestion that this restraint might be desirable, because in his view any United Nations force would be bound to protect Nasser. He argued that they must abide by their original intentions. Israel would be soon forced by its own victory to accept the cease-fire; then there would no longer be any valid excuse for continuing military operations. Landings had to begin, preferably on Sunday, but not later than Monday.

Pineau's mission succeeded. Later that evening, at about the same time as the Canadian Ambassador in Washington was informing the State Department and the White House that the British government had indicated it would not undertake landings before Monday night, Defence Minister Antony Head took off in a Canberra bomber for Cyprus. He arrived on Sunday, at 4:00 A.M. local time, approximately as Pearson was telling Hammarskjold in New York that the British might not carry out landings before Monday night. And by 9:00 A.M. Head was breakfasting with Keightley and his deputy commander, Admiral Barjot, having accepted the French plan to land paratroops on Monday morning. In New York the Assembly had just approved the Canadian resolution, which, as Pearson explained, "has as its purpose the bringing to an end of the fighting and bloodshed at once."

There was cynicism to say the least in these political strata-
gems. Arnold Heeney, referring to the talks in London between
Norman Robertson and Selwyn Lloyd, said: "I was authorised
to inform the State Department that as a result of Robertson's
conversations in London we were confident that the British
[and French] would not begin landings before Sunday night
[November 4], and further we believed that if the Assembly
took action along the lines of our resolution, no landing would
take place during the period that recommendations for an international police force were being worked out. This I took to be
the forty-eight hours mentioned in the draft resolution. . . . This
important information was communicated immediately to the
Acting Secretary of State and the President."

Head himself said later in the British House of Commons,
"I went to see General Keightley to see whether the airborne
drop could be made earlier, to overcome the beach defences
and eliminate the naval bombardment. . . ."

Further comment would be pointless.

V

THE British press was overwhelmingly in favour of a United
Nations force, stressing that the Canadian proposal provided
an opportunity not only for a fresh start in the Middle East,
but also for an upward turn in the fortunes of the United
Nations itself. It was suggested that Eden should resign, so that
the pieces of Britain's shattered reputation could be put back
together again by someone less prone to bellicosity.

Some thirty-odd Conservative members of the British Parliament, who felt they had reached a point beyond which they
were unable to give either tacit or voting support to Eden, were

told by reliable Labour Party sources that Hugh Gaitskell, Leader of the Opposition, would be willing to co-operate in some measure with the Conservative administration if it chose a new Prime Minister. Had a Cabinet minister of stature resigned to offer a cure for their political malaise, these Conservative fears might have been translated into action. As there was no such doctor in the House, the group remained inactive, their antagonism really too vindictive and petty to present a serious threat to the Prime Minister.

In Paris, the Canadian Ambassador was summoned to the Quai d'Orsay and asked to inform "Mr. Pearson and his friend, Mr. Hammarskjold," that France insisted upon being included in any United Nations force, and insisted further that the Soviet Union should not be. "We have not gone to all this pain and trouble to solve the situation out there just to open the door to Russian intervention," said the Director General of Political Affairs.

The first informal planning committee for the creation of an international force met at 10:00 A.M. on Sunday in New York in the Secretary General's suite on the thirty-eighth floor of the Secretariat building. It consisted of Hammarskjold, refreshed and enthusiastic now that there was something challenging and positive to execute; his assistant, Ralph Bunche, who had drawn up the Israeli-Arab demarcation lines in 1949; Pearson, with Holmes and Murray as advisers; Engen, Arthur Lall, and Ambassador Uruttia of Colombia, with their advisers. Between them they represented North America, Latin America, Western Europe, and Afro-Asia.

In an environment such as this, Hammarskjold's incisive brilliance, inexhaustible capacity for subtle, tortuous legalistics, and driving energy could be displayed to their best advantage. No man was better suited to serve Pearson's purposes at that time; precise executive ability was harnessed to broad political vision.

Convinced (while attending a futile Security Council meeting on Hungary that had started at 3:00 A.M., immediately following the Assembly, and had not ended until dawn) that
Pearson had found a means to break the chain of tragedy in the
Middle East, and armed with an exacting mandate for action,
Hammarskjold was driven by a consuming determination to
prove that the United Nations could react quickly and effectively.

"As we're got to have the consent of the governments
which will contribute to the force, we have to know which they
are going to be," he said, according to the minutes of the meeting. "I suggest you inform your governments as quickly as
possible that they may be asked to supply troops. We have to
get a temporary, short-term force between the Israeli and
Egyptian armies, then we can worry about the transition to a
larger, long-term force to police the demarcation lines.

"I propose asking General Burns to take on the job of force
commander. He can select a couple of dozen of his Truce
Supervisory officers to form his staff. I called him an hour ago,
and, if the Assembly approves, he's ready to move from Jerusalem to Cairo. I propose to keep this thing moving by putting
an initial report before the Assembly tonight, one setting up a
command in Egypt. That way the belligerents can see we mean
business.

"But it's going to take two weeks at least to get troops on
the ground out there. Some people have been suggesting that
in the interim we should take on small units of British and
French forces which are in the area and attach them to Burns."

Lall was at once provoked. "My people – in fact, not a
single Afro-Asian country – will not accept British or French
troops in a U.N. force," he said. "You'll run into all sorts of
trouble if you give the impression that the whole idea is to
cloak an Anglo-French occupation of Egypt with U.N. respectability."

"What do you suppose we should do if Britain and France proceed with their plan to land troops in the Canal Zone?" asked Hammarskjold. "Should we declare war on them?"

Lall smiled appreciatively. "Not quite," he said. "It will be difficult, I know. But you have to understand this. With respect to a U.N. force, the British and French are untouchables."

Lall was not being obstructive. His listeners understood that he was expressing moderately what other Afro-Asians would denounce violently.

"Until yesterday," said Pearson, "I didn't have even a resolution. I've gone ahead with this because I think it's the best way of preventing any landings at all, and of discouraging the Israelis from thinking they can settle down permanently in the Egyptian territory they've occupied. Britain and France didn't oppose the resolution, nobody did. That's why Canada is prepared to offer troops. We're looking for political settlements, not a return to the status quo.

"I know some delegations voted on the assumption that the United Kingdom and France would not be involved. But that's not necesarily my assumption. If Anglo-French troops do land, it might be very desirable indeed to bring them under United Nations command immediately, at least until other forces can be brought in. However, we're not going to deadlock on this issue. If there's a profitable alternative, Canada will go along with it."

"If it's known that we're even contemplating Anglo-French participation," said Lall, "it will be tantamount to inviting them to land their troops. They have to be convinced that there is going to be a United Nations force, and that they are not going to be part of it. On the other hand, I see no objection to American troops. They have the Sixth Fleet also immediately available. It seems to me to be a question of persuading President Eisenhower to release them."

Engen objected on the ground that if one or more Great Powers were untouchable, then all the permanent members of the Security Council should be excluded. Hammarskjold and Pearson agreed with Engen, as they did with Uruttia, who suggested they were thinking too narrowly in terms of NATO countries.

The meeting ended at 1:00 P.M. with a preliminary list of countries drawn up as possible contributors, and Pearson invited Hammarskjold to join Engen and himself at the Drake Hotel, where they could work undisturbed on the draft report for a command set-up.

This was diplomacy of a unique order. Only six hours earlier, the Security Council had invoked the "Uniting for Peace" procedure to transfer the Hungarian crisis to the Assembly, and the first of these sessions was scheduled for 4:00 P.M. When it finished, there would just be a short break before the Assembly reconvened to continue its sessions on the Middle East. Television, press, and public were being treated to the spectacle of two critical dramas played out consecutively on the same stage by the same cast.

The deadline for a second and final report establishing an international police force was thirty-six hours away; no one could foresee what action the Assembly would take on Hungary; the Anglo-French armada was less than two days' steaming from Port Said; and there was the danger that a seaborne assault would be preceded by a paratroop drop.

Then – almost casually, it seemed in so grim a climate – the delicately drawn division between the crisis in the West and the crisis in the East began to blur as the two threatened to coalesce. NATO headquarters in Paris issued a laconic warning that the Royal Navy was tracking two Soviet submarines passing through the Straits of Gibraltar into the Mediterranean.

CHAPTER ELEVEN

Time Limits

DURING the Sunday morning meeting in New York, Pearson received an encouraging telegram from Selwyn Lloyd assuring him that the proposed police force was receiving urgent and serious consideration in London – encouraging because it indicated there would be no quick Anglo-French rejection. It implied, too, that as the United Nations was acting fast to produce a blueprint, this might prove reason enough for delaying the actual invasion of Egypt.

Pearson telephoned Ottawa, informed Prime Minister St. Laurent of the previous night's events, and suggested the Cabinet should consider calling an emergency session of the Canadian Parliament to approve the allocation of forces for service with the United Nations.

On Sunday morning, therefore, the Prime Minister, as well as the Minister for External Affairs, considered that what they were doing would provide London and Paris with an alternative for their own military operations. In this context the curious aspect of the telegram from Lloyd was its timing. It was sent at approximately 5:30 P.M. London time.

Early that morning Eden had telephoned Mollet in Paris

to say that in his view the second United Nations cease-fire and withdrawal resolution and the decision to establish a police force for the Middle East made it urgently necessary to consult. Mollet agreed, and by lunchtime Pineau and Bourgès-Maunoury had arrived at Downing Street to meet with Eden's inner cabinet. The French Defence Minister was there to reinforce Pineau should the British reveal signs of wishing to postpone or abandon military operations.

To Pineau, Eden appeared calmer, more confident, than he had the previous day, and seemed quite willing to accept the military argument that, preparations being as advanced as they were, postponement of any kind might prove disastrous. The French visitors were not so happy about Lloyd, who gave them the distinct impression of having reservations about the wisdom of proceeding with hurried operations while the United Nations was acting upon the Canadian resolution. They sensed that he might be accepting decisions with which he was not necessarily in agreement.

In the afternoon a crowd of ten thousand or so demonstrators gathered in Trafalgar Square, carrying placards emblazoned with such slogans as "Eden Must Go" and "Law – Not War." A large number of them marched down Whitehall to besiege Downing Street, providing the Prime Minister's guests with ample proof that he was indeed being subjected to formidable pressures under which his self-discipline – or self-induced hypnotic calm – might crack at any time.

Such a moment threatened shortly after 4:00 P.M., when a cable arrived from Hammarskjold which, because it virtually cancelled out Eden's hopes of having Anglo-French forces placed under a United Nations hat, may have decisively influenced subsequent events. It said:

. . . The Assembly did not accept the establishment of a United Nations Force as a condition for the cease-fire. The statements made prior . . . to the resolution on the United

Nations Force made it clear that it was a widespread view that none of the parties engaged in the present operation in the area should participate in the Force. This has a direct bearing on any possibility of stationing Anglo-French troops between the combatants. . . . I must assume the decision . . . would exclude such an arrangement. . . .

The time limit for acceptance of the cease-fire was given as 8:00 P.M. London time, giving Eden only four hours and Mollet three in which to consult. This was realized in New York by Pearson who, after speaking with Arthur Lall and Sir Pierson Dixon, suggested to Hammarskjold that there would be no objection by the sponsors of the Indian resolution, which had set the deadline, if it was extended to avoid laying the United Nations open to the charge of being unreasonably arbitrary. Hammarskjold agreed, and added nine hours by changing the deadline to 5:00 A.M. Monday.

At this point Eden had everything to gain by accepting the cease-fire. By bending a whole sequence of interlocking facts, he could proclaim that by their action Britain and France had awakened the world to the dangers of a deteriorating situation; had shown Nasser in a salutary manner that he could not tear up international agreements, flout world law, and dishonour national obligations with impunity; and, having inspired the conception of a world police force, provided the right conditons for United Nations intervention. Therefore, both governments would uphold the Charter, desist from further use of their own forces, and assist other interested nations in negotiating a peaceful settlement of Middle East problems. It is probable, too, that as the bombing had not inflicted much loss of life it would have been quickly forgotten by all but the Arab states, which might have regarded the Anglo-French show of strength with thoughtful respect.

France had everything to lose. Far from enjoying the same close ties with the United States as did Britain, it had been in political conflict with Washington since the end of the Indo-China disasters and the beginning of the North African war. Widening of the Paris-Washington breach was, therefore, of minor importance to French leaders. The United Nations had never been a major consideration in French foreign policy, as it had not in the past made any effort to ease the pains of France's withdrawal from empire.

France, however, did care about Algeria. It was the calculated conviction of all Frenchmen that Nasser was the primary obstacle to peace in North Africa; Nasser must therefore go. Such relentless pursuit of a single objective gave French leaders a strength of purpose that was less evident in British leaders, whose objectives tended to blur under pressure.

Lloyd had said at the outset that Britain's aim in the Middle East was "to bring about an early cessation of hostilities and to safeguard the free passage of the canal," because the United Nations could not possibly do it. Sir Pierson Dixon had claimed later that the safety of traffic in the canal was an overriding purpose of Anglo-French intervention; and in the Assembly on Thursday he had reaffirmed that it was necessary to separate the belligerents in order to secure the safety of the canal.

Then Eden had told the British House of Commons that he would welcome "the participation of many other nations in bringing about a settlement," a remark that was taken to refer to the canal-user nations which had met earlier in London. By Saturday, however, he was so astonished by the speed with which the United Nations had reacted to Pearson's police force proposal that suddenly he was making it a condition for accepting a cease-fire, and trying hard to become part of it. On Tuesday, Britain and France had issued an ultimatum because the United Nations was ineffective; on Saturday, the United Nations was being invited to finish off what Britain and France had started – on condition that the Anglo-French action received implied approbation in the acceptance of their troops in the United Nations force.

Eden was either misinformed or completely uninformed about world opinion and the strength of its hostility, which is inconceivable; or he desperately sought relief from a demoralising sense of guilt by contriving to give his actions respectability, which is conceivable.

Hammarskjold's cable, almost contemptuous in tone, made it unmistakably clear that the United Nations would not have the terms of its intervention dictated by Eden; that he could disabuse himself of any illusions about becoming an agent of the United Nations; and that he should call off his disreputable war immediately. By the grace of Pearson's persuasion in New York, he had until Monday morning to do it.

Such a message from a man many British political leaders and newspapers then saw as a pro-Arab friend of Nasser's, who could not be relied upon to deal fairly with British interests, would certainly anger Eden, and it is understandable that he should have readily agreed with Pineau and Bourgès-Maunoury that the cable represented nothing, that they must return to, and abide by, their original objective – the overthrow of Nasser.

Once the French ministers were satisfied that they had succeeded in their purpose of injecting the British leaders with new confidence, that the paratroop attack would be launched as arranged from Cyprus at about midnight that Sunday, and having reassured Butler that they were as concerned as he that loss of life should be kept to a minimum, they left Downing Street for the return flight to Paris at 5:00 P.M.

The British leaders remained at Number 10 while the mob, thinned down by rain, cold, and boredom, eventually dissipated, and discussion must have taken a new and sudden switch almost at once, presumably at the insistence of Selwyn Lloyd, who would not openly criticise his Prime Minister in the presence of representatives of a foreign government. After the French ministers left, however, British militant decisiveness seems to have faded, at least sufficiently for Lloyd to send his telegram to Pearson only thirty minutes later.

Referring to these meetings in his memoirs, Eden said: "It was clear to me that a postponement could not be accepted. . . . Postponement would, in fact, have meant calling off the operation. . . ." That was precisely why a police force was being planned in New York; the whole essence of Pearson's concept was to produce a credible and acceptable alternative to Anglo-French military action. All it required from London that Sunday afternoon to avert calamity was faith in the friendly intentions of Lester Pearson, faith in the ability of Hammar-skjold to carry out the mandate handed him by the Assembly, and faith in the dedication of both men to the removal of the fundamental causes which had led Britain and France to under-take, at incalculable risk to prestige and reputation, operations which in other circumstances would have been repugnant to them.

Selwyn Lloyd may have understood these needs better than most of his colleagues. If so, he must have argued his misgiv-ings forcibly enough to persuade this gathering of hard, experi-enced, professional politicians and soldiers that a postponement should not be entirely ruled out while there were dramatic events yet to unfold in New York.

Despite the tone of unswerving purpose in Eden's assur-ance, years after the event, that postponement was not seri-ously considered, a message did in fact go out in the early evening from Downing Street to Cyprus asking Keightley to state ". . . in the event of postponement of the airborne assault for twenty-four hours for political reasons, what is the latest time by which a decision must be made?"

The General, who had just arranged the timing of the para-troop attack with Defence Minister Head, was encouraged by the ebullient, irrepressible extrovert, Admiral Barjot, to reply that only three hours remained.

In New York, the advocates of emergency shirt-sleeve

diplomacy kept exhaustion at bay with a continuing diet of sandwiches, coffee, Scotch, and aspirin; in London, traditional diplomacy was being beckoned to the edge of an abyss by the spectres of dead dictators.

II

THE Assembly, meeting on Sunday, November 4, in its second emergency special session under the "Uniting for Peace" procedure, which meant that two such sessions were running together even as the Russians clawed the heart out of the Hungarian revolt, made a patently futile attempt to persuade them to cease and desist. The words were brave, the sentiments noble, and the delegates cynical. The superficial mating of the United States with Communism was seen to be blessedly temporary as Cabot Lodge lashed Sobolev with harsh and angry accusation. Things were getting slowly back to normal at the United Nations.

Pearson, speaking in the first debate and recognising an opportunity to draw attention to the merciful nature of the Anglo-French action compared with the savagery of the Russian, taunted Sobolev by saying: "The governments of the United Kingdom and France have stated firmly and publicly that they are prepared to hand over what they claim to be solely their police role to a United Nations force, a force we are now trying to organise. It is quite true that there remain differences . . . on the conditions in which a transfer can take place. Nevertheless, a transfer has been accepted as necessary . . . and a promise has been given that it will take place.

"Will the Soviet Union give us the same promise . . . ? I put this question directly to the Soviet representative. . . . Yesterday, my government proposed the intervention of a United

Nations force for peaceful purposes in the Middle East. . . .
Why should we not now establish a United Nations mission . . .
of an appropriate kind for the situation in Hungary?

"So I ask the Soviet Union to accept this chance . . . to prove
its good faith. . . ."

Sobolev may not have been terribly impressed, but the
killing and maiming of fifty thousand Hungarians made the
deaths of fewer than two hundred Egyptians seem a little less
criminal.

Lester Pearson enjoyed a degree of intimate friendship
with Sir Pierson Dixon that lessened the abrasive effects of
those difficult days. The vast majority of delegates agreed with
Pearson that the Englishman's quiet, philosophical defence of
Britain's lapse into bellicosity deserved unqualified admiration.
Dixon understood the immense effort that Pearson, Hammarskjold, and Engen were making to repair the damage to the
Atlantic alliance and the Commonwealth and to restore confidence in the United Nations. The same exchanges between
New York, Ottawa, and London that had convinced Pearson
of British and French sincerity in their proclaimed intention to
uphold the Charter by complying with its terms, thereby giving
force to the rule of moral law, had also convinced Dixon that
an end of the crisis was in sight, that the ultimate disaster of
actual invasion had been averted.

He expected, as did Pearson, to hear from London at any
moment that, in view of the United Nations' obvious intention
to put together a police force in the shortest possible time, the
cease-fire would be accepted. He joined Pearson, Engen, and
Hammarskjold on the thirty-eighth floor in an atmosphere of
relaxed, shared relief for the hour's break before the Assembly
reconvened at 10:00 P.M. to take up again the Middle East
emergency.

They discussed the next stage of the planning for a police
force, Egypt's acceptance of the cease-fire and the principle of
physical intervention by the United Nations, and Israel's curi-

ously persistent refusal to halt military operations.

Abba Eban had told the Assembly the previous day that Israel would observe the cease-fire if Egypt did the same; this morning he had hedged by telling Hammarskjold that his government required clarification on five issues concerned with Israel's rights in territory it now occupied; and only an hour or so earlier he indicated Israel could not possibly accept a United Nations force in conquered Egyptian territory without "mature consideration." The Sinai campaign was obviously finished, but no Israeli leader would admit it.

Israel, in fact, was continuing skilfully to sustain the fiction of armed conflict to provide the British and French with legal justification for further operations against Egypt, even to the extent of sacrificing some of the sympathy and goodwill that had been steadily growing at the United Nations and in Washington since Nasser had concluded the Soviet arms deal. The pressure being exerted by Bourgès-Maunoury in Paris through Peres in Tel Aviv was proving effective.

By midnight the Assembly had approved Hammarskjold's first report, and Burns, appointed United Nations Force Commander, was instructed to establish a headquarters consisting of staff officers drawn from members of the Truce Supervisory teams of any nationality but those of the permanent members of the Security Council. Canada, Norway, and Colombia had offered to contribute troops to the proposed force, and Egypt had formally accepted that they should take up positions in the Canal Zone.

Pearson and Engen adjourned with Hammarskjold to his office suite overlooking the East River, to begin work on the second report which had to be ready for the Assembly within twenty-four hours. The lights that burned for the peacekeepers on the thirty-eighth floor never went out during the days and nights of the race against the invasion fleet in the Mediterranean. Feeling that the finish was in sight, they waited for the reply from London and Paris telling them that they had won and that, with the United Nations intervention replacing their own, Britain and France would accept a cease-fire.

Shortly after 1:00 A.M., Monday, November 5, the Anglo-French reply to Hammarskjold's cable rapped out on wire service teleprinters in an adjoining office. Paratroops were being dropped on Port Said and its suburban satellite town of Port Fuad. The invasion of Egypt from the air had begun – and three men who thought they had all but restored peace to the deserts of the Middle East were momentarily silent, shocked by the implications.

There had been Lloyd's earlier telegram: the ambiguously worded but clearly implied British undertaking to Ottawa that landings would be postponed while the United Nations established a police force. There had been Cabot Lodge's appeal in the Assembly for Britain and France to "honour their obligations under the Charter, and as loyal members of the Assembly to call off the fighting"; Dixon's comforting statement that his government's reply was "likely to have considerable bearing on the conception of an intervention force"; and Eisenhower's discreet intimation that he would forgive and forget if Eden abandoned further use of force.

This concerted diplomatic effort to inject a little sanity into aberrated disorder had been reduced to a meaningless exchange of political niceties by the stark realisation that throughout it all planes had been loaded, troops put aboard, and the airborne assault delivered to its targets.

Pearson, in particular, was deeply affected.

He deplored American hostility to Britain and France no less than he did Anglo-French methods of resorting to military action. In his opinion the narrowly aimed, self-righteous wrath of the United States administration was negative, at a time when positive intervention in the interests of peace and Western unity was both urgent and vital. On the other hand, his efforts to assist London and Paris in their difficulties were being thwarted or brushed aside too often. He sympathised to some extent with Anglo-French objectives and, had even a token gesture of faith in the Canadian government's willingness to be helpful been made by at least giving private warning of what might happen, whatever course he took to prevent further military involvement would have been coupled with constructive alternatives designed to reach similar ends by more peaceful means.

But paratroops! *After* a United Nations command for Egypt had been formally established! *After* the United States had proposed, with some support, the eventual appointment of commissions to negotiate settlements designed to secure Israel's borders, and to introduce measures ensuring freedom of navigation through the canal. Through their initial action, Britain, France, and Israel had achieved an invaluable objective by making the United Nations more conscious than ever before of its failings in respect to the instability that plagued the Middle East. It seemed inconceivable that there should not now be a genuine and general urge to resolve the situation once and for all.

Instead there was a paratroop invasion, street fighting, and a war that could explode from the confines of the Nile Delta to engulf the entire region, if not the world. It was not easy to understand or forgive.

And still, somewhere at sea and converging upon Egypt were a hundred and thirty warships and a hundred thousand men.

III

FROM early Saturday, the feeling that a world war was uncomfortably close began to pervade the major capitals of East and West. The coincidence of three Great Powers – France,

Britain, and the Soviet Union – being involved simultaneously in suppressive actions against weaker states was too portentous to be shrugged aside. Much has been said in the intervening years to publicly depreciate the likelihood, but the hidden official fears were real enough for many diplomats to have believed then, as they still do, that the world has not in the last two decades been so finely balanced between war and peace. In Korea, they argue, American atomic power ruled out ultimate commitment by the Soviet Union; and mutual nuclear deterrence confined the confrontation on the arming of Cuba with Soviet missiles to super-power politics.

During the weekend of November 3-4, events in Hungary and Egypt were less precisely etched. The situation, as seen from New York, was so confused that Pearson, Hammarskjold, and Engen were, with the exception of about three hours' sleep, in constant conference among themselves or with their respective governments and attending meetings until 7:00 in the morning. And the next twenty-four hours saw the same process repeated: a more or less continuing Assembly on either the Middle East or Hungary, with hourly reports of new developments serving to complicate their efforts to secure a cease-fire in Egypt.

There was evidence that Syria, fearing it might be next on Israel's list for conquest, had turned to Moscow for help. British and French pilots reported an efficient radar system operating from Syria, and air reconnaissance photographs showed MIGs lined wing-tip to wing-tip on Syrian airfields. Some Western embassies in Damascus were placed on twenty-four-hour notice to leave the country, and the British and French Embassies in Cairo burned their secret documents.

NATO Headquarters reported that a bonfire burned throughout Sunday in the courtyard of the Soviet Embassy in Vienna, that the Soviet early warning radar lines had been brought to the highest state of alert, and that the volume of military electronic communications traffic had trebled across the Warsaw Pact nations.

The British and French Defence Ministries issued a warning that certain areas of the eastern Mediterranean and the Red Sea were closed to merchant shipping until further notice, and the Soviet Union replied by placing "responsibility for all possible consequences" upon the allied governments. Moscow then announced that fifty thousand reserve officers had volunteered for service in the Middle East, and an intelligence analysis considered that "while a proportion of these can be expected to be sent to Egypt, the majority are likely to go to Syria where stores of Soviet arms are far in excess of the needs of the Syrian army."

FROM AN ACCOUNT BY HANS ENGEN: *Many delegations at the United Nations felt a major world conflict was approaching. The fact that Britain, France, and the Soviet Union were already committed meant more than the official diplomatic exchanges. The decision to commit forces is always the most crucial for a government, as everything that follows becomes relatively more simple. The temptation to go a step further than initially intended is greater. A political ambition is more readily extended to achieve whatever is proved to be militarily feasible. We had three governments committed – three governments which might actually attempt to go further than they intended, or further than they were publicly admitting.*

The probability of Soviet intervention in the Middle East with volunteers and the magnitude of Soviet activities in Syria combined to provoke grave concern. There was every reason in New York to suppose that we had until Monday night to stop the fighting – and the only acceptable troops in the area were the United States Marines of the Sixth Fleet, which was protecting the evacuation of United States citizens from the Levant and Egypt. It may sound ridiculous now to think of American troops going into Egypt to stop the British and the

French, but by Monday morning we were pretty desperate. And it was, after all, only two years since Americans had been the principal United Nations force in Korea.

We shared – Pearson, Hammarskjold, and I – a sort of despairing hope that if Britain and France could be persuaded American troops had been ordered in, they would stop rather than allow the situation to collapse into impossible chaos. The alternative was to let Britain and France get so involved that Israel would exploit the situation, as General Burns expected it would, by attacking Syria. But that would have brought the Soviet Union in with volunteers, so in the end we decided neither course was acceptable. We had to find another way.

The Hungarian crisis was ominous because it could be linked directly with Suez. We knew there had been a political decision in Moscow not to use the Red Army to crush the Hungarian revolt, a decision which had been opposed by the Soviet General Staff. While the new liberal de-Stalinisation policy prevailed, there was no political objection to Hungary gaining a measure of freedom as Poland had done. The military argued, however, that the Red Army could not risk losing a country of such strategic importance as Hungary, from where it controlled the Danube, during a state of war in the Middle East. The General Staff viewed with horror the prospect of the Hungarian revolt being repeated in other satellites, thereby undermining the political and military structure of Eastern Europe in a time of high international tension.

There was evidence that the Soviet leaders expected the Anglo-French landings to take place any time after Friday. When Britain and France failed to accept the cease-fire, they located the invasion fleet and decided landings would, in fact, take place despite the delay. On this basis the generals won the argument and the decision was made in Moscow to retain Hungary by force.

The moral aspect was immediately an issue at the United Nations. Everyone asked what was the difference between the

*Soviet Union crushing Hungary, and the British and French
assaulting Egypt? Was it because an attack on an African or
Asian country was more acceptable than an attack on a European country? The Afro-Asians and the Latin Americans were
particularly influenced by this.*

*Typically, however, neither Pearson nor Hammarskjold was
diverted from the conviction that Britain and France should
at all costs remain untarnished by the brand of aggression. They
were quite determined that the more vehement anti-colonialists
who were gaining support should not succeed in persuading the
Assembly to aggravate the crisis by adopting harshly worded
resolutions. . . .*

Paradoxically, the United Nations was receiving more
reliable information about developments in Hungary than about
those in Egypt. Radio broadcasts, intelligence reports, and the
accounts of refugees already beginning to stream across the
Austrian border combined to place Soviet propaganda in perspective.

If the Iron Curtain in Europe was showing signs of wear
and tear, another drawn across the eastern Mediterranean was
proving exasperatingly effective. Tight security measures and
objectionably stringent censorship in Cyprus prevented any but
the barest details of Anglo-French operations being disclosed.

While Nasser boasted that British and French aircraft were
being shot down in droves as they bombed what he claimed to
be cardboard replicas of MIGs previously flown to Saudi Arabia
for safety, that the Egyptian army had been "withdrawn" from
the Sinai to defend the homeland against more dangerous
enemies than the Israelis, and that enemy paratroops were being
killed in the air before they could land, there was nothing from
the allied side upon which balanced assessments of what might
actually be happening could be made.

General Keightley even declined to admit officially that he

was fighting a war. All references to "the war" were blue-pen-cilled from news copy wired from Cyprus, and correspondents attempting to leave the island to free themselves from these irksome restrictions were searched before departure and their notes confiscated. The inevitable effect was to foster the growing belief that something far more sinister – political or military – than the war itself was being carefully concealed.

It was rumoured in New York on Monday morning that Port Said and Port Fuad had surrendered, but by lunchtime official denials were being published. In fact, the local Egyptian commanders did attempt to surrender, and a cease-fire was ordered while negotiations were progressed. Fighting resumed after the Egyptians received orders by telephone from Cairo to defend the twin ports to the last man.

Describing the incident in his dispatch, General Keightley said: "On the resumption of hostilities, the Garrison and populace were encouraged to resist by loudspeaker vans, which toured the town announcing that Russian help was on the way, that London and Paris had been bombed, and that the Third World War had started. At the same time, arms were distributed to civilians, some from lorries and some from piles dumped in the streets. . . . The subsequent tribulations which were suffered by Port Said were entirely due to the local commander being overruled and instructed to continue the battle."

While Hammarskjold, Pearson, and Engen were having lunch on Monday in New York, Foreign Minister Fawzi called from Cairo to say that Egypt intended to continue fighting for as long "as the aggressors are on Egyptian soil." Hammarskjold recognized that behind the contrived excuse of informing the Secretary General personally of the paratroop attack, Fawzi was appealing for United Nations intervention in time to save the Egyptian government from downfall.

Hammarskjold told Pearson and Engen of the conversation and added: "If it wasn't for you, Dulles, and Lodge, I think the U. N. may not have recovered from the damage caused by the British-French action." His listeners were equally certain that their own efforts would have been futile but for the ability and energy of the Secretary General. He had thrown off the lethargy that had followed the collapse of his hopes in October that the six principles so laboriously arrived at would lead to a Suez settlement.

After lunch, Pearson sent a cable to Prime Minister St. Laurent in Ottawa: "Hammarskjold and his colleagues are enthusiastic about the response to our initiative. They feel something important has begun, the advantages of which may be in the long run far more significant than the setbacks the U.N. has recently received because of the Anglo-French action. Discounting some of their enthusiasm, there is no doubt that under the impetus of an immediate and critical situation, steps have been taken which might have been difficult, if not impossible, to take in normal circumstances. Hammarskjold is particularly pleased that we have already secured approval for a resolution restricting the force to non-permanent members of the Security Council, as this will keep the operation in the Assembly and also keep out the Russians as well as the British and the French. The inclusion of the first would make American co-operation impossible, and of the latter, Arab-Asian co-operation.

"The greatest difficulty will be to overcome Israeli opposition to the whole idea. Of course, the Anglo-French landings have complicated matters. The Arab-Asians will be violently emotional and may wish to take action by condemnation and sanctions against the British and the French."

Pearson was too caught up in the turmoil of events to perceive that by rapidly exploiting the United Nations police force concept, he, Hammarskjold, and Engen were within sight of a way out of the difficulties besetting the West, had already saved the United Nations from the disastrous setback that would have resulted had it proved impotent in the crisis, and were also paving the way for United Nations progress in the entire field of collective international response in times of crisis.

Their difficulties were in no way helped when Krishna Menon arrived in New York from London bringing the threat of mischief and trouble.

For a cabinet minister intimately involved as the contact between Nehru and Nasser, he was singularly uninformed about what had been happening. He stormed into an Arab-Asian caucus meeting being held in one of the United Nations committee rooms, proclaiming that the idea of an international force was quite impossible. His own permanent representative, Arthur Lall, quietly informed him that the Asian bloc had voted for it *en masse* and that Nasser had accepted it.

In the early afternoon Menon called on Pearson at the Drake Hotel to comment wearily upon the wickedness of the times and add: "This force of yours is all very well, you know, but the United Nations is not supposed to wage war."

"Have you a better proposal?" asked Pearson. "We are open to any suggestion."

"No, not yet," replied Krishna Menon. "But we are going to have to keep an eye on how this force is formed. It seems to me that the Secretary General can choose almost anyone he likes to contribute troops. I wouldn't be surprised if it ends up all white."

"Oh, I don't think that's the case, Krishna," said Pearson. "I'm sure we would welcome an offer of troops from India."

Krishna Menon evaded the issue, saying: "You can be sure of one thing. We cannot allow this U.N. force to become a sort of successor to the British-French aggressors. I intend to introduce a draft resolution tonight condemning them for the aggression and demanding that they withdraw from Egypt immediately."

When he had left, Pearson telephoned Hammarskjold. "Menon was here," he said. "He says the present mood of the Assembly is to have Britain and France condemned as aggressors. We don't want that to happen. We'd better do something."

IV

NIGHTFALL in Egypt. French paratroops had captured Port Fuad and were heading south along the canal toward Ismailia; Egyptian defences held out against the British in Port Said, particularly on the sea front. Israel, not daring to procrastinate any longer, accepted the cease-fire and, as Egypt had done so already, there was no longer official justification for the Anglo-French intervention. The canal was blocked at both ends, the combatants were separated and had nothing to fire at, and what was left, in a moral sense, was an Anglo-French war against Egypt, which was not really anyone's intent.

Sir Edward Boyle, a junior minister at the British Treasury, following Anthony Nutting's example, resigned because "I do not honestly feel that I can defend, as a minister, the recent policy of the government, and I feel bound to associate myself with that body of opinion which deeply deplores what has been done."

Shortly afterwards the British government made a long-overdue gesture to world opinion by announcing that the bombing of Egypt would "cease forthwith," thereby ending five days of almost non-stop air bombardment.

The Security Council met at 8:00 P.M. on Monday, November 5 in New York to deal with a spurious Russian bid for Arab-Asian applause by demanding that as the General Assembly was proving ineffective, the United States and the Soviet Union should drive the British and French out of Egypt with their air forces and navies.

"The United States of America and the Union of Soviet Socialist Republics," said the Moscow proposal, "as permanent members of the Security Council having powerful air and naval forces at their disposal, should give military and other assistance to the Republic of Egypt . . . by sending naval and air forces, military units, volunteers, military instructors, and other forms of assistance, if the United Kingdom, France, and Israel fail to carry out this resolution within the stated time limits."

These time limits were twelve hours to cease firing, and three days in which to withdraw from Egyptian territory.

Cabot Lodge replied: "Yesterday we learned of the butchery which Moscow was in the process of carrying out against the people of Hungary. . . . Now we have this Soviet proposal. I submit, in all candour, that it sets a sombre record of cynicism and indifference to the values of international morality. The Soviet resolution embodies an unthinkable suggestion. . . ."

Sir Pierson Dixon said: "The idea is that two permanent members of the Security Council should combine against two other permanent members. . . . Of course, it has been the Soviet Union's failure to co-operate . . . which has rendered the United Nations . . . an ineffective organ for international peace and security. That explains why the United Kingdom and France felt obliged to intervene in the emergency created by Israel's invasion of Egypt . . . obliged to intervene in the interests of preventing a conflagration and preserving peace and security. . . ."

Here was another shift in British rationalisation for the Anglo-French action. Instead of safeguarding freedom of passage through the canal, the principal basis for intervention was the hypothesis that it had been necessary because the United Nations was ineffectual.

During the two hours the Council spent discussing the Soviet proposal, the United Nations building was filled with rumours that the Russians were ready to take action alone if it were not accepted. But apprehension gave way to relief when, confronted by prompt, outright rejection by Cabot Lodge, Sobolev smiled and nodded his head as if he were more interested in having an example of strong Soviet pressure on the record than in pressing on with a desperately serious proposal.

Krishna Menon, believed by many delegates to be pathologically jealous of the central roles in the crisis being played by Pearson and Hammarskjold, carried out his threat to produce a strongly condemnatory resolution for the Assembly session due to begin when the Security Council meeting ended. Backed by the Arab-Asian bloc, it described Britain and France as "imperialistic aggressors" guilty of "crimes against humanity by waging a criminal war."

Hammarskjold and Pearson were working on the final police force report in the Secretariat building when a copy of Krishna Menon's resolution was brought in by John Holmes. They called the President of the Assembly and explained what was happening, and as a result the Assembly session was called off on the excuse that the Council meeting had continued too late into the night. In fact the Security Council threw out the Soviet proposal at 10:00 P.M. and adjourned thirty minutes later, early enough to allow the Assembly another all-night session if need be.

It was realised in the Secretary General's office that Krishna Menon, having been out-manœuvred temporarily, could introduce his resolution the next night. But by then they hoped it would be too late, that Britain and France would have accepted their plan for a United Nations force and the fighting stopped. This meant that the blueprint for the force would have to be in London and Paris in the early hours of Tuesday morning to enable the British and French governments to use it as their reason for complying with the cease-fire demands.

Pearson thought extra pressure might be needed. He telephoned Prime Minister St. Laurent, suggesting that he address a personal appeal to Eden asking that the basic principles of a United Nations force be accepted unconditionally, and the war brought to an immediate end. If not, there was almost no hope of Canada, the United States, or any other of Britain's friends being able to stave off disastrous consequences.

As a result, the British High Commissioner in Ottawa was called to the Prime Minister's residence and asked to convey to Sir Anthony Eden a warning that, in the Canadian government's view, further delay in complying with the wishes of the United Nations would result in irreparable damage to the cause of international peace and justice.

Eden replied in a telegram to St. Laurent the same day, saying that after discussions with French leaders he had decided that the Anglo-French operation should continue as planned. He argued that if Britain and France withdrew, the Israeli-Egyptian war would drag on and the danger of a wider conflict would be increased. "The whole area," he said, "will relapse into chaos."

The Anglo-French decision had been an agonising one, but they were sure it was the right one. He hoped Mr. St. Laurent would understand how vital it was to protect the canal, while avoiding any mention that the canal was by that time hopelessly blocked and wholly out of service.

Eden warmly welcomed the Canadian initiative in New York and expressed "my personal indebtedness to Mr. Pearson for the skill and energy with which he has sponsored this idea [the United Nations police force]." In his view it was all the more imperative to "come to grips" with the situation, in order to create the conditions under which the United Nations force could relieve Britain and France of their joint responsibility.

It may be that St. Laurent would have replied to this rather meaningless telegram with a brief acknowledgement, had it not been for the final paragraph in which Eden trusted most sincerely that he could count on the deep and real value of Canadian support.

St. Laurent, determined to make it clear beyond question that Britain might enjoy a measure of Canadian sympathy but not wholehearted Canadian support, telephoned New York, spoke briefly with Pearson, and then sent a reply that same night to Eden, which began: "I think we have a sympathetic understanding of your and France's position, but we still regret that you have found it necessary to follow the course you are taking." The Canadian Prime Minister felt it unfortunate that the events in the Middle East had served to cloak with a smokescreen the renewed brutal international crimes of the Soviet Union in Hungary. He pointed out that, just as Eden had said the Anglo-French action was designed to restore order and peace, so the Soviets were saying that they had acted to restore order and peace in the face of the inability of the local authorities in Hungary to do so. And just as Eden had announced that Britain and France would give adequate warning of air attacks so that local populations might submit without suffering from military operations, so the Soviets were warning the Hungarians to stay off the streets and refrain from supporting the rebels.

St. Laurent acknowledged that these comparisons were not necessarily valid, but added that in both cases disregard for the United Nations Charter made it difficult for Canada and others to use world opinion to check the Soviet Union.

He added that Canada was also concerned about the reactions of the Eastern members of the Commonwealth and hoped to seek a solution in the Middle East through the United Nations, which would minimise the damage to the Common-wealth and the Western Alliance. In conclusion, he said: "We will continue to do our best to be of whatever assistance we can in a positive way, but I would not wish to leave with you the impression that as seen from here the situation appears other than tragic."

This message was in every sense that of one friend speaking to another in sorrow rather than in anger and, as such, could have given little comfort to Eden who was more in need of active support.

Pressure was also bearing in on him from another direction. The Soviet Union, now firmly in control of Hungary, moved with serious and ponderous menace from the background of the Middle East drama to deliver an ultimatum.

Bulganin's similarly worded notes to Eden and Mollet, received in London and Paris late on Monday night, referred first to the "dangerous consequences" of their "aggressive war in Egypt," warned that London and Paris lay under the threat

of Soviet missiles, and then concluded: "We are fully determined to crush the aggressors . . . through use of force. We
hope at this critical moment you will show due prudence and
draw corresponding conclusions from this."

A letter was sent at the same time to Ben-Gurion, saying:
"Israel is acting as a tool of foreign imperialist forces in continuing this senseless adventure, challenging all the nations of
the East who are carrying on the struggle against colonialism
and for peace. . . ." Ben-Gurion was advised that he "played
with the destiny of your country and people," and then told:
"The Israeli government will duly understand and evaluate
this warning of ours."

Yet another Russian letter was received in Washington
which called upon the United States to join with the Soviet
Union in the use of their respective air and sea power to expel
the aggressors from the Middle East.

It mattered little any more whether the Russians were making a powerful, concerted effort to establish Communist pro-
tectorship of Arab nationalism. The gravest danger now was
that, even if the shadow of nuclear war cast from Moscow was
filled with propaganda rather than might, there could be a
serious intent to send volunteers armed with conventional
weapons to Egypt's assistance. Four months earlier Eden had
told ten Commonwealth Prime Ministers gathered at Downing
Street that it was the duty of all nations to avoid provocative
acts in major areas of conflict. Far from avoiding it, he had
invited upon himself the very consequences he had, in his wisdom, so accurately foreseen.

Eden and Mollet, after consulting by telephone at approximately 1:00 on Tuesday morning, were probably relieved to
find they were equally determined not to be intimidated by
Soviet pressure. In such a highly charged situation, com-
pounded by a tense atmosphere of midnight drama, it seems
that Mollet and Pineau on the one hand, and Eden and Lloyd
on the other, were impressively calm and controlled in their
assessments of the Russian threat.

In Downing Street, at least, the façade of political steadiness was supported by the conviction that in the last analysis the United States would throw a protective umbrella of nuclear authority over its allies. Wisely, however, both governments asked Washington to confirm that this would be the case. A brief message from the State Department, however, shattered the façade and let disintegration set in.

"The Government of the United States," said the message, "will respect its obligations under the North Atlantic Treaty arrangements. . . ."

Official exchanges at times of crisis are seldom what they seem. Beneath harmless exteriors there are explosive intents hidden from all but the few statesmen who may be aware of the background of events and the contexts in which they are drafted. In this case, Eisenhower was angry and exasperated, weary after an arduous election campaign, and faced with a day which would decide if the American people had confidence in his administration.

The message was deliberately designed to be interpreted in two ways: the United States guaranteed the security of Britain and France if they were attacked wherever Western interests were at stake; or the United States guarantee under NATO was valid only if there was an attack in Europe.

Downing Street and the Hotel Matignon were gripped by quick uncertainty. The Soviet threat would be dangerous indeed if Moscow intended to attack not England, not France, but "by God," as Mollet put it, "the Suez Expeditionary Force."

Eisenhower, not intending to be re-elected on a peace platform and have to make war the theme of his victory speech, dispatched a curt rejection of Bulganin's proposals, and informed Eden and Mollet in personal messages that "relations between people should be governed by the Charter of the United Nations. . . . The resort to force, condemned in our enemies, should not be permitted by our friends. It is a question of conscience before God and men."

Eden, failing to reach the President by telephone, sent a personal message to the White House asking for immediate assurance that the United States would retaliate against the Soviet Union if Britain and France were attacked. While the long night of grand drama dragged on, the Prime Minister kept vigil at Downing Street, waiting for the reply that never came. Instead, there was a message from the British Ambassador saying that the State Department had hinted that if a run on the pound sterling developed, Britain would have difficulty keeping bankruptcy at bay. It is hardly surprising that Eden should mention obliquely in his memoirs: "The United States . . . used every resource at their command, and there were many."

At 3:00 A.M. in Paris the United States Ambassador, Douglas Dillon, was called to the Hotel Matignon and asked for reassurances of the American position in the light of the Soviet threat. He was unable to be any less ambiguous than the State Department's earlier assurance that the United States would stand by its NATO obligations. An hour later in Washington, the French Ambassador, Hervé Alphand, called at the White House to seek clarification from the President.

Eisenhower, obviously under the immense climactic strain of domestic electioneering, and self-admittedly overwhelmed by the chaotic state of world affairs produced by the Anglo-French action, said with heartbreaking sincerity: "You must stop this war. You must withdraw from Egypt. Our position is that of the United Nations Charter. It is inviolate for all nations, all men. Mr. Ambassador, let me tell you this. Life is a ladder which mounts up to Heaven. I am near the top of that ladder, and I wish to present myself with clean hands before my Creator."

It was a painful interview. Alphand left the White House knowing he had been confronted by a question of principle, a moral position so utterly unassailable that it was impossible to argue against.

A few minutes after midnight in New York, Pearson and Hammarskjold, assisted by the senior Secretariat under secretaries Ralph Bunche and Andrew Cordier, completed the report on the formation and composition of an international police force. While copies were cabled to London, Paris, and Washington, they relaxed in Hammarskjold's office, praying fervently that Eden and Mollet would recognize that they were now "off the hook," that they could comply with the cease-fire and allow the United Nations to restore order and negotiate a peace.

But by then it was dawn in Egypt, and the invasion armada had arrived. Big naval guns were already pounding the beach defences at Port Said.

CHAPTER TWELVE

The Cease-Fire

BY threatening two major powers with rocket war, the Soviet Union had taken what constituted the gravest and most aggressive diplomatic action in its history. Propaganda, obviously one motive, was too glib to be the only one, and Western political-military intelligence analysts worked throughout the night to uncover undertones they knew would be less simple, less benevolent.

There was convincing evidence that the Russians were sincere in their warnings. As a principal military power, the Soviet Union could not neglect an opportunity to pose as the defender of peace against aggression; it might also wish to lessen the risk of the fighting in Egypt developing into a major war while the Red Army was preoccupied in restless satellites; mention in the letter to Eisenhower of joint sea and air forces – and not ground forces – was significant because it indicated willingness to be committed within the restrictive framework of police action rather than of war; and there was also the consistency of the approach: typical impatience with the United Nations, and an equally typical preference for bilateral dealings with the United States.

There was evidence, too, of insincerity. By involving the United States in joint police action, the Soviet Union would invite increased American influence during subsequent peace settlements in the Middle East, which would run counter to Soviet policy; there was no intelligence of specific Russian preparations for war; and it seemed hardly likely that Russia would act alone as sea forces would have to pass through NATO-controlled waters, and air forces would have to over-fly Turkey, a NATO country in which there were United States missile and Strategic Air Command bases. There was also the possibility that prompt United Nations action in the Assembly, which clearly contained a threat to Russia's expansionist ambitions in the Middle East, might prove successful. Awakening to this prospect somewhat belatedly, the Soviet Union was now attempting to blanket it.

Conceivably, therefore, the Soviet Union was trying to bully, in order to extract maximum political capital by seizing upon what was a superficial split between the United States and the United Kingdom. The delivery of these notes obviously opened the way for the formation of a volunteer force.

It was highly unlikely that the Soviet Union intended to use force, but it wanted to be in a position to act if the United Nations police force failed to take over rapidly. The Soviet Union could have delivered aicraft, and airlifted volunteers. Bombers at existing Soviet bases could be used against targets in Israel, as well as the Anglo-French fleets in the eastern Mediterranean. As has often been the case, the Soviet leaders miscalculated Western reaction and underestimated the fundamental strength of Anglo-American solidarity. But Anglo-American disarray was such, in fact, that there was still no reply from Eisenhower to Eden.

An early morning meeting of the Presidential Council of Ministers in Paris unanimously endorsed the government's actions in Egypt, then gave Mollet, Pineau, and Bourgès-Maunoury authority to proceed with military operations until the Canal Zone was occupied. In London, where the pressures were great and complex, the pendulum of power swung away from war. Each of the issues facing the British Cabinet was in itself sufficient, in more ordinary circumstances, to influence policy. In the abnormal, supremely testing conditions which existed then, these issues combined to become overwhelmingly decisive.

There was Hammarskjold's cable showing that a United Nations force was being formed at speed; a strongly worded appeal from Prime Minister St. Laurent that Britain and France should hand over to the international force and withdraw from Egypt; an imminent collapse of the Commonwealth; a lack of any assurance that the United States would retaliate against a Soviet attack on the Anglo-French expeditionary force; a strangely disquieting silence from the White House which could be interpreted as revealing a frightening degree of Presidential disapproval; the unenviable predicament of fighting a war for which all justification had ended with the cessation of hostilities between Israel and Egypt; and mounting opposition to the government's policies, not only from the Socialists, but from all sections of public opinion and from within the Conservative party itself.

There was, too, the legacy of Sir Edward Boyle, which Macmillan brought with him to Downing Street from the Treasury – a report revealing that Britain's gold and dollar reserves were vanishing at an alarming rate, and a run on the pound sterling was developing in New York and other financial capitals, as the State Department had hinted might happen. The United States Federal Reserve Bank had begun to offload sterling at a discount, and in New York sterling was being offered in blocks of $1 million to $5 million at a time. It had cost the Bank of England $300 million to maintain the exchange rate during Monday alone, and $1,000 million was said to be needed to avert devaluation. The Treasury had already applied to the International Monetary Fund for a withdrawal of sterling capital, but the State Department was reported to be obstructing the process. Macmillan immediately telephoned Washington to say that unless Britain was given a loan to save sterling, it faced a bad financial crisis.

Other factors contributing to the débâcle about to take place were Eden's health and the uncontrolled emotionalism of the British Labour party.

As Eden, suffering from weakening after-effects of the severe fever that had held him helpless in its violent heat only a few weeks earlier, neared mental exhaustion, he was bewildered and dismayed by the partisan intensity of the abuse thrown at him from across the floor of the House of Commons.

Confronted by economic, political, and military threats from friends as well as from enemies, the full Cabinet met at 9:45 A.M. on Tuesday, November 6 to decide between peace and war, most of the ministers hostile to the actions being carried out in their name, and a smaller number, perhaps, openly dissatisfied with the quality of the Prime Minister's leadership.

The meeting continued throughout the morning, punctuated by the occasional absence of one or more ministers required briefly in the House of Commons to answer questions. A gallery correspondent was so shocked by Eden's appearance that he wrote:

> The Prime Minister sprawled on the front bench, head thrown back and mouth agape. His eyes, inflamed with sleeplessness, stared into vacancies beyond the roof except when they switched with meaningless intensity to the clock, probed it for a few seconds, then rose again in vacancy. His hands twitched . . . mopped themselves in a handkerchief, and were never still. The face was grey except where black-ringed caverns surrounded the dying embers of his eyes.

The choice facing the Cabinet could be reduced to these

essentials: fight on in the shadow of Soviet threats and economic ruin, or halt immediately and use the United Nations police force as the instrument for ordering a face-saving withdrawal.

On rare occasions, generally when a slide toward war is discernible in world affairs, the Swiss Federal Council issues appeals for peace and invites belligerents to meet in a neutral country such as Switzerland for a final attempt to resolve their differences. The Council considered these exceptional circumstances now existed, and at 10:00 A.M. issued an appeal in which the Great Powers were urged to hold peace talks in Geneva.

"The shadow of a third world war hovers over mankind," it said. "Peace can and must be saved."

A few minutes later SHAPE (Supreme Headquarters, Allied Powers, Europe) broadcast a warning to all NATO commanders which read:

FROM SACEUR [Supreme Allied Commander, Europe] MESSAGE BEGINS STOP RELIABLE SOURCES ANKARA REPORTS TURKEY FLOWN OVER BY JETS STOP TURKISH AIR FORCE ON HIGHEST ALERT END OF MESSAGE.

By over-flying Turkey the Soviet Union was accepting the risk of involving NATO. The aircraft could be "on delivery" to Syria or Egypt, they could be carrying volunteers to unknown destinations in the Middle East, or they might be bombers heading for the Anglo-French fleets lying off Port Said. More than ever, Eden needed reassurance from the White House; and more than ever there on election day the silence was like an impassable moat surrounding a moral redoubt.

II

PINEAU, doubting the strength of British determination, wanted desperately to be in London, where he suspected crucial decisions were being made. Instead, he was at Mollet's side, welcoming Chancellor Adenauer to Paris. The German leader had come to discuss a French proposal for European economic and political union, but more immediate matters demanded attention at the Hotel Matignon that morning, among them the United Nations police force report.

This document, consisting of beautifully obfuscated Hammarskjold, could be interpreted more or less as the reader wished. An Arab-Asian could be persuaded that Britain, France, and Israel were to be driven out by an international force with the consent of Egypt. A Frenchman or Englishman could presume that having stopped the spread of war and awakened world opinion to the perils of inaction in the Middle East, he could now hand over the task of securing lasting settlements to the United Nations and withdraw with honour and dignity.

There was a tendency among some Cabinet members in Paris to regard the police force idea as a device being used by an anti-French Hammarskjold to disparage France in the eyes of the North-African Arabs. Pineau, as sharply pointed as the Secretary General was obtuse, says today: "It was widely thought during this period that Hammarskjold was anti-French, anti-British, and interested solely in furthering the Arab cause. He was, of course, very friendly with Dr. Fawzi, and this was probably the reason for these misconceptions. I never once saw him allow personal bias to affect his position in the slightest. The General Assembly was almost unanimously hostile to our operations and, being Secretary General, he probably reflected this enormous majority opinion."

Pineau recognized that so much in the report might prove

tempting to members of the British Cabinet who had little taste for further military operations that it could be dangerous for France. He knew of the pressures upon Eden, and the memory was still fresh of his last visit to Downing Street when the British Prime Minister had appeared "exhausted, with trembling hands betraying that perhaps his nerves were not completely under control."

French troops were already twenty miles down the canal and, if given their head by the British command, might reach Suez within forty-eight hours. Pineau decided to advise that Hammarskjold's report be accepted on condition that parts of it were clarified. By this means he hoped to satisfy British sensibilities and so delay final acceptance that by then it would be too late for the United Nations to save Nasser.

Before lunch the telephone rang, and a secretary announced that the Prime Minister of England wished to speak with the Prime Minister of France. Ironically, a German leader in Paris was about to witness a British surrender.

By midmorning the outcome of a war which the British government described as a police action was in doubt, the government itself unsteady. Nasser's downfall was unlikely, and occupation of the Canal Zone, according to British estimates, was four to five days away, though the French considered forty-eight hours a more reasonable time limit. The difference in estimates was caused by British preference for advancing armoured columns along the canal, and the French conviction that paratroops should be dropped at key centres all the way to Suez.

The most serious question facing the gathering of ministers at Downing Street was whether the war against Egypt – now nakedly exposed as such – could be morally justified for even an hour longer than necessary, let alone days. To prolong the agony might invite drastic intervention by the Soviet Union, by the United States, or by both. There were those ministers who, though disapproving of the war in principle, thought it would be even worse folly to fail to achieve the objectives for which so much in national reputation and honour had been sacrificed already. Others wanted an immediate, unconditional cease-fire on the ground that Hammarskjold's report provided a means of salvaging a measure of national self-respect. They argued that by complying with the Assembly's resolutions, by accepting an international police force, Britain and France could show themselves to be supporting, however belatedly, the rule of law in world affairs.

The blows that fell in the decisive hour between 11:00 A.M. and noon were crushing in their combined effect.

Nehru sent a personal message to Eisenhower proposing, with majority Afro-Arab-Asian support, that the United States Sixth Fleet should be sent to Port Said at once to enforce, as the vanguard of a United Nations force, the cease-fire resolutions of the General Assembly. Nasser announced that he would allow United States Marines to land, and simultaneously appealed for volunteers from any nations "believing in the cause of freedom and justice" to enlist at Egyptian embassies for service in Egypt.

Washington responded by informing Nehru that the President was unable to commit United States forces to an "area of conflict" without the consent of Congress, and with a warning to United States citizens that service with the Egyptian armed forces might cost them their citizenship.

Then SHAPE issued a third warning of Russian intervention. The Turkish defence ministry had reported that the Soviet Union had formally applied for Turkish permission to pass a cruiser and three destroyers through the Dardanelles into the eastern Mediterranean. The following signal was sent from the British War Office to General Keightley's headquarters in Cyprus:

RUSSIA MAY INTERVENE IN THE MIDDLE EAST WITH FORCE.

At Downing Street, Macmillan was summoned from the cabinet room to take a telephone call from Washington. He was told in effect that a United States loan of $1,000 million would be immediately available if Britain and France agreed to cease fire at midnight. Aid while Britain was fighting despite United Nations recommendations might be misinterpreted in other countries.

The ethical, moral, political, and legal issues no longer predominated. With the unanimous consent of the full Cabinet Eden placed his call to Paris. Chancellor Adenauer and Pineau waited in silence while Mollet listened to Eden's plea for understanding and co-operation. According to the French version of the conversation, Eden said in effect: "My dear friend, I am overwhelmed by all kinds of pressures. The Labour Party has divided the country, two of my colleagues have resigned, and other ministers are threatening to follow suit. I cannot count upon the full support of the Conservative party any longer. There are pressures too from the Commonwealth and from the President of the United States. Nehru may sever relations . . . and Canada is not with us. I cannot go on alone without the United States, that is impossible. We must stop this afternoon."

Mollet, shocked by the grave implications of the British decision, replied: "But that is absolutely impossible. We cannot stop so quickly. If we wait a little longer our troops will reach Suez. I strongly urge that you reconsider."

"I cannot wait," said Eden. "I am under pressure here to bring hostilities to an end today. The best I can do is to postpone it until tonight. We must stop at midnight."

"I shall consult with my colleagues at once," said Mollet. "You may expect me to telephone you with our decision."

Bourgès-Maunoury arrived suddenly from the Defence Ministry and Adenauer withdrew to allow the three French leaders to discuss freely a surrender that could topple the government.

Mollet, making his position clear from the beginning, said: "I am not prepared to continue the military operation without Great Britain. France and Britain have co-operated through all this crisis. Our solidarity has been fully in play since the loss of the canal. We have shown that the *Entente Cordiale* is a reality. The English are in a difficult situation, and if we went on alone it would break this Franco-British solidarity and put us in a bad position in the eyes of the world."

Pineau has since said that his own position was precisely the reverse. "I saw no harm in discussing a termination of hostilities, but it was quite clear that having started the operation we had to finish it. We were within two or three days at the most of occupying the canal, and Nasser's flight from Cairo would then have been inevitable. To abandon the operation when we were so close to success was, in my view, a capital political error. We had accepted the role of aggressors, and having done so we were now asked to renounce the essential benefits we could derive from it. I explained that no matter what the English did, our Algerian problem meant that for us there could be no question of abandoning the operation under any pretext. I felt, too, that we would have fewer difficulties with the United Nations if we succeeded in our purpose than if we failed. I warned that if we stopped in the middle, the United Nations would force us to evacuate Egypt. Then the success of the entire operation to date would be turned into failure."

Bourgès-Maunoury, in qualified agreement with Pineau, said, "We can occupy the length of the canal in a couple of days. If the English stop then, the agreement we have with them and with Israel is rendered null and void. We can simply ask the Israelis to go to the limit with us to finish the campaign."

Mollet, loath to part company with Eden, was unconvinced. They agreed to place the issue before the Cabinet that evening. Significantly, Eden had not asked that France should join Britain in a cease-fire; he had merely informed Mollet of his own Cabinet's decision.

At 12:30 P.M. in London on Tuesday, November 6, Norman Robertson called on Eden at the House of Commons.

"I've asked you to come here," said the Prime Minister, according to notes made later by the Canadian High Commissioner, "because we have given serious consideration to the Secretary General's report which reached us this morning. In the light of this, the governments of the United Kingdom and France will notify the Secretary General today that we agree to a cease-fire.

"I should like you to tell your Prime Minister that we are grateful for Canada's steadying influence in the councils of the United Nations, and I should like further to ask that the Canadian government help us in seeing to it that the canal is cleared of blockships as quickly as possible. There will probably be all kinds of political and psychological objections in the U.N. to allowing our own and French technical services doing this job. But if you people and the Americans can persuade a majority of the U.N., particularly Egypt and India, to let us make a start, then the canal will be cleared that much sooner. We have the finest salvage equipment in the world available. Our information is that it may take three to five months, so that this is an urgent and sensible follow-up to the cease-fire."

Robertson reported this conversation by telephone to Pearson at the Drake Hotel in New York, where it was about 8:30 A.M., and added: "The Prime Minister wants you to know that he hopes you will be able to get a really effective U.N. force set up as speedily as possible. He thinks it important, probably because he doesn't want to have to withdraw from Egypt until an international force is there to take over. That way it will appear as if the United Nations is completing the operation he started."

Later that morning, Arnold Heeney telephoned from

Washington to report: "I spoke with Hoover, the Acting Secretary of State, a few minutes ago. His view is that the British can't expect to get an undertaking that their salvage fleets will be used to clear the canal until they've actually announced an unconditional acceptance of the Assembly resolutions. He means by that, withdrawal as well as cease-fire."

"When does he think the cease-fire will come into effect?" asked Pearson.

"He seems to be pretty certain it will be midnight London time. When I asked what made him believe that, he was vague, but implied that the State Department more or less expected it. It's my impression that contacts between the U.K. and France on the one hand, and the United States on the other, are far from normal. But he did say that the President had received a message from Sir Anthony Eden yesterday, which was the first of its kind in over a week.

"Somewhat obliquely, I thought, he mentioned that for a variety of reasons the President had not been able to reply yet, and the effect of this silence may have been to accelerate British acceptance of the cease-fire."

The "moat of silence" technique may have been a harsh form of diplomatic pressure to exert against a Prime Minister who was exhausted and physically enfeebled. It had, however, combined with other pressures to produce a necessary result. When peace is threatened in a nuclear age there is not much point in being politely concerned for the sensibilities of wayward friends.

III

PRESIDENT Eisenhower was re-elected; Eden announced in the House of Commons an unconditional cease-fire; Mollet concurred; and Anglo-French advance units came to a halt twenty-odd miles south of Port Said.

Bourgès-Maunoury, Thomas, Peres, Israeli staff officers, and French staff officers searched frantically for a way to keep the campaign moving just long enough to reach Ismailia, a few hours away. There were signs of panic among the Egyptians, and it seemed that, if Nasser should be overthrown, it would be by his own defeated army officers or by being forced to flee Cairo – if the Allies could give a little extra push.

The Israelis, their front line against the eastern edge of the Canal Zone all the way to Suez, suggested putting their troops into French uniforms and moving them forward to occupy it. Admiral Barjot and French paratroop commanders tried to mount air drops along the canal before the cease-fire came into effect, but they couldn't find enough aircraft. The Israelis then proposed sending their forward units into Ismailia to hold it until French flying-columns could take over during the night. Their units would be withdrawn back to the Sinai by dawn, when they could be seen, nailed innocently to the desert by their own cease-fire.

Any one of these schemes might have proved feasible had a French officer held a key command. But at every level of the Expeditionary Force the French were deputies to the British – and there was no escaping the British soldier's scrupulous regard for obeying orders.

General de Gaulle, who threw from the sanctum of his country retirement a long shadow of authority over all things political and military in France, had been informed of every development since London and Paris had decided to intervene.

He had warned the French General Staff, "Beware of having British leadership at all command echelons."

The army of France, haunted by withdrawals from empire, seeking to release itself in Egypt from past frustrations, was denied at the last moment the victory it needed. Naturally, the General had been right; the British were to blame – and the politicians.

The politicians were by then trying to repair the rifts between them. Eisenhower broke his silence to telephone Eden congratulating him on the wisdom of the cease-fire, proposing close consultation on Middle East affairs, and pleasantly remarking upon the clarity of the new telephone link.

Eden, spirits revived, sent a personal message to Prime Minister St. Laurent, which referred to the urgent message he had received from Ottawa the night before and said:

I must tell you that I understand your feelings and anxieties. Here we have been living with them from day to day, and our decisions have been taken only after we have weighed the moral considerations with scrupulous care and with the thought of the strain upon our friends in the Commonwealth always first in our minds.

From the moment this war broke out, it has been clear to me that every Arab country would be involved and set about Israel under Egypt's direction, unless the war was stopped at once. Our operation was thus a life-saving one.

A war of that kind would be fought backwards and forwards across the canal and it would be lost to all of us for months and months. There is little doubt that Israel would have decisively defeated the Arabs one by one and that by our intervention we have saved them.

The only possible way of stopping hostilities was for someone to get there quickly and be on the ground. The ideal would have been an international force from the start, but there isn't one and in the nature of things couldn't be one for a time. . . . We are ready to . . . hand over responsibility to a United Nations force.

I know we have incurred much criticism . . . but I hope you whose Government have played a leading part in encouraging acceptance of proposals for a United Nations force will regard what we have had to do as paving the way for it to become a reality. I hope you will press ahead with the force plan which I believe may yet give the United Nations strength, which is the only hope of preserving international law and peace in the world. . . .

A strange letter. Militarily, the Israeli army would not have remained alongside the canal if Israel was attacked in the north by Jordan, Iraq, and Syria. More probably, it would have attempted to hold the Egyptians in the Sinai while defending other borders. So in the event of an all-Arab war against Israel the canal would hardly have been a major battleground. To predicate that the Anglo-French operation was "a life-saving one" designed to rescue Israel read oddly, as nobody had yet considered such a possibility. Even more curious was the next proposition that as Israel would have defeated the Arab states, "by our intervention we have saved them."

Most significant was the suggestion that Britain and France could hand over responsibility to the United Nations force. In propaganda terms this was the face-saving interpretation Pearson had made possible, but in the context of a letter from one head of government to another it implied that the British had convinced themselves already that this was the United Nations intention.

In order to persuade the General Assembly to accept the concept of an international force, Pearson had deliberately avoided all reference to the possibility that one of the subsidiary benefits would be its propaganda value to Britain and France. The only colleagues to whom he admitted his concern about helping Britain and France were Dulles, Hammarskjold, and

Engen, because they were, in varying degrees, as interested as he in constructive rather than condemnatory proposals.

It was still early afternoon in New York when the contents of this letter were telegraphed to Pearson for his information. He was immediately depressed. Hammarskjold's final report was to be presented for Assembly approval the next morning, and if the British and French made their withdrawal conditional upon handing over responsibility to a United Nations force, the Assembly would never approve it. The Arab-Asians were already suspicious that the force would be a device designed to serve Anglo-French interests; Nasser was suspicious that by consenting to a United Nations force entering Egypt he might be inviting a new form of white imperialism into the Middle East; and the Soviet Union knew that the presence of a United Nations force would prevent further Communist penetration into the area and would try hard to sabotage its establishment.

If the police force idea was to survive, there could be no suggestion that it was merely a substitute for the Anglo-French Expeditionary Force.

Pearson's first visitor in the afternoon confirmed his fears. It was Krishna Menon, seeking clarification of the functions of the force. Pearson had no intention of being specific at this stage, and the Indian eventually left after saying: "We may consider contributing a battalion, once we know what the force is going to do. At the moment I'm concerned that the British and the French will twist it to serve their own interests."

India's support in the Assembly was essential for Pearson. The primary obstacle was personal rather than political, as he was aware of Nehru's animosity toward Eden. The Indian Prime Minister had told a small group of diplomats in New Delhi that he blamed Eden for "the aggression against Egypt, not the British or French people." India would remain in the Commonwealth, he had said, if Eden were to be replaced as Prime Minister.

In Pearson's view a personal message from St. Laurent to

Nehru might help win support for the police force proposal, allay Menon's fears, encourage India to contribute troops, and at the same time serve to draw the Commonwealth closer together. After he suggested this to Ottawa, St. Laurent sent a letter to Nehru saying:

> In these difficult days through which we are passing India has never been far from my mind. I hope that our friendship has given me some understanding of, and sympathy for, India's position in the present Middle East crisis, and I know that you appreciate our situation here. . . . The restoration of peace to the Middle East and the hope of achieving, under the auspices of the United Nations, a permanent settlement of the prolonged strife which has rent this troubled area are, I am sure, the objectives of both India and Canada. I am therefore particularly pleased that you have agreed in principle to participate with us in the . . . United Nations force which is being organised. It is my earnest hope that none of us will be diverted from our common purpose and our long-term interests by the unhappy events which have led to the present crisis in the affairs of the world.

It implied a Canadian-Indian identity of interests, which in any event St. Laurent believed to be the product of a meeting with Nehru during his earlier world tour. Canadian understanding for the sense of outrage prevalent among Asian states invited India to avoid being "diverted" from the Commonwealth by events, and frankly appealed for Indian co-operation in the forming of a United Nations force.

Pearson's second visitor that afternoon was Sir Pierson Dixon, obviously relieved at developments in London and Paris, who wondered whether the United Nations would use Royal Navy salvage crews to clear the canal.

"I don't think so," said Pearson. "You have to face two inescapable consequences to the way this force is shaping up.

British and French troops will have to leave the Suez, and the Israelis will have to draw back to their original borders."

"I thought that might be the case," said the British representative, and his thoughtfulness hinted that it was not a reply he relished sending to London.

Dixon was followed by de Laboulay, the French minister in Washington on loan to his delegation in New York, who said his government had just announced the cease-fire in Paris and it was not quite in the same terms as the British.

"We do not accept that Israeli forces should withdraw from the Sinai until there is a political settlement," he said. "Nor do we agree that the British and ourselves should leave the Canal Zone unless the Egyptians also withdraw. That way the U.N. police force can occupy the zone and remain as a buffer between the Israelis and the Egyptians until a settlement is reached. It may be that Egypt will have to cede to Israel some of the territory now occupied by Israeli forces."

"Neither of these positions is tenable in U.N. terms," said Pearson. "The Assembly certainly won't support you, and the functions of the international force depend upon you withdrawing, not the Egyptians. In my view it will be unfortunate if you and the British speak in the Assembly from different positions. Perhaps you had better see them now and get together on what you will be saying."

"Perhaps you are right," said de Laboulay, "but Paris is not willing to concede as much as London on this issue."

At the same time in Paris the Quai d'Orsay, which knew nothing of the secret agreement signed at Sèvres by its political chief, issued a statement which had the effect of neutralising it anyway, without objection from Pineau.

When asked by the Canadian and American Ambassadors whether the accusation by French deputies in the National Assembly that they had been let down by Britain, that British promises were "scraps of paper," were true, Daridan, the Director General, replied, "These feelings certainly represent a

majority opinion. We started out to inflict a resounding defeat
upon Colonel Nasser; we did it, but we did not continue until
the final objective was achieved. That was Prime Minister
Eden's decision, not ours.

"When the British decided to stop, we had no alternative
but to stop also. Should a similar state of affairs ever arise
again you can be sure we in France will go about things differently. However, we believe now that the Russians were preparing to take over Syria and use it as a platform from which to
mount an operation against Israel. We have, at least, prevented
that happening."

On Wednesday the General Assembly approved Hammarskjold's report, instructed him to proceed with the formation of
a United Nations police force consisting of approximately six
thousand men, and accepted his recommendations for an advisory committee, a "peace force cabinet."

The composition of this committee had created additional,
unexpected problems. At previous informal meetings with the
Secretary General there had been Canada, Norway, Colombia,
and India. But when the time came to form a proper committee
to assist Hammarskjold with the political questions arising
from the formation of UNEF, India had not actually offered to
contribute troops, but Pakistan had.

"We knew there would be trouble if we nominated one and
not the other, so we agreed that the fourth member should be
Iran," said Murray. "When Arthur Lall heard about this he
stopped me in the corridor and in great excitement demanded
to know why India had been excluded. He even threatened to
withdraw India's support of the force if it were not on the
committee. He could see no reason for including Iran and
called the dropping of India an insult.

"I reported this to Mr. Pearson, and there were further
meetings with Hammarskjold. We asked the Pakistanis if they
would mind serving alongside India and they agreed, somewhat reluctantly. So then we had six members on Tuesday. But

Lall further objected, on the ground that as Iran and Pakistan were members of the Baghdad Pact and Canada and Norway were members of NATO, the committee was not sufficiently 'non-aligned.' We added Brazil, but then Menon entered the picture to say that Egypt would not accept Iran and Pakistan and that there should be more Asian members.

"On Wednesday morning he suggested Burma or Indonesia and then changed his mind to say that Burma had close ties with Israel and was therefore unacceptable.

"Menon then suggested Yugoslavia, but we managed to head off this proposal and Mr. Pearson suggested that we should accept any uncommitted country Menon cared to propose. He came back with Ceylon, and we agreed. During this furore Poland tried to nominate Czechoslovakia, but we organised a successful move against this, mainly because the Iranian Ambassador, Mr. Entezam, bowed out of the committee so gracefully."

Once the Assembly approved Hammarskjold's report and recommendations, peace was able to arrive in Egypt on the same day as major war. The United Nations had been seized of the crisis on the night the invasion armada sailed from Malta. They had both taken six days (though some slower ships had sailed three days earlier and actually taken nine days) to reach that point on a ribbon of road south of Port Said where the French General Massu had halted his advance; and if peace was a few hours late in arriving, most of the world was impressed by the speed with which the United Nations had proved itself capable of acting.

Pearson, Hammarskjold, and Engen had known from the beginning that their unremitting efforts were not obstructed, mainly because the United States was behind them and the Soviet Union was not inclined to hinder them. But their critics – and these were many in Canada, Britain, France, Australia, New Zealand, Belgium, and the Netherlands, to name the countries which were most divided – were beginning to level

severe criticism against the United Nations generally, and
Pearson and Hammarskjold particularly, for applying double
standards of morality – intervention in Egypt, but none in
Hungary.

The reasoning was specious. The Soviet Union dealt cyni-
cally in double standards by scornfully assailing Britain and
France on the one hand, and rejecting any form of United
Nations presence in Hungary on the other. To have imposed
intervention by force would have meant a declaration of war
by NATO against the Warsaw Pact, which, in the climate of
1956, would have entailed a nuclear holocaust. Peace then
was a matter of expediency – what could be done in practice
rather than what should be done in theory.

No doubt both situations were ideally suited for similar
measures. In practice, however, the United States was prepared to give, and did in fact give, wholehearted support to the
Middle Powers – Canada, Norway, India, and Colombia – in
their efforts to contain the brushfire in Egypt, while it was not
prepared to engage in a test of strength in the vastly different
conditions prevailing in the Hungarian situation. The British
and French were equally prepared to accept United Nations
intervention, which they hoped would in some measure assist
them to achieve their objectives, but the Soviet Union was
determined that such action should not prove effective in its own
private satellite domain.

Events in Hungary haunted the peacemakers in New York,
causing some of them even greater anguish than events in
Egypt. But the Soviet Union was untouchable, while Britain
and France would respond to the moral persuasion of world
opinion. By accepting the cease-fire, they had given strength
to the United Nations which it had lacked before; now they
had simply to withdraw unconditionally and the victory of
peace over war would be complete.

They baulked.

IV

ISRAEL was the first. For many years Ben-Gurion had proclaimed that Israel would never fight a preventive war against the Arabs, and only three weeks before, on October 15, he had reasserted his peaceful intentions. He was, of course, planning preventive war then. He had accepted the cease-fire, after procrastinating for as long as possible, in order to hold on to whatever sympathy for Israel's grievances existed at the United Nations, and now, unaccountably and irascibly, he almost threw it away.

Speaking in Jerusalem, he announced that Israel would not withdraw from the Sinai or the Gaza Strip, that there were no old borders to withdraw to because they no longer existed, and had always been fictional anyway. He praised his soldiers for winning a clean, decisive victory over Egypt, the strongest Arab state, and made disparaging comments on the Anglo-French intervention, saying that Israel had won its war without them, and would have preferred that they had stayed out of the Arab-Israeli dispute. He was bitter about the American pressures that had been exerted against him, and denounced the United Nations for failing to stop Egyptian fedayeen raids.

The kindest interpretation is that Ben-Gurion was weaving the first strands of the cloak of secrecy that would hide the fact of collusion in the years ahead, that he was establishing, too, the basis for an Israeli claim that it had won a clean victory — by itself. But in New York, where no one was aware that there were secrets that had to be hidden, it was a speech guaranteed to re-ignite simmering enmities at a time when the success of United Nations negotiations depended upon the cooling of passions.

Pearson, who spoke with the Israeli representative, Abba Eban, in the corridors of the United Nations, told him that the speech must have been as offensive to the British, the French, and the Americans as it was to the Arabs. "If you people persist with this," he said, "you run the risk of losing all your friends."

Several hours later Eban telephoned to say he had been in touch with Jerusalem, where the Foreign Office was perturbed by the Canadian reaction and by the atmosphere the speech had created at the United Nations. He hoped that "I shall be authorized soon to say something which might improve the situation."

Eisenhower's rebuke that night to Ben-Gurion indicated that the United States was quite willing to isolate him if he refused to comply with United Nations recommendations. It coupled the threat of economic sanctions with the promise of fair and just consideration of Israel's complaints during subsequent peace negotiations. The President's message was accompanied by an even more strongly worded letter to Mrs. Golda Meir from Acting Secretary of State Hoover, which envisaged "complete severance of United States–Israel relations and a powerful movement within the United Nations to expel Israel" if it failed to withdraw from Egypt.

Next day the Israeli Foreign Office announced that the army would be withdrawn as required, but few of the governments principally involved were convinced of Israel's sincerity. Pearson noted prophetically in a memorandum to Ottawa: "The critical point in our difficulties is going to be Israel's intransigence about returning from the lands she has just occupied. . . ."

In Washington, the State Department was thinking much the same about Britain and France.

Eisenhower's telephone call had so induced Eden to believe that Anglo-American relations were returning to normal that on Wednesday, November 7, he returned the call, suggesting to the President that they should meet to discuss problems that had been left in abeyance during the silent period between the White House and Downing Street. Eisenhower agreed, authorized Eden to extend the invitation to Mollet, and arrangements were made for the British and French leaders to leave by air that night.

Eden then telephoned the Hotel Matignon and said, according again to the French version: "We can breathe a little easier now. The President would like to see us both in Washington tomorrow. However, in view of the hostility toward us at the United Nations he asks that we make no formal announcements, and travel with minimum staffs. I think you will agree that it is important now to realign ourselves with the United States and NATO. You will see. Our policy has been right all along."

An hour later Eisenhower telephoned Eden to ask what, specifically, they would be discussing. When Eden replied in the most general terms, the President said he had no wish to argue the merit of the United Nations resolutions. The United States had voted for them, and would not be persuaded to undertake any action that ran counter to their terms.

Eden assured him that there was no intention on his part to challenge the United Nations position. It seems more than likely, however, that any talks at the White House would inevitably have ended in some sort of argument about them. Eden could not afford to withdraw immediately, before an international force had been formed, as to do so would create the impression of being kicked out of Egypt, a humiliation he was trying desperately to avoid. The survival of his government depended upon his being able to give the impression that Britain and France were in fact handing over to a United Nations force. It was equally important for Eden that a Western summit meeting should take place in Washington as quickly as possible to create an aura of Anglo-American amity that would dispel popular belief that the United States, and Eisenhower personally, strongly disapproved of Anglo-French actions. Eden's purpose was to minimise the crime by minimising the consequences.

Eisenhower obviously failed at first to perceive this. However, he consulted with Dulles, then recovering from his operation at the Walter Reed Hospital in Bethesda, Maryland, and with Cabot Lodge in New York, both of whom immediately recognised the dangers for American policy. The United States would become suspect in Arab-Asian eyes the moment Eden and Mollet arrived, and its rigid moral position would be compromised. India, in particular, would probably interpret the visit as showing that beneath all its superficial self-righteousness, the United States was really in sympathy with the colonial powers.

In New York, Cabot Lodge had carried the correct and unassailable hostility of the United States administration to the British and French armed intervention into his relationships with their representatives at the United Nations. One of the reasons so many delegates admired Sir Pierson Dixon and M. de Guiringaud during that critical week was that they had withstood with considerable fortitude and charm Lodge's implacable refusal to even speak with them. Pearson and Engen went out of their way time and time again to entertain and meet with them simply to counter their isolation from the United States delegation.

Lodge's behaviour, which certainly achieved the effect of emphasising American impartiality, would have appeared ludicrous had the Prime Ministers of France and Britain been welcomed at the White House.

On Wednesday evening Eisenhower telephoned Downing Street for the third time to explain that, as he would be involved in discussions on domestic problems with leaders of Congress for the next few days, Eden and Mollet should defer their visit until a more convenient date – preferably after their troops had been withdrawn from Egypt.

Eden has since written: "I did not foresee . . . that the United States government would harden against us on almost every point and become harsher after the cease-fire than before."

There was, however, still no question of Mollet or Eden withdrawing immediately or unconditionally from Egypt. Selwyn Lloyd at that time believed the Americans were wrong in exerting pressure on Britain to withdraw when the emphasis should be upon the need for getting United Nations forces on the ground in Egypt. The presence of Anglo-French troops in the Canal Zone was a bargaining point he had no intention of abandoning either lightly or prematurely.

Any earlier doubts he might have possessed about the wisdom of the Anglo-French course had been dissipated to some extent by news from Israel confirming the capture of huge stocks of Communist arms and revealing that an Egyptian plan had been uncovered signifying that Egypt, with Russian connivance, intended to attack Israel the following spring. He had convinced himself that this information indicated that a world war had been averted by the Anglo-French action.

He appears to have been oddly influenced at this stage by the Israelis, accepting without reserve their statements of what had been found in the Sinai and in Gaza, although there was no actual confirmation of the Egyptian intention to attack Israel. He was also prepared, so it seems, to accept the Israelis' further claim that Syria was preparing to attack them, one that in retrospect was transparently false. Somehow, as with Eden, he had become convinced, too, that the establishment of a United Nations force would be a moral victory for Britain, that the quicker it was put into Egypt the sooner he would have a viable excuse for the intervention. In view of his statements later in New York, it is also probable that he really believed that United States preoccupation with the withdrawal aspects of the Assembly resolution might serve to obstruct creation of the United Nations force.

During a meeting with United States Ambassador Aldrich in London, Lloyd referred generally to Nasser as an angry man because his army had been so soundly defeated and his air force destroyed on the ground; that the Russians must also be angry because their protégé had suffered so severely, and added: "All of this will result in great pressures being brought to bear upon us to withdraw without a satisfactory settlement." Apparently concerned about the seriousness of the Syrian threat to Israel, he said, "I've already told the Israelis that they must avoid providing any excuse." He thought the Israelis would be unlikely to withdraw from the Sinai quickly, and as their possession of it "is one of the two bargaining counters possessed by *us*, I hope they are not going to be bullied out too fast." Lloyd was also concerned that the British and American delegations in New York were no longer speaking to each other and said, in effect, that "when I get there I may not be listened to in the same friendly atmosphere as on previous occasions."

In this reflective mood he flew to New York, hoping for an opportunity to breach the silent redoubt in Washington.

The shooting had stopped, the canal was blocked, and Nasser could with good reason announce that "God is with Islam." There were approximately fifty thousand Israeli troops and an Anglo-French force of some twenty-five thousand on Egyptian soil. The equivalent of another army wallowed about at sea off Port Said.

No one would withdraw – unless and until a United Nations force appeared.

CHAPTER THIRTEEN

The Force

PEARSON had worked closely, ceaselessly, with Hammarskjold through tumultuous nights in the Assembly, bleak and
silent dawns seen by a handful of drawn-faced men from the
solitude of the thirty-eighth floor, and through wearisome,
often frantic days, in the United Nations corridors when events
unfolded with cruel inexorability to try tempers already frayed
and tender. He had discovered that the Secretary General's
cold, metallic manner was a self-imposed façade, that it concealed a solitary personality prone to seize upon challenges,
metaphysical and practical, as safety valves for restless energy
and intellect.

The United Nations police force concept had been one
such challenge, one that had required their concerted efforts to
overcome. But once the executive machinery of the United
Nations took control, it became the Secretariat's responsibility
more than that of individual members, and in consequence it
was deprived of its partisan enthusiasm and political momentum. The sense of urgency may have been undiminished but
dispersal of responsibility had a dissipating effect. Pearson

could do no more than keep a watch in brief on its development; Hammarskjold, the burden of achievement now shared by civil and military assistants, slipped back into the soft, yielding world of Fawzi's challenging subtlety.

"All through this affair Nasser has been asking me why the United States doesn't do something," said Ambassador Raymond Hare of the United States, who had replaced Henry Byroade in Cairo. It was Friday, November 9, and he was discussing with diplomatic colleagues the last-minute possibility that Egypt would refuse entry to a United Nations force.

"Before the cease-fire, when the bombs were falling, he kept summoning me to make plea after plea for United States or United Nations intervention. First it was could we not expedite action on a U.N. force? Then before the landings he wanted to know could we not do something on our own, such as use the Sixth Fleet? I told him that by openly taking a position against our two traditional allies, the United States government had gone further than it had ever gone or cared to go again.

"Now that a U.N. force is being formed, he's suspicious of it. The Secretary General sent him a cable asking for permission to land an advance guard, and he's quibbling. I think Soviet offers of volunteers and material help have made him feel his position is so strengthened that he can dictate to the U.N. instead of acquiescing."

On Saturday morning, November 10, Canada's Ambassador Norman was confronted by the resurgence of Egyptian dictate when Dr. Fawzi called him to a meeting at the Foreign Ministry to say: "I would like you to convey to Mr. Pearson how much Egypt appreciates the independence of Canadian policy. However, we have now decided that it might be wiser in the interests of both Egypt and Canada if there are no Canadian troops in the United Nations force. You are a member of the Commonwealth, also a member of NATO. We are opposed

to participation in the United Nations force of countries belong-
ing to regional groupings, alliances, or associations of such kind
as these."

Fawzi added that his government had no wish to detract
from its recognition of Canada's independent role in the crisis,
for which it was "very grateful," but a question of "form is
involved."

"Troops of Canada owe allegiance to the Queen of England," he continued, "and wear British-type uniforms. President Nasser does not doubt that the Canadian offer of troops is
an honourable one and is quite sure that Canadian troops will
not be sent here to occupy. There remains, however, in the
conscious, or perhaps sub-conscious, of us all that Canada is a
member of the Commonwealth."

Ambassador Norman considered the Foreign Minister's
attitude unreasonable, but Fawzi continued imperturbably,
saying he was worried about demonstrations outside the Canadian Embasy which would prove "embarrassing to both our
governments."

Fawzi said he had discussed the problem with General
Burns, who had replied that if Canadian troops were barred
from serving with the international force he would resign as its
commander.

"We would regret that very much," Fawzi continued to
Norman. "General Burns is a United Nations official and
therefore in a different position."

"Surely you would regard a national contribution of troops
in the same light," said Norman.

"No. An individual can become an international official.
An army always remains national. The countries who want to
send troops here with our consent must be free from all
entanglements."

When Pearson received a report of this interview, he
recognised that the insertion of the "consent of all parties
concerned" clause into the force resolution, which he had

thought would prove a "minor concession to the Americans," could lead to all manner of complications which had to be somehow avoided. He was considering Norman's telegram when the Canadian Minister of National Defence, Brooke Claxton, telephoned from Ottawa to tell him: "Our people here are pretty keen on this idea of yours, Mike. This is a first-class operation and we've got a crack battalion all ready to go."

"Which one?"

"The Queen's Own Rifles."

"Good heavens, Brooke," Pearson exclaimed. "The Egyptians are determined to get regiments with names like that out of their country. How do you think they'll react when we tell them we're sending in the Queen's Own? They'll raise all sorts of objections, and we've got enough of those already. Why don't you change the name?"

Claxton, believing Pearson to be serious, asked: "To what?"

"The East Kootenay Anti-Imperialistic Battalion."

Unimpressed by Pearson's humour, Claxton replied: "If you people in New York think that for the sake of anyone, the United Nations or that guy in Cairo, we're going to make a famous regiment masquerade under a damn silly name like that, you're mistaken. It's a good Canadian regiment with a proud history, and that's the way it's going to stay."

"All right, Brooke," said Pearson, adding a lighthearted touch, "but haven't you got another regiment you can send, one that resounds a little less of the British Raj?"

"Sure, the Black Watch."

'That's worse from the Arab point of view," said Pearson. "You'd better leave it with me for a while. I'll fix things up."

By then, however, the Queen's Own Rifles were on their way to Halifax, Nova Scotia, where their equipment was already being put aboard the aircraft carrier *Magnificent*.

FROM THE ACCOUNT OF LESTER PEARSON: *There was a possibility that the international force idea might break down at*

*the last minute. Work had proceeded almost incessantly for
a week on translating the concept into a feasible, practicable
proposition, and we just couldn't allow it to be frustrated. I
have rarely in my life seen a man operate with such tireless
precision as Dag Hammarskjold did in those days. Even so,
the objections were formidable, largely due to a gradual
divergence of views on the mandate given by the General
Assembly.*

*The Americans had led the cry for a cease-fire, and the
Indians were in the van of the clamour for an immediate
withdrawal by the belligerents. The danger in both approaches
was that neither went any further. If Britain and France failed
to comply, or were in any way dilatory, the next step would
have been to brand them as aggressors and to institute against
them some collective action such as economic sanctions. We,
in the Canadian delegation, could not permit them to be
placed in so humiliating a position. The United Nations force
concept was designed to avoid it, while at the same time
providing a means of keeping the peace while political settlements were negotiated. If it failed, then the chances of the
Commonwealth actually breaking up, and of the Anglo-American alliance being completely severed, would be considerably
increased.*

*The first obstacle was Hammarskjold's doubts about
General Burns as the Force Commander. There had been
some difficulties in his relations with the Secretariat during his
command of the Truce Supervisory Organization* [it is possible,
if his book *Between Arab and Israeli* is any guide, that he was
not always as impartial as Hammarskjold would have wished],
*and Hammarskjold hoped to introduce someone new. My feel-
ing was that we had no time to hunt around. We had a first-
class field officer on the spot with United Nations experience;
therefore we should use him. The time factor persuaded Hammarskjold to agree. Then the Indians, who had supported our*

idea throughout the Assembly negotiations, began to get suspicious that Canada was just trying to make things easier for the British and the French.

We ran into trouble with the Egyptians because the Assembly had gone on record as recognizing Egypt's unlimited sovereignty over its own territory and had agreed that a force could not be put on the ground without the consent of the parties concerned. The Secretary General exchanged some twenty-odd cables with the Egyptian government on this point during the next three days and finally reached the conclusion that there was virtually nothing we could do, within the terms of the Assembly mandate, without Egypt's consent. In his view, and I agreed with him, the only course was to keep on negotiating with them while in fact getting troops out there. Interpretations, under these conditions, were inevitably flexible and ambiguous and by the time the Advisory Committee met with Hammarskjold to discuss what he had done, and was doing, he had been forced by Egyptian objections and Indian pressure to move away from my original concept. There was even a strong likelihood that Canada would have to withdraw its participation. There was a danger, a very real one, of this whole operation collapsing, and if it did, then police action by the United Nations in the future would have been quite impossible. There were people who would have been quite happy about that, and there would be a strengthened tendency on the part of certain governments to rely entirely for their security on their own arrangements. My preoccupation was to do what I could to see this did not happen. . . .

When the advisory committee met for the first time on the thirty-eighth floor at 10:30 A.M., November 14, the divergence of views became immediately apparent. Hammarskjold opened proceedings by saying: "The starting point for my whole operation is the full and unlimited sovereignty of Egypt. At this stage only Egyptian consent is necessary to the establishment and arrival of the police force. I have undertaken with the Egyptian government that after the withdrawal of Anglo-French forces, the international emergency force will have no function in the Canal Zone, or in Port Said. It will follow Israeli forces back from the Sinai and the Gaza Strip to the original demarcation lines.

"The line taken by the government of Egypt was that its consent was necessary for each single unit in the force. . . . I agreed that a special unit of it cannot be placed in a country without the consent of that country. It is quite obvious that it is impossible to include a unit without the agreement or consent of the government where the force is stationed.

"To sum up . . . on the basis of Egyptian sovereign rights it is recognised that entry and presence depend on their consent. It is recognised *de facto*, although it is not a restriction on the right of the Secretary General to set up the force, that no single national unit should come without their consent. It is recognised that the United Nations Emergency Force shall have no function in the Canal Zone after the Anglo-French withdrawal, and that the force will in no way take over from Anglo-French forces."

Pearson, with the Queen Own's Rifles boarding the *Magnificent* in Canada, was suddenly confronted by the humiliating prospect of having them publicly turned back by the Egyptians when they attempted to land.

"If Egypt makes good its claim to determine by its own decision all the powers and functions of the United Nations Force, then I think we will be in great difficulty," he said. "They say the Assembly resolution means that Egypt can exercise a veto over every contingent in that force. That is intolerable, because what sort of force do we have then? To admit for a minute that the Egyptian government will decide that a force from country A is admissible and a force from country B is not, is something that I cannot accept. It would not be a United Nations force; it would be an Egyptian force in the sense that the Egyptians would be permitted to decide who should be in it.

"Some governments, including my own, are collecting forces now, and the revulsion of feeling against this whole operation by public opinion in a country which had sent a force forward and then was told by the Egyptian government that it could not land, would be very great indeed."

"We have on the one hand the need to get going with the force quickly," said Hammarskjold, "and on the other, these conditions mentioned by Mr. Pearson. I regard them as matters for negotiated agreement with the Egyptians."

Arthur Lall of India, suspicious of Pearson and determined that "the invaders" should not gain anything from their "aggression," said: "It is equally intolerable to me that the decision on who should compose the force should be reached without the consent of Egypt."

"This is an *ad hoc* emergency force formed to deal with specific conditions," said Hammarskjold. "If they insist upon deciding who should make up the force, then we can discuss this with them."

Pearson tried again. "We're overlooking something that's important here," he said. "There seems to be some idea in the Secretary General's exchanges with the Egyptians that the United Nations force merely consists of national contingents operating as national contingents once they are in the United Nations service. That is not true.

"Once you send your contingent to a United Nations force you lose complete control of it. Insofar as the operations and functions of the force are concerned, you put it under another command. Its own commander takes no orders from his own government. By putting it under United Nations command, you accept United Nations responsibility."

Engen added his objections. "Our understanding of the whole thing," he said, "is that we are sending a Norwegian unit to a United Nations force. We are not sending a unit to a force

picked for a specific purpose. The status of the force is that
of a United Nations force, and the Egyptian government must
recognise the principle of it being a United Nations force. They
cannot feel free to propose their own criteria in selecting the
components of a United Nations force."

"There is no general decision of the United Nations to set
up a long-term emergency force," said Lall. "The Assembly
has not created an arm of the United Nations. Here is a force
set up for a specific purpose or situation."

"The only way forward," said Hammarskjold, "is to negotiate
and see how they hang the flag."

Lall said: "Let me say this, Mr. Secretary General. I cannot
see how the United Nations should wish to impose conditions
upon a country which has been aggressed against."

"We are not imposing terms," said Pearson. "We are trying
to help Egypt, and Egypt has accepted certain conditions itself.
It accepted the Assembly resolution, and we are operating
within that resolution, that's all."

"I intend going to Cairo within the next couple of days,"
said Hammarskjold, "so why don't we wait and see how the ball
bounces there. Now we must get back to the practical side, the
question of how we are going to press the button. Ralph can
give the military picture as it hangs today."

Ralph Bunche had assumed the technical administration
of the force, referring to himself as the Secretary General's
"Minister of Defence." He said: "We have twenty-one offers
of troops. We have in Naples, waiting for transport to Egypt,
advance base personnel from Norway, Denmark, Canada, and
Colombia. More will arrive in Naples from India and Sweden
tomorrow. The Canadian air force is carrying its own contingents, the United States air force is carrying a majority of the
rest, though we have also signed a contract for Swissair to take
in some. The Yugoslavs intend travelling by sea in their own
transports if we accept their offer.

"General Burns has pointed out that nearly everyone wants

to send infantry units. The force cannot be composed entirely of infantry units. It needs specialist units – transport, maintenance, signals, engineers, etc.

"We are giving the troops blue armbands, and we have purchased a considerable supply of what are called helmetliners, the liners that go inside steel helmets. They will be painted United Nations blue, and they will look quite nice with the letters 'U.N.' in white on each side and the United Nations seal in front."

At the end of the meeting, Pearson telephoned Ottawa to recommend, after consulting General Burns, who urged it, that as technical and support units were needed more than infantry, and as Canada, of all the contributing nations, was probably in the best position to supply them, the Queen's Own Rifles should be disembarked from the *Magnificent* and replaced by units of this nature. In effect, this proposal removed at least some of the Egyptian objections to Canadian participation. Once again, practical steps in New York were serving the cause of political compromise in Cairo.

II

PEARSON'S refusal, supported by Engen, to admit that Egypt had any right to decide which national contingents should make up the United Nations force, had the effect of hardening Hammarskjold's attitude toward the Egyptians. He informed the Egyptian government by cable that Canadian participation had to be accepted, and on his instructions Burns saw Fawzi in Cairo to explain that Canada would be willing to provide technical units, not "bayonet-carrying infantry."

Krishna Menon in New York, anxious that continued

Egyptian hostility to Canadian contribution might anger the United Nations, where Pearson's stature had immeasurably increased, telephoned Cairo, and later intercepted John Holmes in the corridors of the United Nations to inform him that Egypt would accept Canadian field ambulances or air transport. "Their stand is cracking," he said. "They'll expand this to include other units." Krishna Menon was actually helpful on this occasion.

A few minutes later Holmes was called to the Secretariat and shown a cable from Fawzi which said: "After careful reconsideration of the composition of the United Nations force in the light of new developments, the Egyptian government has decided to accept Canadian participation in the form of air transport."

When Pearson read it he reacted angrily, telling Holmes: "Tell the Egyptians their position is quite unacceptable. General Burns has asked for a self-contained contingent, and that unit is now under way. We will not allow the Egyptian government to determine the nature of our contribution."

Inescapably, however, Egypt did determine to some extent the composition of the United Nations force. Caught between the dangers of a deteriorating situation, the likelihood of the force being defeated at birth by too many obstacles, and the improbability of any alternative being as attractive to the British and the French, Pearson arranged for more acceptable Canadian units to be made available. To have retained a rigid attitude, especially as General Burns wanted the Canadian composition to be altered, would have simply complicated Hammarskjold's difficulties to an impossible degree. Egypt also managed successfully to bar Pakistan's participation on the excuse that membership in the Baghdad Pact made it objectionable; India, Indonesia, and Yugoslavia, however, were welcomed by Cairo; and there were no arguments concerning the Latin-American countries, Brazil and Colombia, or the Scandinavians – Norway, Denmark, Sweden, and Finland.

During the day, ten United Nations officers arrived at Port Said from Haifa in a British landing craft to establish command headquarters, and Swissair landed sixty-five Swedes, Danes, and Norwegians at Ismailia, who were then taken to a base camp in the desert and placed under what was officially termed "the supervision of Egyptian military guard for their own protection." The Egyptian liaison officer who met them said: "Now you are here, you will go where we tell you and do what we tell you to do."

The Egyptian government then announced that as the "aggressors are not complying with the withdrawal resolutions of the General Assembly," it would continue to fight, and accept all help offered. And a Moscow statement said: "The Soviet Union cannot any longer tolerate the delaying tactics of the aggressors. Unless they withdraw from Egypt immediately it will not be possible to stand in the way of large numbers of Soviet citizens, amongst whom are reservists, pilots, tank operators, artillerymen . . . to leave for Egypt as volunteers."

Incredibly, it seemed, at a time of cease-fire, at a time when United Nations advance troops were already arriving in Egypt, the crisis, already abating, began to climb again toward a new peak of tension. Alarmed by Washington's silence now that the dangers were perceptibly increasing, Pearson instructed Arnold Heeney to find out why the State Department had failed to pursue its earlier proposals for setting up special negotiating commissions to reach settlements on the Suez Canal dispute and the entangled Palestine issue.

We are at a critical moment [his message said], *and a strong stand by the United States is indispensable to success. An unequivocal and forceful position against Communist "volunteers" is the first necessity. If the Russians and Egyptians are bluffing in this, their bluff should be called, and in a way that will impress the Arabs. If they are not bluffing, then it is all the more important that Washington acts firmly to halt their fatal course. This is all the more important now because of inevitable delays and difficulties in getting the United Nations force into operation, and hesitations, delays, and difficulties in the British, French, and Israelis withdrawing at once from their present positions. We can deal at the United Nations and through diplomatic channels with this latter difficulty, but only the United States government can take adequate steps to counter, in Moscow and in Cairo, the "volunteer" threat.*

These difficulties . . . underline the necessity of pressing ahead with the United States resolutions here on a Suez and Palestine settlement. There seems to be some feet-dragging at the moment in New York on these two matters. I hope the United States delegation will get orders to counteract this attitude here.

We must take advantage of present opportunities without delay, or we will soon be in trouble again.

Pearson's fears were quickly confirmed by diplomatic intelligence reports from Washington that the Egyptians were seriously contemplating asking the Soviet Union to send volunteers. Referring to this attitude, the reports said: "There is deep apprehension here that the Anglo-French command will soon spring another surprise. The Egyptians are convinced that the primary goal of the British and French is to remove Nasser, and since this has not been accomplished they fully expect some move, however desperate, to achieve it."

Referring to the Egyptian statement that if hostilities resumed Egypt would "accept help from anyone," the reports continued: "This is not bluff. It is a faithful reflection of present Egyptian intention, and as such, pretty basic stuff. In my opinion, if a United Nations force does not quickly arrive in sufficient strength, a combination of morbid suspicion of Anglo-French intentions, and mounting restlessness in army circles, will make it increasingly hard for Nasser to exercise complete control."

The cause of this critical development was persistent Anglo-French-Israeli reluctance to withdraw until, according to their public statements, an "effective United Nations force" could take over on the ground. Rapid clearance of the canal, which Nasser had blocked by sinking forty-seven ships and destroying two bridges, and an early resumption of traffic were the official and most important reasons. There was, however, a third, more immediate, and strictly practical reason for remaining in Egypt as long as possible.

The same reason was one of the incentives which drove Nasser to quibble about the composition of the United Nations force and obstruct Canadian participation.

At stake was the bulk of Egypt's Communist bloc arms – tanks, guns, ammunition, spare parts, and workshops – sitting in the Sinai desert under Israeli guard.

The elated Israeli army had never seen so many modern arms in one place or such a vast network of underground storage dumps, huge concrete workshops, and fortifications. To remove so immense a quantity of arms from the various bases would require weeks, perhaps months.

The main site was east of the canal-crossing at El Kantara, and lay astraddle the tarmac road to Rafah and Gaza, where subsidiary dumps were situated. British and French forces occupied El Kantara and could provide a screen for the mass movement of arms from the Sinai into Israel via the Gaza Strip, the shortest and most accessible route. To cover so massive a transfer of arms by road convoys, which the United Nations might not have allowed, it was vital there should be no withdrawals – from the Canal Zone or the Gaza Strip.

Pineau has since said: "During the months of November and December we had to face at the United Nations pressures of every kind in order to force us to evacuate Port Said and the canal. We sought to gain time. We sought to gain time not because of procedure, such as phasing our withdrawal with United Nations arrival, but because time was needed to permit the Israelis to rid the Sinai of all arms deposited there, and to take them back to Israel. From our positions we were able to protect the operations of the Israelis, and this was well worth the trouble, even if it became increasingly hard to justify."

The two means of justifying continued occupation – canal clearance and effective United Nations takeover to avoid a vacuum in the area – may have been difficult for the British and the French to sustain. The Israelis, acknowledged by everyone to be aggressors, had no justification.

The Assembly, now in its eleventh regular session, with the various committees engaged upon normal business, was nevertheless dominated by the two major issues, the Middle East and Hungary, which had brought many foreign ministers to New York, among them Shepilov, Lloyd, Pineau, and Mrs. Golda Meir. When Ambassador Eban introduced Mrs. Meir to Pearson, she said: "There can be no question of a return to the status quo. We cannot allow the Egyptian army to reoccupy the Sinai and re-establish the bases and armed strength from which the threat of war first arose. We cannot allow the Egyptians to return to the Gaza Strip to reactivate their fedayeen bases. Nor can we permit them to reoccupy the islands controlling access to the Gulf of Aqaba. We have occupied them to open up Elath, our vital southern port."

Pearson replied that it was Canada's intention to try to achieve peaceful solutions in the Middle East, not to allow the whole region to remain in a state of political impasse. "Surely," he said, "the military defeat which Nasser has suffered will have lowered his prestige in the Middle East."

"Oh, he'll find some way to capitalize on it," Mrs. Meir replied. "He's already saying the British and French forced him to withdraw his army from the Sinai because he was being stabbed in the back. And he's looking for scapegoats. Our information is that he's already executed the chief of the Egyptian air force, and forty-three other senior officers are under arrest. The Soviet Union's backing is making him braver, and Syria too."

Pearson replied that it was not Canadian policy to bolster one side in the Palestine dispute at the expense of the other and said: "I don't believe anything we've said or done in New York will have that effect."

"Well, why are you pushing us so hard to withdraw?" asked Mrs. Meir. "There's nothing to guarantee that Nasser will allow Israeli shipping in the canal, nothing to guarantee an end of fedayeen raids, nothing to guarantee our use of the Gulf of Aqaba to open up Elath. And I warn you he will impose so many conditions on your United Nations force it will probably end up ineffective."

"We won't accept all his conditions," said Pearson.

"He's not even allowing your own troops in the force."

"He will," said Pearson.

He gave no indication then of the anxiety he actually felt. The canal was blocked along its entire length; the United Kingdom and Western Europe were either under gasoline rationing or about to be; NATO's military capability was declining as gasoline reserves dropped, the threat of eventual immobilisation of its air and ground forces in a prolonged emergency diminishing its credibility as a defensive alliance; an effective United Nations force was not yet formed, and there would be no withdrawals until it was; and the appearance of Soviet volunteers, reinforced by the sudden offers of more from Indonesia and Red China, was increasingly probable. The French in Port Fuad seemed unmolested, but the British in Port Said were suffering a heightening tempo of guerrilla attacks, and the forces all the way down the canal to El Kantara were being sniped at and raided. The cease-fire was becoming more precarious by the day.

The situation called for strong, unequivocal initiative and leadership from the United States, but the White House remained stubbornly silent.

III

BY Tuesday, November 20, the United Nations Emergency Force, as it was now officially designated, numbered seven hundred in Egypt, with three thousand-odd more on their way by sea and by air. There were more soldiers than equipment, and Burns, there to preside over the Anglo-French retreat, had to borrow jeeps and trucks from the British army, then paint them white and blue with paint borrowed from the French army.

Lloyd was accompanied to New York by Rear Admiral Peter Dawnay, Royal Navy, suitably attired in the guise of a diplomat, whose role appeared to be that of persuading the Secretariat that as the canal had to be cleared of blockships quickly, British and French salvage fleets could do it more efficiently than anyone else, mainly because they had the best equipment and the most know-how.

When President Eisenhower heard of this he remarked caustically: "That's nonsense. The Italians know more about salvage operations than anyone else. I know that from my days in North Africa."

Apart from their normal naval units, the British and French governments had contracted, prior to the attack, the services of the largest Dutch, German, and Danish commercial salvage firms, and had in fact collected a combined fleet of thirty-six of the most modern salvage vessels in Europe. But Nasser was adamant – the British and the French would have to withdraw before any canal clearance work could be started. Then it would have to be done by Egypt, with the assistance of the United Nations. During this deadlock, oil supplies to Western Europe dropped by nearly 30 per cent, and the position was bound to get worse. There was, however, no indication that the United States intended to implement emergency plans for maintaining a safe level of supplies to NATO countries.

The United States, trapped by its own rigid policy, could

not supply the United Kingdom and France until their troops were withdrawn from Egypt for fear of alienating the Arab countries. It would be inconsistent with its stand in the United Nations, and by not rushing to shore up Europe's dwindling oil reserve position the United Kingdom and France might be persuaded to take the hint and hurry up the evacuation of their troops from Egypt. There was little doubt that inaction resulted from a deliberate lack of high level policy to pursue the matter, a quite different attitude from that displayed in September, when Arthur Flemming, head of the Office of Defence Mobilisation, and others seemed to be chafing to rise to a challenge.

The consequences of American inaction on oil were the possibility of so weakening Western Europe economically that it would provide fertile soil for home-grown Communism, and even create the conditions which would encourage the Soviet Union to push westwards. In any event, it would have been plain bad business for the United States to write off something in the region of $20 billion in assistance programs over the previous ten years by refusing to act when the Suez "war" seemed all but over.

Commercial firms were beginning to act independently. European oil distributors were already buying in small quantities from Gulf Coast oil companies, and sales inquiries were being received by the Canadian and Venezuelan governments. Prices offered were, in general terms, 20 per cent higher than normal rates, and United States companies considered laying down special pipelines to meet the European demand.

Washington ignored this activity to the extent that when the Italian Ambassador approached the State Department for a declaration of United States intentions, Hoover told him: "The problem is a European one rather than one for individual nations to negotiate. We have not yet decided what action we should take and, though you may have seen press reports to the contrary, we have not disbanded the Middle East Emergency

Committee. We've merely decided not to reactivate it. We're certainly going to have to do something eventually, but I can't tell you at this time when that will be."

The Ambassador reported to Rome that he interpreted this as meaning "the United States is employing the device of inaction to place additional pressure on the governments of the United Kingdom and France to withdraw their troops from Egypt."

At approximately the same time, the Organisation for European Economic Co-operation in Paris reported that additional oil supplies available in North America could maintain Europe's needs at 75 per cent of the pre-crisis level. This would be sufficient to sustain most national economies until the canal was cleared and Middle East supplies resumed, but "failure to undertake such assistance may so affect the various balance of payments situations in Western Europe that widespread austerity and lowering of living standards will inevitably result."

Flemming, who had co-ordinated the work of the Middle East Emergency Committee and the Military Petroleum Advisory Board, had alternative plans ready, but it seemed as if nobody wanted them. King Saud complained about Washington's inaction as he had, for political reasons, announced that Saudi-Arabian oil would not be sold to Britain and France, the two biggest oil purchasers in Europe. He had felt safe because Aramco, aware of Flemming's plans, had assured him that arrangements would be made for Europe to continue purchasing oil through American companies so that he had no need to worry about diminishing royalties. Now it appeared that no arrangements were being made, that he would have to make do on something less than $1 million a day.

IV

SELWYN LLOYD, knowing that the attitude of official Washington toward the British and French Embassies was frosty, and actual contact confined to unavoidable formal functions, was nevertheless encouraged to expect a thaw by the paradoxical friendliness of President Eisenhower when the new British Ambassador to the United States, Sir Harold Caccia, had presented his credentials a few days earlier. According to the Ambassador, the President began by saying that he had just had to deal with an announcement made by the French that the British and French Prime Ministers were coming to Washington on an official visit. In his view it was quite the wrong moment to make any announcement. He had, therefore, instructed a statement to be issued that no firm plan had yet been fixed. Eisenhower felt that the first essential was to get the United Nations plan moving. Until the United Nations force began to arrive and actual withdrawals by the Israelis on the one side and the French and the British on the other had started, the whole position might be prejudiced by an overt getting together of the heads of government of the United States, France, and Britain. In particular, he feared that this might give the Russians an excuse for claiming that the three principal Western powers were ganging together to bulldoze something through the United Nations. On the basis of such a claim they might then take independent action to support the Arab states and carry an uncomfortable amount of world opinion with them.

What was important was that some United Nations troops should get in as quickly as possible and that this should be accompanied by some significant withdrawal. When Caccia asked whether the time for a visit by Prime Minister Eden would be right as soon as this process had begun, Eisenhower repeated that the first priority was to get the United Nations plan going as a means of forestalling any Russian initiative.

The President then asked Caccia to convey to Eden his warmest message of personal friendship, and to say that because he had "sharply differed from the Prime Minister on tactics on a single point" did not mean that his views about the "vital need for an Anglo-U.S. alliance" were changed in any way. There was only a divergence of method. He "shared the Prime Minister's views about Nasser," but he had felt from the beginning of the Suez crisis that this was "difficult ground to choose for bringing Nasser down." Rightly or wrongly, a great deal of world opinion did not share "our views" about Nasser's seizure of the canal. "He [the President] could not personally have been more friendly or indeed more forgiving," said Caccia.

Any illusions Lloyd may have harboured that Anglo-American relations might be improving at last were soon dispelled when, attempting to arrange a courtesy call on Eisenhower, he was told that the President would be too busy to see him. Pineau, who also tried to arrange a meeting at the White House, was rebuffed in similar terms.

Eden has since recorded that Lloyd met with "expressions of disapproval" in Washington, that "United States officials refused to co-operate at any level of policy-making" until the withdrawal from Port Said was completed. "One senior American authority," he wrote, "frankly declared that it was not possible at this stage for the Administration to talk with Her Majesty's Government."

The hostility Lloyd had feared he might have to face at the United Nations was accorded in full, devastating measure to Pineau and himself. Because of the alphabetical order of seating in the Assembly, the British and American delegations had to sit side by side, so close, in fact, that they were almost cheek by jowl, yet when Lloyd arrived in New York they were avoiding contact and conversation with each other in the Secretariat building, where they occupied adjoining offices, and in the elevators and corridors and other public places of the main United Nations building.

One of the senior American advisers, Samuel De Palma, confessed to Murray that "I personally feel it a tragedy that we should be under instructions not to talk to the United Kingdom delegation. We're just as concerned as you Canadians that this rift should be healed as quickly as possible."

In spite of these perversities, there were signs pointing toward improvement. Nehru announced that to quit the Commonwealth would be an angry gesture that could serve no useful purpose, the Prime Minister of Pakistan said his country was "in the Commonwealth," and even the Ceylonese spoke less of leaving. The Israelis were said to have withdrawn some troops from the Sinai, the French were known to have embarked troops for the return voyage to Algiers, and the British had announced their intention to begin withdrawing.

Eden, too weak to influence events any longer, consulted with his inner cabinet for the last time and acquiesced to the advice that he should take a rest. He flew to Jamaica, leaving Butler to act as caretaker of a litter of shattered loyalties and a disorganized, disillusioned government. As Britain's economic prospects were becoming increasingly serious, another appeal was made to Washington, and this time it was United States Secretary of the Treasury, George Humphrey, who telephoned London to tell Butler he could not help or support Britain financially until after an unequivocal undertaking to withdraw from Egypt by an early date had been given. Butler's reaction was to inform the House of Commons on November 22 that withdrawal was "about to begin," an undertaking that apparently did not go far enough for Washington.

At a time when circumstances required calm detachment to avoid reversing a perceptible cooling down of overheated emotionalism, Krishna Menon stirred the dying embers of the crisis – and the Anglo-American alliance threatened to collapse among the ashes.

CHAPTER FOURTEEN

War Vacated

THE resolution Krishna Menon circulated on November 22 with the support of twenty Afro-Asian states, including Egypt, castigated Britain, France, and Israel for failing to comply with earlier resolutions, called upon them to do so forthwith, and in effect accused them of bad faith in such harsh terms that the fragile structure of negotiations toward peace was endangered. It was becoming evident and accepted that withdrawal would have to be phased with the arrival of UNEF, but Krishna Menon would not tolerate anything less than public condemnation of their transgression.

Shocked by the implications, Selwyn Lloyd spoke to Pearson, who assured him: "We and our friends will not support it." He also spoke with Cabot Lodge in the corridors and was told "it would make all the difference" if he could announce that at least one British battalion had actually been withdrawn. That same afternoon, Acting Secretary of State Hoover informed Ambassador Caccia that the United States would "at least abstain." It seemed the United States would not break with Britain entirely.

Next day the announcement Lodge had asked for was

made: a British battalion was to leave Egypt immediately. The French government then disclosed that a third of its forces had already left; and the Israelis issued a statement saying that two battalions had been withdrawn from the Sinai. By noon on the 23rd the withdrawal had begun; the three governments were complying with the wishes of the United Nations.

Lodge suggested to Krishna Menon that his resolution was no longer necessary, and when the Indian Defence Minister replied that he had no intention of abandoning it, protracted argument resulted in the wording being changed from a hard expression of concern that there was failure to comply with the United Nations to "notes with regret that intervening forces remain in Egypt." Instead of stating the facts baldly, the effect was to imply non-compliance, a minor concession considering that the information upon which it was based had been overtaken by events.

On Friday afternoon, Pearson told the General Assembly: "The withdrawal, as we see it, has begun. Now, resolutions reiterating previous resolutions are, I think, useful and often necessary when the original resolution . . . has been treated with contempt and has been defied, as is the case with the United Nations resolution on Hungary. But when a resolution deals with a matter on which action has begun in compliance with a former resolution . . . then I do not think myself that it is . . . positively helpful. . . .

". . . This is not a time for recrimination among those who are anxious to find a solution. . . . It is not a time for recrimination between delegations . . . it is a time for restoration."

On Saturday morning the delegates were aware that a new crisis had arisen, one which could produce more alarming effects than the Anglo-French ultimatum three weeks before. There were some thirty speakers on the list, a considerable number of whom were hoping to postpone a vote until after the weekend, to give time for wiser counsels to prevail.

Lodge, the fourth speaker, talked for approximately fifteen minutes on such non-controversial subjects as the clearance of the canal, the necessity of giving the Secretary General authority to negotiate with salvage companies, and Hammarskjold's initial reports on the functions of UNEF. He reserved the last few seconds for Krishna Menon's Afro-Asian resolution, saying: "Although we do not think it necessary, the . . . resolution expresses sentiments which are in every respect consistent with our policy, and we shall therefore vote for it. . . ."

Now assured of United States support – there is a possibility that he had always been sure of it – Krishna Menon broke through the ripple of astonishment welling up around the hall to propose a snap vote. Paul-Henri Spaak, Belgium's Foreign Minister and a respected elder United Nations statesman, intervened hastily. "I am somewhat surprised . . . even somewhat disturbed," he said, "by the Indian representative's sudden proposal that we cut short the debate. Yesterday . . . a draft resolution . . . was circulated. This morning we received a revised text of that initial draft. We received the French translation . . . scarcely an hour ago. Consequently, my delegation has not had an opportunity to give the text careful and undisturbed attention. I should like to announce that I have just presented an amendment to it. There has not been time yet to circulate this amendment, therefore I shall read it out."

His amendment took note of the withdrawals that were taking place, noted that Britain, France, and Israel were complying with the United Nations resolutions, and called upon them to expedite matters in the same spirit with which the United Nations was acting on the swift creation of UNEF. It was a summons for action, which the Assembly wanted, but the impeachment was soft, delivered chidingly, without animosity.

Rushing angrily to the rostrum, Krishna Menon shouted insultingly: "There is no amendment before the Assembly. The representative of Belgium may have an amendment in his head, or it may be on its way upstairs, but the General Assembly is not seized of it."

He demanded an immediate vote, threatening to withdraw India's support for another resolution submitted by the advisory council members which gave Hammarskjold authority to continue with the building up of UNEF.

The Assembly was stunned. India was in a position to turn Afro-Asian opinion against UNEF and so stultify its growth. Krishna Menon was virtually forcing the delegations into making a choice – harsh condemnation of Britain, France, and Israel, or Asian rejection of UNEF.

It was after 1:00 P.M., and the President, anxious to avert an immediate showdown for which most of the delegates were unprepared, adjourned the Assembly for lunch. The respite was too brief for corridor diplomacy to affect the outcome. After lunch, Lloyd rose, relaxed and calm, and referred to the need for rapid clearance of the canal, to the facts that the Anglo-French salvage fleet was already at work unblocking Port Said, that the Secretary General intended contracting a United Nations salvage fleet from private firms in countries outside the conflict, and that the United Nations fleet would not begin operations until after the withdrawal.

"The United Kingdom," he said, "has firmly given its full support to the efforts of the Secretary General to organize a salvage team under the auspices of the U.N. It has declared its willingness to release any salvage ships now under charter to the British Admiralty or to the British government. We shall do everything within our power to help, and we welcome the assumption of the United Nations responsibility. . . . We are ready to lend our resources to work in any way wanted in this task. . . ."

This persuasive and reasoned speech convinced many delegates that despite their own instructions on voting, there would be a swing towards the Spaak amendment. Spaak, in fact, made a long, brilliant appeal for a lessening of passions and an expression of faith in the fundamental sincerity of the French and British undertakings. The struggle against the Krishna Menon resolution was pressed hard throughout the afternoon until 5:00 P.M. when the votes were taken.

The United States abstained on Spaak's amendment while other NATO countries which were also members of the United Nations, including Canada, voted for it. The United States voted with the Afro-Asian and Communist blocs for the Menon resolution in its entirety, though most of its Western European allies and Canada abstained.

It was, for Britain in particular, tantamount to being openly accused by the United States of bad faith and of deliberate deception of the Assembly. In the opinion of an Australian representative, "the United States administration has now told the world that it no longer trusts Britain and France."

The condition Lodge had laid down as being necessary to "make all the difference" had been met and had made no difference at all. Lodge gave no apology, avoided Lloyd and Pineau, and excused himself to other delegations by saying that Krishna Menon's tactics had made it impossible to abstain without being misunderstood. Most of the delegations discounted this on the ground that Canada had abstained without suffering loss of political independence or prestige among the Asians.

Robert Murphy has since commented on Lodge's "curious acquiescence" when it came to dealing with Menon's rough tactics. "Menon seemed at times to hypnotize Lodge," he said. "It was fantastic to reject the Belgian amendment."

In Washington, Hoover sent his apologies to the British Ambassador through Robert Murphy, who had the unenviable assignment of calling Caccia to explain that the United States was a "prisoner of our own policy."

On Monday, the Australian Foreign Minister, R. G. Casey, reflected in the Assembly the widespread alarm and despondency caused by the American actions. Referring to relations between the United States and the United Kingdom, he said: "Those relations do not affect only those two countries; they are of vital importance to every non-Communist country in the world. . . . If United Kingdom–United States relations are less than 100 per cent good, practically every one of us is adversely affected, and the peace and stability of the world are menaced. . . . We in Australia say to our mother country, the United Kingdom, and to our great friends in the United States: Put first things first and get together in confident relations of mutual trust for the good of the whole democratic world."

Few of his listeners could recall a time when relations between the United States and Britain had been so bad.

Though many attempts were made to bring Lodge and Lloyd together during the next three days, they proved futile; and the British Foreign Secretary left New York cold and angry, while Lodge departed for Washington in answer to a summons from the White House.

The United Nations had never seen the British representatives so depressed and bitter. In inter-delegation conversations they referred scathingly to what they described as the evident wish of the United States to play a role on colonial issues uninhibited by the Western alliance. They were alarmed at the prospect of the Afro-Asians, now unrestrained by the United States, adopting tactics on the problems of Algeria and Cyprus which would make it difficult for Britain and France to remain members of the United Nations. They questioned, too, whether the United States actually wanted Britain and France to remain Great Powers in any sense.

The French delegation made no attempt to hide that they considered the débâcle had been contrived not by Lodge alone, but with the connivance of Senator William Knowland, an observer with the United States delegation. William Rountree, the recently appointed chief of the State Department's Near East Section, was also, in the French view, at least partly responsible.

According to a senior British official, relations between Lloyd and Lodge had become "icy." It seemed to the British delegation that the United States was prepared to ruthlessly "alienate its true friends in order to curry favour with peripheral countries who will never be their friends."

The American delegation were also worried, one adviser admitting that Lodge had received instructions from Washington to abstain on the Krishna Menon resolution, but had been unable to comply because he had already committed the United States in support of it. He deplored "the coolness between Mr. Lodge and Mr. Lloyd" and added that Dulles had decided to attend the NATO Council meeting being held in Paris in December in an attempt to repair the damage.

Pearson responded to what he considered to be a crisis of confidence between Western Europe and the United States by urging in both London and Washington that, instead of indulging in recrimination and constant "digging in the past," the United States and Britain should concert their efforts to mend the rift in the interests of Western unity and security. He was concerned that the NATO Council would become so divided and undermined by suspicions that the alliance might eventually collapse.

The State Department was evidently just as concerned, and on Wednesday, the 28th, Hoover called Ambassador Heeney with a request for Canada's help in healing the breach. The Ambassador said that Canada, and Pearson in particular, was gravely worried, that the United States vote for the Afro-Asian resolution and failure to support the Spaak amendment had come as a severe shock to the Canadian government. The "personal coolness between Lloyd and Lodge" was highly unsatisfactory, and he was instructed by Pearson to say that Canada hoped the United States would now concentrate on enabling the United Kingdom to "work their passage back."

In comments on the Lloyd-Lodge relationship, Hoover explained that he realized how difficult it had been for Lloyd,

in view of the political situation in London and the isolation
of the British delegation at the United Nations. However, he
said, Lloyd had made some sharp, personal criticisms of Lodge
in briefings of Commonwealth correspondents in New York
which had been reflected in a mounting volume of anti-
American press publicity in the United Kingdom. Hoover had
himself deliberately refrained from contact with the American
press during recent days because it was his purpose to "keep
down tempers." Hoover confessed that the President, as well
as Dulles, was deeply upset, that few things since he had first
taken office four years ago had hit him so hard as "this public
deterioration in relations between Britain and the United
States."

II

BRITAIN was moving swiftly toward an acute political up-
heaval. Divided, isolated, and abused as the island was, the
decision of the United States to associate openly with those
ranged against it carried the hostility of an ally beyond acceptable limits. Lodge's rejection of the appeals for reason made
by Spaak and Pearson exerted a unifying force that cut across
party political loyalties to produce an emotional upsurge of
latent anti-Americanism rooted in national frustration.

The government, feeling it must soon submit to world
opinion by withdrawing quickly from Egypt, enjoyed too late
the wide support for the objectives it had used force to achieve
and which it had lacked since the beginning of the crisis.

The Labour Party in the House of Commons was re-
strained, and more than a hundred Conservative members of
Parliament tabled a motion bitterly assailing the United States.
The Cabinet, resigned to withdrawal, and in search of a means

to put failure in the guise of victory, could no longer count upon a Parliamentary majority. Ahead was the bleak prospect of defeat and downfall, leaving the country without a government, and an army suspended upon the shores of Egypt.

Hoover aggravated their distress by replying to the Conservative motion with a telephone call to Ambassador Aldrich in London, instructing him to protest to the Foreign Office on the ground that the revolt within the government's own ranks was being construed in Washington as a direct attack on the President. The United States Administration, he said, was forced to conclude that the motion had been organized with the connivance of the British Cabinet.

France, shocked by what appeared to be American disregard for the self-evident fact that French troops were leaving Egypt – there were press accounts of the men embarking at Port Said, and it was known that experienced troops were urgently needed in Algeria – returned to the immediate postwar mood of intense anti-Americanism which had never been completely dissipated.

Mollet gave an angry speech in Paris in which he expressed in vigorous terms the government's regret that allied military action had ceased before the main objectives had been achieved – occupation of the Canal Zone and the removal of Nasser.

American rejection of the Spaak amendment also irritated Belgium, the Netherlands, Luxembourg, and Portugal – NATO allies who interpreted it as signifying a lack of confidence in Western Europe.

Many consequences began to flow from the two votes cast by Cabot Lodge on November 24, not the least of which was an almost unanimous verdict of the Western alliance – the United States and Canada excepted – that they heralded the ultimate end of NATO.

The Foreign Office and the Quai d'Orsay, reflecting the attitudes of Lloyd and Pineau, let it be widely known that in their judgement, as one highly placed official described it at a lunch in Paris, "an important factor in the American attitude is the President's personal pique at not being consulted prior to the Anglo-French ultimatum." He said it was official Anglo-French opinion that United States foreign policy was, due to the absence of Dulles, largely in the hands of Lodge in New York. And a diplomat who was present commented to his government that the British and French "seem to find themselves in the strange situation of hoping for the return of Dulles to the State Department, where his presence used to cause them such anxiety."

The ripples reached Ottawa, where the Liberal government came under an attack of renewed ferocity from the Opposition for not having backed Britain and France from the outset. Pearson, involved by then in delicate negotiations to bridge the chasm between London and Washington, was severely criticised by elements within his own party for placing them in what appeared to be a vulnerable position politically. He gave it scant attention, preoccupying himself with the most dangerous crisis that had arisen since the advent of the "cold war" – complete Western disunity at a time when the Communist world was rapidly restoring unity within itself.

The crucial factor was the Anglo-American stand-off.

Faced with a new alliance of the United States with the Afro-Asians, Britain and France were unable to move forward; their governments were unable to move backward because of the impact on domestic politics. Faced with Anglo-French immobility, the United States could move ahead no faster than the United Nations which, in turn, could move no faster than the perpetual suspicions of the Egyptians would allow. Canada, uncommitted, unhindered, and as yet uncompromised, could manœuvre. Pearson contrived, in the days of chaotic aftermath, to produce a "four act play," as the United Nations named it, to break the deadlock, and inspire a resumption of dialogue between the major Western powers. In diplomatic terms it was a delineative *tour de force* which rivalled his parental responsibility for the international police force. As that had served to prevent the spread of war, so his response to this new danger freed the Western alliance from its deadlocked state.

The acts were these:

ACT ONE

Hammarskjold should announce the actual strength of UNEF *to show that it could perform its functions effectively.*

ACT TWO

Lloyd should follow soon afterwards with an announcement that the British government, now convinced of UNEF's *competence, would withdraw its troops from Egypt by December 14 if possible. Lloyd would also hint that the talks between himself, Pineau, and Fawzi in the Secretary General's offices during October, which had produced the six principles for a canal settlement, would be resumed from the point where they had been left off prior to hostilities.*

ACT THREE

Nasser should follow in one or two days with an announcement that in view of Lloyd's statement of British intentions, Egypt would agree to co-operate immediately on clearance of the canal, without waiting for the last allied soldier to leave.

ACT FOUR

The Secretary General would report to the General Assembly that work on clearing the canal could begin by December 15, the day after the withdrawal.

Hammarskjold, his principal colleague in the forming of UNEF, was brought into close association with him once again for the staging of the "play." While Pearson urged it upon London and Washington through Canadian diplomatic representatives, Hammarskjold negotiated directly in New York with Fawzi, Sir Pierson Dixon, and James Wadsworth, deputy head of the United States delegation, who had taken over for the period of Lodge's absence in Washington.

During these discussions Dixon asked Hammarskjold to give an assurance that he would be free to use Anglo-French resources for the clearing operation. Hammarskjold asked Fawzi for the Egyptian view on Anglo-French salvage crews remaining in the canal after the withdrawal, and was told he would be "free to use any equipment he considered necessary," but the question of crews remained open. Fairly, it seemed, the Egyptian government was willing to give Hammarskjold wide latitude for a successful operation, providing non-Egyptian forces withdrew. Dixon appeared satisfied.

The British Cabinet seized upon the proposals, as they offered an opportunity of placating the Conservative back-benchers with a plausible pretext for evacuating Egypt; Washington seized upon them because they offered an opportunity to use the British withdrawal as the basis for realigning Western policies. Egypt had to accept them as they conformed with the United Nations resolutions it had accepted. Lloyd undertook to persuade France to agree, and arranged to discuss the timing of the withdrawal with Pineau.

By noon on Wednesday, the 28th, the "play" was ready for production, and Hammarskjold performed Act One the same evening by announcing that UNEF would consist of six thousand men within two weeks. Next day in London, Selwyn Lloyd informed the House of Commons that the government was satisfied with the competence and projected strength of UNEF, and would accordingly arrange the withdrawal of British forces as quickly as possible. This was an interim statement, he said, which would be expanded on Monday, December 3, after he had spoken with the Foreign Minister of France.

There was some anxiety in New York and Washington as this tended to throw the "play" off schedule, postponing Nasser's appearance until after the weekend and stretching the links of the interlocking acts to a dangerous degree. Lloyd, however, completed his role as promised on the Monday, Pineau and Mollet made similar announcements in Paris, and the subsequent acts were performed with minor delays and only one major alteration – Nasser refused to commit himself to the six principles as the basis for resumed three-power discussions under the Secretary General's auspices.

Lloyd's part was the most difficult. Unlike Mollet and Pineau, who enjoyed the popular support of the French Parliament and their country, he had known that whatever the methods used to extricate British forces from Egypt it would be his duty to confront a hostile House of Commons. His attempts to present the military operation as a success were contrived from flimsy material – UNEF, a turning point in United Nations history, would not have been possible without the Anglo-French action, and a Communist plot to ferment war in the Middle East had been exposed – and, not surprisingly, Conservatives as well as Socialists were subdued and shocked by such specious reasoning. The Communist arms build-up in Egypt and Syria had been known before the Suez crisis, and if its formidable extent had been previously obscured it was the Israeli attack, rather than the Anglo-French, which had revealed the truth. And the creation of a United Nations police force was hardly, by any stretching of the imagination, the work of Britain and France. Nor could Lloyd rationally claim that the officially expressed aims – safety of traffic through the canal and the security of oil supplies – had been accomplished. The canal was blocked, and Britain's oil supplies had already dropped by nearly 40 per cent.

Aneurin Bevan, his customary vitriolic wit replaced by gentle irony, replied to the Foreign Secretary for the Socialists. "We sympathise with the right honourable and learned gentleman in trying to sound the bugle of advance to cover his retreat," he said. ". . . I feel I would be a bully if I proceeded any further."

Sir Ian Horobin, one of the Conservative "Suez Group," asked without humour: "Can my right honourable and learned friend assure us, now that we have agreed to withdraw our army from Egypt with no effective safeguards for our vital interests, that the necessary American consent will be forthcoming, in due course, to bringing back our Prime Minister from Jamaica?"

Then another member urged Lloyd to "consider putting forward the Prime Minister's name for the Nobel Peace Prize on the grounds that he has given a conclusive demonstration that aggression does not pay."

Yet three days later when the House divided on a Socialist motion criticising the government, the Conservative majority remained intact, but only after Cabinet ministers had privately assured backbenchers that there would be no ignominious retreat. The government proceeded then to refute Selwyn Lloyd's undertakings to the General Assembly.

On December 7, Dixon called on Hammarskjold to inform him that "the Anglo-French salvage fleet, with its administrative support, is a single unit which must either stay as a whole or go as a whole." This position was confirmed by a letter from Butler the next day and Hammarskjold was confronted by a serious qualification of Lloyd's promise to the Assembly on November 24, one which compromised his own verbal agreement with Fawzi that he should use whatever equipment was necessary while leaving open the question of British and French crews until after the withdrawal of troops.

Butler aggravated the difficulties on December 13 by announcing that no British salvage ships would serve under the United Nations flag without British crews. There were six special heavy-lift ships in the Anglo-French fleet which the United Nations engineers needed to drag sunken vessels to the sides of the canal, and Hammarskjold planned to man them with Dutch, Swedish, and Norwegian crews. But Lloyd's unconditional offer of British resources was now hedged around with conditions, and as the troops had not yet withdrawn, there was no chance of the Egyptians allowing Royal Navy crews to operate down the entire length of the canal. The British government was not only reneging on Lloyd's solemn assurances, but seemed to be obstructing the very process of rapid clearance which it was also constantly demanding.

Lloyd himself would not have been party to this, as he knew better than some of his Cabinet colleagues perhaps of the efforts being made in New York to reconcile the host of enmities that had arisen in the aftermath of the military action. Nevertheless, he was bearing the brunt of the accusations and recriminations then flowing in full spate. More cruel thrusts were ahead for him to endure.

The meeting of Lloyd and Pineau with Dulles at the NATO conference in Paris the next day could hardly have been more ill-timed. It was December 14, the day on which, according to the agreed "play," British and French troops should have withdrawn from Egypt. They were still there, and their presence was preventing the United Nations canal clearance operations. Furthermore, British insistence on the retention of British crews was depriving the United Nations salvage fleet of equipment it needed and could not get elsewhere. Dulles, who had intended originally to use the occasion for making peace with his allies, was naturally angry already at what he considered to be yet another instance of Anglo-French duplicity, and further explanations by the English and French that the withdrawal was being delayed because of concern for the safety of their nationals living in Egypt merely exasperated him. In Britain's case the majority of these nationals were Cypriots, and Cyprus was in revolt against the British. Understandably, he suspected this explanation to be one more pretext for hanging on in the Canal Zone against the will of the United Nations, evidence enough for him of a careless disregard for the consequences in terms of Western unity. He regarded Lloyd's statements at the United Nations and in the House of Commons as placing Britain under an obligation to withdraw, an obligation from which the United States at any rate could not release the British government. To do so, he said, would constitute "in some sense a breach of faith on the part of the administration with Congress and United States public opinion." He added that the Anglo-French action had caused revulsion throughout the United States.

Eden said in his memoirs: "This was strong language and at variance with the reports of our own representatives, who considered that the sharp feelings displayed at the time in Washington had not really represented American public opinion."

The British Ambassador in Washington was then a comparatively recent arrival and a hardly more competent judge of American opinion than Dulles, though it was equally true that Ambassador Aldrich and High Commissioner Norman Robertson never really believed that Eden's resort to force represented British opinion.

The "play" succeeded in restoring contact between London and Washington, and Washington and Paris; it also set in motion the protracted process of creating the conditions in which friendly relations would be encouraged. But after painful examination of the damage, senior officials on both sides of the Atlantic, in Ottawa as well as Washington, in Paris as well as London, felt that the re-establishment of mutual trust and confidence might take a generation to achieve.

The British and French commanders handed over Port Said to General Burns on December 22, and the last Allied troops sailed away from Egypt. UNEF, some four thousand strong, including Canadian technical units, was established on the canal facing Israeli positions in the Sinai. In compliance with United Nations resolutions of six and seven weeks earlier, no members of the British or French armed forces remained, not even salvage crews. The British government, more so than the French, had forfeited a considerable measure of international sympathy and understanding by its obstructive tactics, which served to delay clearance of the canal and resumption of oil supplies to Western Europe.

On the other hand, the United States held to its promises of help once the withdrawal had taken place. Arthur Flemming's Middle East Emergency Committee was reactivated in Washington to begin the formidable task of redistributing North American oil supplies and rerouting Middle East oil by tankers round the Cape. Britain was offered an immediate United States loan, and the International Monetary Fund released $1,300 million in two instalments to bolster the British economy.

Eden returned to London from Jamaica in mid-December, rested but still physically weakened. One afternoon in New York just before Christmas, the telephone rang in the Secretary General's office. Shortly afterwards, Hammarskjold conveyed the gist of the conversation to a close friend among the permanent representatives to the United Nations, who was present in his office at the time. It went as follows:

Hammarskjold	Who? Yes, put him on.
Eden	This is Eden here. I am calling from my office now with the First Sea Lord of the Admiralty, Admiral Mountbatten, and we were discussing this ship of ours down in Port Said.
Hammarskjold	What ship?
Eden	You know, that salvage ship. It is a very good ship. There is only one problem. Mountbatten says it has got a gun on board.
Hammarskjold	Then they can't use it, because they are not permitted to take any ships with guns through the canal. Because of the cease-fire there can be no weapons.

Eden	Yes, I understand that. But you see this is one of your guns.
Hammarskjold	I beg your pardon. A U.N. gun?
Eden	I don't mean the U.N. I mean a Swedish gun. It is a Bofors gun.
Hammarskjold *(visibly astonished)*	I see. But after all, I am sorry, the ship cannot be used even if it is a neutral gun.
Eden *(his voice fading)*	I thought it would be of use to you, this ship. As I said, Mountbatten and I were talking this over now. I felt I should give you a ring and tell you about this. Would you please consider it . . . ?
Hammarskjold	It is difficult for me to consider.
Eden	Well, goodbye.

After further attempts to see the President in Washington had failed, Eden resigned early in the New Year, and was replaced as Prime Minister by Harold Macmillan. Eisenhower reacted by breaking the White House silence to arrange an Anglo-American summit meeting in Bermuda during March, and the process of mending the alliance, which Pearson had started in November, proceeded smoothly toward a successful conclusion.

Then once again Pearson faced the dismaying prospect of UNEF's imminent collapse.

III

ISRAEL was stuck firmly and obstinately in the Gaza Strip, and at Sharm el-Sheikh, at the entrance of the Gulf of Aqaba, refusing to withdraw until its ships were guaranteed freedom of passage to and from the port of Elath, and given assurances that fedayeen raids would not be resumed. No one, least of all the Arab states, was prepared to give specific guarantees, and another deadlock appeared inevitable. UNEF could not move forward to the Israeli-Egyptian demarcation lines where it was supposed to be. There was an ever-present danger of Israeli-Egyptian hostilities recurring, an event that would require contributing countries to risk being involved in a spreading war or to pull out their contingents from UNEF.

Mrs. Golda Meir and Abba Eban travelled constantly between New York and Washington, resisting blandishments, threats, promises, and appeals. Hammarskjold pointed out that Israel's failure to comply with United Nations wishes was resulting in a steady loss of sympathy and prestige; Eisenhower announced that the future of the United Nations hinged upon its ability to persuade the Israelis to return behind their own borders; Egypt threatened to obstruct the clearance of the canal and so set back a resumption of the flow of oil to Western Europe; and Syria denied the Iraq Petroleum Company permission to repair its pipelines until Israel had withdrawn.

In a ninety-minute interview in Washington, Dulles told Mrs. Meir that Israel's only hope for the future lay in better relations with the Arabs, and in his opinion, no efforts had been made in this direction for some years. There was little rapport between the Israeli government and the United States administration, he said, mainly because nobody knew what Israel's long-term objectives were. A more sympathetic attitude would be given to Israel's immediate problems, he added, if the United States had a clearer conception of where Israel thought it was heading.

Only France remained a staunch friend. On each occasion a massive majority of the General Assembly condemned Israel, France was the one nation that voted against the motion. For three months France and Israel were so often a minority of two that even their most implacable enemies began to express admiration for France's refusal to be separated from its ally.

Critically aggravating the withdrawal issue at this stage was the Israeli belief that Hammarskjold was negotiating with a pro-Arab bias, that he delineated his responsibilities too legalistically and narrowly. There seems little doubt that the aloof, austere Secretary General probably preferred dealing with Fawzi, whom he found more flexible than the obdurate Mrs. Meir, and that he interpreted the Assembly mandate to mean, in its strictest sense, that there should be an over-all return to the status quo ante and no infringement of Egyptian sovereignty by the United Nations. He was too personally dedicated to United Nations ideals, too rigidly ethical in the conduct of his duties, and too meticulous in adherence to the authority conferred upon him by Assembly instructions, to be guilty of bias. Since the inception of UNEF he had been solely responsible for negotiating in the tense conditions of a war to produce what the majority of the Assembly demanded – cease-fire and withdrawal. He had not, at any time, worked against France or Britain; but on the contrary he had earned spontaneous expressions of appreciation from their representatives who regarded his handling of the delicate negotiations with the suspicious, affronted Egyptians as nothing short of magnificent.

Israeli leaders were alone in their distrust of his methods of implementing his instructions, an attitude that hardly served to reassure those who were trying to ease Hammarskjold's difficulties.

On February 11, while Eban was in Washington seeking a United States commitment to guarantee the freedom of the Gulf of Aqaba, Mrs. Meir called upon Pearson in New York for a disturbing interview. After implying that the Secretary General was more concerned with Arab than with Israeli sensibilities, she said: "We have made it very clear to the Secretary General that our ships will never again be turned back at the Straits of Tiran by Egyptian guns. We will shoot our way through."

Mrs. Meir added that Israel would not tolerate an Egyptian return to the Gaza Strip from where fedayeen raiding could be reorganised and once more launched to spread terror among the border villages. If Israel had to withdraw its forces, it would be on condition that the Strip was demilitarised or placed under United Nations administration.

When Pearson warned that such intransigence invited economic sanctions, she expressed surprise at the strength of the pressure being exerted on Israel. Acknowledging that the military operations had produced a psychological reaction, she mentioned there had been other "aggressions," notably in Kashmir and Hungary, which had not stimulated the same reaction in the General Assembly.

"We have considered this question of sanctions carefully," she said. "And we have decided we cannot give in to such a threat. Sanctions will cause terrible hardship among us, but we cannot forgo our right to self-defence. Whatever happens we shall not give in. But the United Nations should understand that if we are driven too far, made to suffer too much, we may in desperation be forced to fight again."

The warning was too unmistakable to be ignored. Pearson attempted to persuade her that Israel should place more reliance on the arrangements the United Nations might be able to make along the demarcation lines, in the Gaza Strip and at Sharm el-Sheikh, to prevent raids and open up the Gulf of Aqaba. If it attempted to remain in Gaza in defiance of the United Nations, he said, Israel would have to expect increasing criticism from the Assembly and a deepening of Arab bitterness and hatred. He felt, when Mrs. Meir had left, that his arguments had made little impression upon her.

The Gaza Strip lies along the Mediterranean coast like the blade of a scimitar with the hilt in Egypt to the south and the point thrusting northwards into Israel. Since the creation of the State of Israel, it had been an Egyptian-administered no-man's-land, some thirty miles long and up to five miles wide in places, normally supporting an indigenous population of some sixty thousand Arabs. When the demarcation lines were drawn, a quarter of a million Palestinian Arabs, uprooted from homes inside Israeli boundaries, were gathered into the Gaza Strip and placed under the supervision of the United Nations Relief and Works Agency.

Egypt administered the area, placing it under military governorship and fortifying it as the forward defence lines of the Egyptian Army. When the Israelis drove out the Egyptians they introduced a civil administration with the obvious intent of placing the Strip under permanent Israeli suzerainty, in direct opposition to the whole thrust of the UNEF intervention, which was aimed at persuading the Israelis to retire behind their borders so that the status quo ante could be restored. Confronted by immense pressures, mainly from the United States, Israel was making United Nations occupation and administration a fall-back position, an acceptable alternative to the return of Egyptian military rule.

When Pearson discussed the substance of the interview with Hammarskjold, they re-examined the proposed functions of UNEF, which was, in terms of United Nations resolutions, an *ad hoc* force created for a specific emergency and for the temporary purpose of supervising the cease-fire and withdrawal. Once Israeli troops were to leave Egyptian territory, Pearson's original concept of UNEF peacekeeping patrols along the demarcation lines while a political settlement was being negotiated between Israel and its Arab neighbours, was their justification for existence.

"We should be able to get UNEF into the Gaza Strip and Sharm el-Sheikh," said Pearson.

"Gaza, yes," replied Hammarskjold, "because we have to patrol the border. But not Sharm el-Sheikh. That's Egyptian territory and we have to accept the *status juris*. UNEF follows the Israelis out, and the Egyptians move in behind us."

"Then the Israelis won't go."

"They have to go back," said Hammarskjold. "UNEF has no other function than that of acting as a buffer between the two armies while the heat cools down and we look for a settlement."

As they talked, the idea developed that Pearson should sound other delegations for a reaction to the concept of a United Nations administration of the Gaza Strip. Within a few days the corridors were alive with open speculation as to whether such a proposal was feasible, and what form so unique an administration should take. Delegates began to think in terms of a United Nations governor, United Nations courts and judges, a United Nations civil police force, and United Nations passport control. Such an administration would combine with UNRWA and UNEF to form an effective United Nations enclave in the Middle East.

On closer scrutiny it proved an impracticable scheme – where would the United Nations find judges, for instance, capable of impartially dealing with a predominantly Arab refugee population – but it provided evidence of sufficient Assembly interest to encourage Hammarskjold and Pearson to use this extravagant reaction as a means for breaking the deadlock with Israel.

At Pearson's suggestion, Hammarskjold agreed to take up privately with Fawzi the proposal that the Gaza Strip provided ideal locations for UNEF command headquarters and for the bases of operational units responsible for patrolling the demarcation lines. However, as the area was desperately overcrowded, there would be barely enough space for both the Egyptian army and UNEF, and under such conditions the risk of irritating incidents taking place between them would be considerably increased. If the Egyptian administration returned and UNEF set up bases inside the Strip, there would be no necessity for the Egyptian army to establish its forward positions farther north than a line south of the Strip from El Arish eastwards across the Sinai. Instead of being formalised by written agreement, such an arrangement should be allowed to develop into a *de facto* situation as the most practical means for UNEF to establish itself adjacent to the demarcation lines.

In less clouded circumstances Hammarskjold would have doubted his right, as Secretary General, to commit the United Nations to so loose an arrangement, but there was an understanding that where no explicit directives were contained in Assembly resolutions he could act in accordance with his own interpretation of a general Assembly attitude. The basis for such action, however, had to be in the record, in order to be supported by evidence that it clearly reflected at least some body of expressed opinion.

He was sufficiently confident that he added to Pearson's formula the proposal that they should include an arrangement for Sharm el-Sheikh, one that would enable UNEF to move into the area to maintain "peace and order" after the Israeli withdrawal.

The State Department, informed of their "conspiracy," became an enthusiastic partner by undertaking to persuade the Israelis to withdraw without clear-cut promises, and to rely upon the good faith of the United Nations and the United States.

Accordingly, Eisenhower announced obliquely on February 20: "We should not assume that if Israel withdraws, Egypt will prevent Israeli shipping from using the Suez Canal or the Gulf of Aqaba." This statement was drafted by Dulles to conform with the understanding that Hammarskjold was reaching with Fawzi at the same time.

As Hammarskjold enjoyed close relations with Fawzi, he was confident of Egyptian co-operation. On the issue of free passage through the Gulf of Aqaba, Fawzi had repeatedly claimed that Egypt's actions were under constant appraisal by other Arab states, which would consider any concessions to Israel as a betrayal of the Arab cause. Israel made informal accommodation difficult by its tendency to complain too often, too loudly. "If they would keep their mouths shut, we would keep our eyes shut," he said.

The first stage of the plan was put into effect on February 22 when Hammarskjold made a brief, three-minute report to the Assembly, each word meticulously chosen in collaboration with Pearson and carefully explained privately to Fawzi and Mrs. Meir.

"The Secretary General states with confidence," he said, "that it is the desire of the government of Egypt that the takeover of Gaza from the military and civilian control of Israel (by UNEF) will be orderly and safe. . . . It may be added with equal confidence that the government of Egypt, recognising the special problems and complexities of the Gaza area and the long-standing major responsibility of the United Nations there for the assistance of the Arab refugees . . . has the willingness and readiness to make special and helpful arrangements with the United Nations . . . for the use of UNEF in the area, which should ensure its deployment on the armistice line at the Gaza Strip and the effective interposition of the Force between the armed forces of Egypt and Israel.

"Similarly, the assistance of the United Nations and its appropriate auxiliary bodies would be enrolled toward putting a definite end to all incursions and raids across the border from either side.

"Furthermore . . . such other arrangements with the United Nations may be made as will contribute toward safeguarding life and property in the area by providing efficient and effective police protection; as will guarantee good civilian administration; as will ensure maximum assistance to the United Nations refugee program; and as will protect and foster the economic development of the territory and its people."

Hammerskjold was declaring a United Nations intention of taking over the area, though his mandate really called for border patrols aimed at preventing raids across it. He implied Egyptian consent, but made no specific mention of it, leaving the Egyptian government uncommitted. It was unlikely that the more vehement of the Afro-Asian bloc and the Communists would permit such intentions to be translated into fact, since they entailed a supposed usurping of Egyptian sovereignty. But Hammarskjold, Pearson, and Dulles would be content if UNEF was permitted in, and the Egyptian Army kept out.

Pearson delivered his studiously rehearsed development of the Secretary General's proposals on the 26th in a speech which explained:

"The military aspects of this withdrawal are relatively uncomplicated. Immediately the Israeli forces leave, UNEF should enter. As the Armistice Agreement limits, in any event, Egyptian forces to 'defensive' elements only, and as UNEF will be already deployed along the armistice line, and as the Strip is is so very narrow itself, the government of Egypt should not in our view envisage the return of its own armed forces to this area. . . . So far as the civil administration is concerned . . . there has already been more than enough murder in the Gaza Strip, and the United Nations cannot be indirectly responsible for more. . . . Therefore, provision must surely be made for a peaceful transition from the administration of Israel to something no less strong and effective. . . . This is all the more desirable because after Israel's withdrawal the United Nations should, in our view and by arrangement with Egypt, accept responsibility to the maximum possible extent for establishing and maintaining civil administration in the territory. The United Nations Relief and Work Agency is already there."

He came, as expected, under immediate attack from Arab representatives. The Syrian spokesman said: "Today the representative of Canada told us that he took an objective stand . . . and he ended by saying his suggestions were admittedly a compromise. Was that intended to set our minds at ease . . . or was it designed to pave the way for their acceptance, although in substance they do not differ in the least from Israel and Zionist proposals . . . ? The representative of Canada is trying to show various faces in various directions. . . . Canada is definitely supporting the Zionist policy."

The Iraqi representative said: "Mr. Pearson has two weaknesses in all his thinking on Palestine. . . . The first is that he has never been to the Middle East nor has he had, as far as I know, any serious discussions with Middle Eastern statesmen . . . his knowledge is only on the side of Zionist propaganda. But ignorance is not the only cause, and we come now to the other one. Mr. Pearson thinks that compromise and expediency are the road to peace in international affairs. . . . A man with these – shall I call them – vacuums in his knowledge and experience cannot be a fair judge or mediator in the Palestine issue."

Then it was the Jordanian representative's turn to assail him, saying: "Mr. Pearson, who was quite active in 1947 in securing support for the partition of Palestine, is trying now, in 1957, to take the Gaza Strip away from its Arab administration and to put it under an international régime. He is not only trying to make a major change in the status of the territory . . . but also to widen the functions and tasks of UNEF in such a way that it will become able to solve territorial problems. . . . The record of the General Assembly . . . proves beyond doubt that nothing of his proposals was incorporated into the resolutions."

Friendly delegates were prepared in advance to speak in support of his proposals: Britain, France, the United States, the Philippines, Australia, New Zealand, and others. By the end of the day the spread of support for UNEF's presence in the Gaza Strip in strength, and the Egyptian army's exclusion from it in strength, was far wider throughout the Assembly than the opposition to it. By the same token, there was a considerable opinion on record that UNEF should maintain peace and order in Sharm el-Sheikh. Hammarskjold now had an Assembly basis, rather than a mandate, for instructing General Burns to follow the Israeli withdrawal by establishing UNEF in both areas.

At 3:00 P.M., March 1, Mrs. Meir told the General Assembly that, in view of certain "expectations and assumptions, Israel would withdraw promptly from the Gaza Strip and Sharm el-Sheikh. By the 4th the handover from Dayan to Burns had been executed, and UNEF was in occupation of the disputed areas – on an emergency basis. It has been in both places ever since, and if the extent of United Nations administration is not as Pearson has publicly proposed it should be, it is precisely as he had always intended it to be.

Since the Israeli army's swift onslaught into the Sinai on October 29 and the Anglo-French ultimatum twenty-four hours later, Pearson had intervened personally and decisively on four critical occasions: first, to implement his belief in the collective action of a community of nations; second, to extricate Britain and France from a dangerous situation with a minimum loss of honour and prestige; third, to inject a sense of purpose and achievement into the United Nations itself, then rendered inactive and impotent by the long years of East-West conflict; and finally to mend the near-fatal wounds in the Atlantic alliance.

The struggle for peace revolved in essence around the opposing philosophies of Eden, the traditionalist whose decisions seem to have been rooted in downy analogies drawn from convenient and superficial historical contexts; and Pearson, the objectivist concerned more with the immediate and the future than with the past. No doubt both these men were sincerely convinced that war should be permissible only in self-defence, and it would be their different interpretations of what constituted legitimate self-defence that would divide them.

Whenever and wherever Britain's vital interests were threatened – in this case Egypt – Eden would react instinctively to apply the well-tried formula for preserving favourable balances of power with the two well-tried instruments of imperial policy – war and subversive intrigue. He would, as in fact he did, draw upon the past to justify military action in defence of interests that were no less vital because they were so widely dispersed. In the case of Suez, the historical context was the Nazi-Fascist era of the 'thirties, which was clever but false.

Pearson, when international peace was threatened, would, by instinct and training, react by seeking to apply effectively the principle of collective security in such a way that the aberrations which caused the convulsion would not be repeated. When he returned to Ottawa from New York, the British High Commissioner called on him to reflect sadly that his country had lost support in Canada and elsewhere by not pressing home with sufficient strength how much it depended upon the uninterrupted flow of Middle East oil supplies. The world had not realised, he said, that Britain would always fight to maintain the flow of oil. It was another way of saying, as Eden had done to Dulles and Murphy in London, that Britain would fight rather than be reduced to the level of a second-rate power.

Pearson's reply was in itself a commentary on the two attitudes. "Canada," he said, "would never support the use of force to keep oil flowing in any direction." For him there was the transcendent obligation of keeping the peace, creating international law and order, and using force only when physically attacked.

Throughout the crisis in New York, the internal threat at the United Nations was Krishna Menon, who, resenting the central roles of Pearson and Hammarskjold, had been determined to prove that progress toward peace was illusory, that first Britain and France should be indicted publicly for first-degree aggression. His final manœuvre was a resolution which would have established a United Nations inquiry into atrocities alleged to have been committed in Port Said.

Pearson, meeting Fawzi in Hammarskjold's office, warned him that if Egypt encouraged Krishna Menon in his trouble-making, it would sacrifice much of the goodwill generated by its co-operation in permitting the stationing of UNEF on its territory. Fawzi, probably not over-anxious to have Egypt's extravagant propaganda claims subjected to impartial examination, used this warning to muster sufficient support in the Afro-Asian caucus to have the Menon resolution rejected out of hand.

The sum of Pearson's successes was immense; but there were failures, too. The enduring political settlement he had considered so necessary from the outset is still nowhere in sight, and not even the first move has been made yet to bring the disputants to a conference table. Neither the United Nations, nor the Great Powers, nor the immediate parties concerned have exerted the slightest effort to reap the profits Pearson had foreseen and spelled out so clearly in his first statement to the Assembly.

It is true that UNEF has been able to maintain an uneasy truce in the area, but it was never stationed on both sides of the demarcation lines to provide a tangible and psychological platform between the Arabs and Israelis, a development which in itself might have helped to create the right conditions for an accommodation.

Pearson tried hard in February to achieve this deployment of UNEF, but without success because the Israelis stubbornly refused to allow the United Nations force to patrol on Israel's side of the border. Israeli leaders continue to resent United Nations activities in the Middle East, yet only the presence of UNEF protects them from further fedayeen raids and allows their shipping to enjoy unmolested passage through the Gulf of Aqaba.

There was also the failure to reach agreement in the United Nations on a permanent formula for the financing of peace-keeping operations, a failure that has bedevilled the organisation in subsequent years.

The overwhelmingly favourable balance of success, not least of which being the blocking of all attempts to have Britain and France formally stigmatised with the mark of aggression, proved of little help to Pearson in Ottawa, where the Parliamentary and press opposition to the Liberal government's independent policy concerning Suez was persistent and petulant. As Secretary of State for External Affairs he could not, at that precarious stage of lingering aftermath, disclose either the power of the forces edging toward general war or how slender were the resources of peace. Others, however, were taking steps privately to bring him international recognition by recommending to the Nobel Committee of the Norwegian Parliament that he should be considered for the Nobel Peace Prize.

These expressions of international respect and admiration appear to have been spontaneously organised by governments whose representatives in New York had reported in detail the tireless precision with which Pearson had guided the United Nations toward restoration of peace. Selected national and international institutions and elder statesmen were briefed by foreign ministries and ambassadors so fully that ultimately between eighteen and twenty recommendations were submitted.

The same accounts indicate that the five judges, all past and present members of the Norwegian Storting, reached their decision unanimously; and later that year, after the St. Laurent government had been defeated and Pearson had left his office, he was formally awarded the Peace Prize for 1957.

Some British sources claim ironically that Eden had been a candidate in 1956, and when his actions automatically debarred him from becoming a Nobel Laureate it was too late for the committee to elect an alternative. By implication, therefore, Pearson received the prize that Eden had forfeited.

Mr. Gunnar Jahn, Chairman of the Nobel Committee, said at the ceremonies in Stockholm: "Since the end of the last war, the situation has never been so dark as during the Suez crisis, and never had the United Nations had a more difficult task to deal with. However, what actually happened has shown that moral force can be a bulwark against aggression, and that it is possible to make aggressive forces yield without resorting to power. Therefore it may be said that the Suez crisis was a victory for the United Nations and for the man who contributed more than anyone else to save the world at that time. That man was Lester Pearson."

Referring to the relationship of peace and people in his Nobel address, Pearson said: "In the end, the whole problem always returns to people . . . to one person and his own individual response to the challenge that confronts him."

The legacy of Lester Pearson's response to the challenge of the Suez crisis becomes more perceptible every year: the era of cease-fire among nations.

The Aftermath

NOW that the smokescreen of secrecy which has surrounded the Suez incident for so long is beginning to lift, we can see more clearly what the noise was all about. The real warriors were not the soldiers, but the diplomats; the real battlefield was not the canal, but the United Nations headquarters in New York. The armies of Britain, France, and Israel hurt Nasser less than the wounds their collusive diplomacy inflicted upon the Atlantic alliance.

When Ferdinand de Lesseps approached the British government for money to finance the building of the canal, he was told that he was asking for "a heavy price for a ditch." The Eden government in 1956 paid a trifle more, in terms of national honour and prestige.

Political relations between Britain, France, and the United States have been strained ever since Suez. In 1962, the Kennedy administration risked world war by imposing the Cuban blockade without prior consultation with the Allies. Six months later General de Gaulle vetoed British membership in the Common Market on the ground that Britain was not yet ready to throw aside the Commonwealth or its Anglo-Saxon relationship with the United States in exchange for Europeanism. Then Britain and France each decided they could not rely upon the American nuclear umbrella and set about the serious business of becoming independent nuclear powers.

Each of these events can be traced directly back to the distrust and disillusionment which came in the aftermath of Suez. Britain and France never wholly forgave the United States for the pressures it exerted upon them. The United States never wholly forgave Britain and France for going it alone. France has never forgotten that it was Britain that capitulated to American pressure; and Britain still resents its own collusive alliance with Israel.

Only Nasser gained. He has the canal; he operates it more efficiently than was expected; he has improved it so that the increase in traffic exceeds the predictions of the old Canal Company; Communist aid bolsters the Egyptian national economy; and he is building the Aswan Dam without Western help.

The most dramatic effects of Suez were felt inside the Commonwealth where the pattern of power shifted drastically.

Britain was not only discredited among the Afro-Asian bloc led by India, but also among huge sections of popular opinion in the old "white" Dominions. Though they officially supported Britain throughout the crisis, Australia and New Zealand were by no means united. Opposition to the Anglo-French action was widespread and vociferous in both countries.

The effect on Canada was profound. Traditional diplomatic association with British policies was severed and replaced by a closer identification with the policies of the United States. The concept of Canada as a North American nation rather than a lingering dependent of European imperialism became a practical reality during the Suez crisis.

The continuing process of making Canada's external policies interdependent with those of Britain, France, and the United States has led to increasing United Nations authority in peacekeeping operations. The gradual evolvement of these undertakings under United Nations auspices from Suez through the Congo to Cyprus has made them a cornerstone of Canadian national policy. Instead of following the lead of a mother country or a big neighbour, we are ourselves taking the initiative in a specific area of international relations.

The ultimate aim of creating a permanent international police force is still out of reach. UNEF remains an *ad hoc* force serving a particular emergency while awaiting political settlements. And the Cyprus force proved beyond doubt that peacekeeping is as much an impromptu affair in 1964 as it was in 1956. But the opportunity for a more imaginative approach exists; and Middle Powers tend to look towards Canada for a solution.

While big powers were practising an obsolete art of war, Lester Pearson seized the opportunity to conceive a new strategy of peace. It can be developed now as yet another permanent deterrent to aggression.

BIBLIOGRAPHY

The following list of authorities is in addition to source material which must remain confidential:

Barraclough, Geoffrey. *Survey of International Affairs: 1956-1958.* Toronto: Oxford University Press, 1962.

Bromberger, Merry and Serge. *Secrets of Suez.* London: Sidgwick & Jackson, 1957.

Burns, Gen. E. L. M. *Between Arab and Israeli.* New York: Ivan Obelensky, Inc., 1963.

Canada and the Suez Canal Crisis. Ottawa: Department of External Affairs.

Childers, Erskine B. *The Road to Suez.* London: MacGibbon and Kee, 1962.

Churchill, Randolph. *The Rise and Fall of Sir Anthony Eden.* New York: G. P. Putnam's Sons, 1959.

Connell, John. *The Most Important Country.* London: Cassell & Co. Ltd., 1957.

Crabites, Pierre. *The Spoliation of Suez.* London: George Routledge & Sons Ltd., 1940.

Damage and Casualties in Port Said. Report by Sir Edwin Herbert, president of the U.K. Law Society, presented as White Paper.

Eden, Sir Anthony. *Full Circle: The Memoirs of Sir Anthony Eden.* Boston: Houghton Mifflin Company, 1960.

General Assembly Records. First and Second Emergency Special Sessions, 1956; Eleventh Session — Plenary Meetings 1956-57, Vols. I and II; Thirteenth Session — Annexes, 1958; Cost Estimates for maintenance of UNEF; Progress Report on UNEF; Summary Study of Experience Derived from Establishment and Operation of UNEF.

Hadwen, John G. and Johan Kaufman. *How United Nations Decisions Are Made.* Dobbs Ferry, New York: Oceana Publications, Inc., 1962.

Hearings Before the Committee on Foreign Relations and the Committee on Armed Services, Parts I and II. United States Senate.

Henriques, Robert. *Hundred Hours to Suez.* New York: The Viking Press, 1957.

Hughes, Emrys. *Macmillan: Portrait of a Politician.* London: George Allen and Unwin, Ltd., 1962.

Impact of the Suez Crisis on NATO Countries. Compiled by NATO.

Johnson, Paul. *The Suez War.* New York: Greenberg, 1957.

Keightley, General Sir Charles F., Commander-in-Chief, Allied Forces. Dispatch.

Lash, Joseph P. *Dag Hammarskjold: A Biography.* New York: Doubleday and Company, Inc., 1961.

Longgood, William. *Suez Story: Key to the Middle East.* New York: Greenberg, 1957.

Middle East Chronology. United Nations.

Murray, G. S. *Political Implications of Peace-Keeping Under the United Nations Charter.* Ottawa: Department of External Affairs, 1963.

Nasser, Gamal Abdel. *The Philosophy of the Revolution.* National Publications House Press, 1955.

Orient No. 1. A Survey of Middle East affairs by the "Society Orient" of France, January 1957.

Orient No. 2. As above. April 1957.

Pearson, L. B. *The Crisis in the Middle East: October-December 1956.* Government of Canada White Paper.

—— *The Crisis in the Middle East: January-March 1957.* Government of Canada White Paper.

Les Prix Nobel—en 1957. Stockholm: The Nobel Institute, 1958.

St. John, Robert. *The Boss: The Story of Gamal Abdel Nasser.* New York: McGraw-Hill Book Co. Inc., 1960.

Schonfield, Hugh S. *The Suez Canal in World Affairs.* New York: The Philosophical Library, 1953.

Security Council Records (Eleventh Year). 734th-755th Meetings inclusive.

Siegfried, André. *Suez and Panama.* New York: Harcourt, Brace and Co., 1940.

The Soviet-Czech Arms Deal with Egypt. Tel Aviv: Israeli Defence Department.

The Suez Canal Conference. Selected documents. London: August 2-24, 1956.

The Suez Canal Report. Suez Canal Authority, United Arab Republic, 1962.

Tillion, Germaine. *France and Algeria: Complementary Enemies.* New York: Alfred A. Knopf, Inc., 1961.

Tournoux, J. R. *Secrets d'Etat.* Paris: Libraire Plon, 1960.

The United Nations Emergency Force. Background paper, 1962.

The Validity in International Law of the Expropriation of the Suez Canal Company. Government of Canada document.

Watt, D. C. *Britain and the Suez Canal.* London: R 11 A. New York: Oxford University Press, Inc., 1956.

—— *Documents on the Suez Crisis.* London: R 11 A. New York: Oxford University Press, Inc., 1957.

Wint, G. and P. Calvocoressi. *Middle East Crisis.* London: Penguin Books Limited, 1959

Zinner, P. E. (ed.). *Documents on American Foreign Relations.* U. S. Government publication.

INDEX

TERENCE ROBERTSON

Terence Robertson, a native Englishman who became a Canadian eight years ago, is a biographer, novelist, popular historian, journalist and traveler of considerable repute on both sides of the Atlantic. His books, most of which have a nautical theme and all of which have been translated into half a dozen languages, include *Night Raider of the Atlantic, Walker, R.N., Channel Dash, The Ship with Two Captains, Full Speed to Heaven* and *The Shame and the Glory*. Mr. Robertson wrote the latter after two years of researching and 80,000 miles of traveling to talk with men involved in the Dieppe Raid of 1942. Mr. Robertson, who lives in Toronto, is a frequent contributor to Canadian and English publications and to the *Saturday Evening Post*.